A State of Depression

# A STATE OF DEPRESSION

Margaret McRae

First published 1986

Published by
MACMILLAN EDUCATION LTD
Houndmills, Basingstoke, Hampshire RG21 2XS
and London
Companies and representatives
throughout the world

Printed in Hong Kong

ISBN 0-333-39981-1 (hard cover)
ISBN 0-333-39982-X (paper cover)

# Contents and Synopsis

# Foreword

*by*

## Dr. T.W. Goldblatt

The central figure in this drama is a young woman who is going through what can only be described as her personal agony. In giving this account, so many years later, of the path she traversed, she has unwittingly provided a picture of indomitable courage and remarkable determination, perseverance and integrity. As a witness of her suffering and of her achievement, I humbly pay this tribute. At the time I was partially aware of these qualities, as it was on the basis of their presence that I knew the work necessary could be done. But it is only on reading her own story, after such a lapse of time, that the full impact of her brave struggle has struck home.

When, a short while ago, I received a letter asking me to write a foreword to a book in which the author had given an account of the traumatic experience of her illness, I was nonplussed because the married name under which she wrote meant nothing to me and her maiden name, while vaguely familiar, stirred no memories. Checking through my files, I found, to my dismay, what I had expected. That after so many years, the notes had long since been destroyed and I had no record of treatment, of its course and development. Indeed, there was not even a history to remind me who she was.

Fortunately, memory returned on reading the manuscript and I recalled vividly the full intensity and poignancy of the treatment sessions described. It is a strange experience to relive meaningful events through the eyes of another person. Some, of course, were seen quite differently by me. Often I did not recognise myself as much of the phraseology used was unlike my own. In any event, when material is condensed it does tend to assume a different aspect. It also became evident that I appeared as having been far more directive than was actually the case. Nevertheless, in essence, her description gave a full and true account of that journey. Of special interest to me, as a therapist, were some of the differences. For example, she described the consultation as one in which I sat behind my desk. I knew this to be factually incorrect as I have never interviewed a patient for consultation other than face-to-face. Any other method would be totally alien to my approach to therapy. Yet her recollection that the consultation took place in this way, although factually incorrect, was nevertheless a true reflection of her emotional experience of me on that day as distant, unapproachable and probably unhelpful.

Equally, the apparently extraordinary game of musical chairs did not take place in fact. No chairs were ever removed from that room or hidden. I needed but to shift their positions a few inches to make them available for face-to-face interview or for reclining on the couch. Yet, once again, this is a true picture of her experience of me as cold, brutal, unfeeling and insensitive. In my own personal analysis, I remember commenting one day on the advent of a new chair, only to discover that it had been an ancient inhabitant of that room long before I first attended.

Reading such an account also makes one aware of one's method, of changes in technique and one's fallibility. Yet, whatever the errors or seeming errors, whatever the inadequacies or apparent inadequacies, the fact remains that on the basis of treatment once a week, this young lady, who arrived in dire straits, was able to leave after eighteen months well and ready to take up her life again and forge a new and healthy future for herself. And I believe it is evident from the account that this was the result of her will to get well, the work she did both in and outside that consulting room and from the events that took place in that room, none of which were haphazard and all of which were carefully thought out, seriously considered and carried into effect.

Despite some qualms, it has given me much satisfaction to read this story. This is not the moment for a technical discussion. Nevertheless, it is appropriate to draw attention to certain developments and psychic patterns evident during the course of therapy. The way in which feelings and thoughts not acceptable to the Self are split off and put into the therapist and experienced as being present in him is clearly visible. Similarly, the consequence of this process of projection, that is, the experience of him as an awful person, even cruel, is also very evident. The manner in which she grows to fear these feelings less, becomes able to tolerate them and eventually comes to terms with them is demonstrated. And finally, the re-integration of these aspects of herself into her own personality so that she begins to feel a whole person again can also be seen.

One is presented with a picture of someone reliving childhood emotional experiences and fantasies together with another person and experiencing these emotions in a different way because of the other person, as a result of which healthier concepts of the Self emerge and healthier modes of living can develop. What is demonstrated is the way in which the technique of psychotherapy based on a psychoanalytic approach can enable a person to live through past experiences and emotions and, with proper guidance and help, relive them differently and thereby support, activate and stimulate those self-healing properties we all possess. And thus begin to find one's own way back to health.

I am truly grateful to the author for this evidence. It is a gift in return, a precious gift, quite unexpected and absolutely independently given. It comes as a confirmation and validation from an unsolicited source of the efficacy and value of psychotherapy. Such a gift gives one encouragement to continue with this demanding, exacting but sustaining work so as to offer others the same opportunity to rediscover themselves and their lives.

*London, 1985* T. W. G.

# Preface

At the end of each psychotherapy session I wrote down everything that I could remember. These notes were originally intended to be used by me as a means of helping me to overcome my illness. It is these notes that form the basis for this book.

It is hoped that those who read this book will be enlightened if they are seeking knowledge, and encouraged if they are seeking help.

For the general reader the book is intended to dispel some of the fears that those who claim to be sane have concerning those who are mentally ill. In one sense this book is a plea to all those who come into contact with mental illness, to regard the sufferer with tolerance and understanding.

This book is also an appeal to those who know that they are under psychological stress to seek professional help, rather than to allow a crisis to overtake them, and perhaps even destroy their lives.

*Billericay, 1985* M. McR.

# Acknowledgements

This book is gratefully dedicated to Dr T. W. Goldblatt, the psychotherapist who treated me throughout my illness from February 1967 to August 1968. Without his patient help and kind understanding I would not have survived.

My heartfelt thanks are also due to 'Rita' and 'Pat' who supported me at a time when others would have fled.

My final thanks are to my husband Francisco who painstakingly read the entire manuscript and gave me invaluable help in improving the writing style. Without his help and guidance this book might never have been written.

# Part 1
# THE DISINTEGRATION OF MY PERSONALITY

# 1 Physical Illness

(April 1966 - October 1966)

In the Easter of 1966 I set off on a three weeks' cycling holiday to Luxembourg, accompanied by two fellow students, Pat and Kathy. We were State Registered Nurses and midwives, training to become health visitors. We welcomed the opportunity to get away from our books and our studies. As we cycled through the beautiful Luxembourg countryside we felt a wonderful sense of freedom. I found that I had much in common with my new friends and we shared many interesting stories with one another as we rode up hill and down dale or, rather, as we pushed our bikes up hill and glided down dale.

As the holiday progressed we drew closer together, and the friendship that was formed became invaluable to me in the coming months. On looking back over that wonderful holiday I realise it was an experience that returned to me again and again during the long period which I am about to describe.

Although at the time I didn't realise it, our three weeks' cycling trip became a symbol of hope and normality, like a life-raft to a person drowning in an angry sea.

The following pages recall the mental terror and anguish which I began to experience from September 1966, and lasted for many long weary months to come. During this dreadful period I gained the support of loyal friends and received expert treatment from a psychoanalyst, Dr Goldblatt. With their help I escaped from the depression and despair which engulfed my life and almost ended it.

The knowledge that there was something wrong came unexpectedly. Two weeks after the holiday I was in college, listening to a lecture, when suddenly I realised I was bleeding.

At first I thought it was the beginning of a normal period, but within a few minutes it was obvious that the bleeding was abnormal. I realised that I was saturated. Blood was dripping on to the floor beneath my chair. I looked around anxiously to see if anyone had noticed. Luckily no one had. I was transfixed on the chair while the lecture became a blurred sound in the back of my mind. I wanted to get up and run.

Fortunately my nurse's training came to the fore and I was able to get a grip of myself. At that moment the lecture ended and I realised the students were beginning to rise from their chairs and make their way towards the door. I stayed where I was, gripping the sides of the desk until my knuckles went white. What on earth is happening to me? I gasped to myself. Then I heard Pat's voice coming to me out of a kind of fog: 'Come on, don't you want any dinner, Margaret?'

'I can't move,' I said, through clenched teeth.

'Why? What's wrong?' said Pat, looking puzzled.

By this time the room was empty except for Pat, Kathy and me. Without saying a word I pointed to the floor beneath my chair. They both gasped in astonishment. Pat went decidedly pale and I could see by the look of shock on their faces that something pretty horrific was happening. Kathy was the practical one of the three of us and within seconds she had taken charge of the situation. I felt myself being lifted up from my chair and being half dragged, half walked, in the direction of the toilets with the two of them supporting me on either side. Once behind the relative safety of the toilet door I sat on the pan and waited until the bleeding stopped. It could have been as long as 15 minutes – I don't know.

Kathy in the meantime very quickly nipped back into the classroom and cleaned up the pool of blood as best she could. She then came back into the toilets and called out to me. My initial panic was now over and I groaned from behind the toilet door that I was not feeling too bad. The flow of blood had stopped. Deathly white, I crept out of the toilet and they undressed me and began furiously dunking my clothes in the sink. By now I looked decidedly forlorn and bedraggled. Pat rushed outside to the lockers and came back with a pair of tennis shorts which I kept at college for the occasional game at lunchtimes. Wearing tennis shorts under my raincoat, no stockings and a bag of wet clothing I eventually made my way home.

At the first opportunity I went to consult my doctor. My own GP was on holiday so I saw his partner. I explained the incident to him as accurately as I could.

'It's probably an isolated occasion,' he remarked. 'Possibly brought on by your career changes and your apprehension about starting health visiting.'

'I m not apprehensive,' I replied. 'I've never had any menstrual problems before and I'm feeling quite settled and happy.'

'Well, you don't look anaemic. Wait a couple of months, and if the trouble doesn't right itself, come back again and I'll arrange for you to be examined thoroughly.'

I left the surgery feeling dissatisfied, since I could not imagine how the condition could right itself. However, there was nothing I could do but wait to see how matters developed.

The next month I was prepared for the worst, so I was not caught out. To my dismay the bleeding was just as bad. I felt reluctant to go back to the doctor straight away in case he thought I was being over dramatic. I certainly didn't look anaemic, so he could be forgiven if he thought I was exaggerating. I decided to wait a few more months until after I was settled in my new health visiting job.

The trouble didn't right itself – in fact it worsened. I started my new job at the beginning of July with enthusiasm, but in my second week I was bleeding so much that I spent most of the day near the toilet in the clinic where I worked. It was obvious that I would not be able to do my job properly in my condition, so I returned to the surgery.

This time I saw my own GP and I described my symptoms to him. He agreed with me that I needed treatment. After examining me he said, 'You need to be seen urgently by a gynaecologist. Have you any preference which consultant or hospital I refer you to?'

I chose a particular London hospital, simply because I had trained there, and I considered that the standard of nursing care was high and the medical facilities were good. While the doctor was writing the letter to the consultant I asked, 'Have I got fibroids?'

'Possibly,' he answered, 'but I can't be certain. You will be able to have more thorough investigations at the hospital.'

'What else could be wrong?' I asked.

'It's impossible to say,' he said, evasively. 'I suggest you phone the hospital and ask for an immediate appointment. It might help if you say that you trained there.'

He gave me the letter. I left his surgery feeling worried. Why had he been evasive? Why the urgency? I decided to read what he had written about me.

Standing on the pavement outside the surgery I nervously tore open the envelope and read quickly. It was the normal letter of introduction, but at the end under the heading Possible Diagnosis it said:

1. Fibroids.
2. Carcinoma of the uterus.
3. Carcinoma of the ovary.

My mind and body froze. I was 25, and at that age cancer could spread very rapidly. I had nursed young women in the terminal stages of cancer of the ovary, and so I imagined the worst.

Without delay I phoned the hospital and insisted that I must have an appointment immediately because my condition was critical. I was told to attend out-patients in two weeks' time.

Not wishing to worry my parents, I simply told them that I was expecting to go into hospital shortly to have fibroids removed.

However, I couldn't shake off the unease inside me. In desperation I confided my feelings to one of my new colleagues, Rita. She was very sympathetic. 'Your mother must be very anxious,' she said.

'I've only told her I'm going to have an operation for fibroids,' I said. 'There's no point in worrying her yet.'

'You are funny,' Rita observed. 'I would want a daughter of mine to tell me her worries straight away so that I could share them with her, and help her to bear them.

'It helps me to tell you,' I replied. 'I don't need to worry my parents.'

The appointment at the out-patients' department was unexpectedly traumatic. There were numerous women in the gynaecology area quietly and apprehensively waiting their turn. Every little while, half a dozen names were called, and those women were led through to another section and instructed to undress and wait in an inner area. Eventually my name was called. After about 10 minutes I was shown to one of the numerous cubicles, and told to get on the couch. A few minutes later a young, harassed looking doctor hurried in, clutching my notes. He glanced at my doctor's letter. 'I have read it, I know what my doctor suspects,' I said, hoping that if I spoke to him he would realise that I was not just another body. I wanted to be treated as an individual.

'Lie down, please, and relax,' was all he said.

The examination was nasty, and I uttered a cry from the pain it caused. 'I'm sorry,' he said. 'It's over now, you can get up.'

As I was getting off the couch he said, 'We'll get you in quickly. We can discuss exactly what we'll do when you are in the ward.' Before I could ask him anything, he had disappeared into the next cubicle, where another patient was waiting.

I wanted to call after him, just to tell him that he was dealing with human beings, not lumps of meat, but a nurse was already hurrying me to the changing room. The cubicle was needed by the next patient in the queue.

I felt sorry for the doctor. It was the system that was at fault, not him. But I felt more sorry for the other patients. They were also experiencing the 'mindless-body-treatment'. . . next please . . . next please . . . next please.

Over the next few weeks I became increasingly convinced that I had a more serious condition than fibroids. A few years back I would have contained my anxiety and fear by trusting in God. Recently I had been questioning the evangelical teaching of my childhood. I hadn't deliberately turned my back on Christianity, but I had become uncertain about my beliefs and I no longer felt that my prayers would be heard.

For the first time in my life I was afraid to die. Afraid because I didn't know what I believed, nor what might happen to me after death. I tried not to think about death, and I did my best to acquaint myself with my new job, but the uneasiness remained, and the sense of dread wouldn't leave me.

I continued to go to work each day. Rita was extremely understanding. She made a point of talking to me as much as possible and she encouraged me to talk about myself. In that way she won my confidence. I needed someone to lean on. My college friends were miles away in different parts of the country in their new jobs, my former friends were scattered far afield, and I was no longer in contact with them. I had only recently moved back to live with my parents, so I had no friends nearby.

By the time I received a letter from the hospital informing me that a bed was available, I was in a very, very nervous state.

It was towards the end of September 1966 when I reported to the hospital ward. The sister showed me my bed and asked me to get undressed and wait behind the curtains, because the registrar was on his rounds and would want to examine me. I waited expectantly. At last I should have an opportunity to talk properly with a doctor about my condition, and about the treatment I would receive.

The registrar appeared. Hurriedly he examined me and then said to the sister, 'We'll operate in the morning.' He turned to go. In desperation I called after him, 'What's wrong with me? What operation am I to have?'

He stopped and looked at me in surprise. 'You have fibroids. It's best to remove them as soon as possible, so we'll perform a myomectomy tomorrow.' With that he was gone.

I was number one on the operating list the next day. That worried me. When I was a student nurse, the more complicated and serious operations were performed first, while the smaller, routine tasks were placed at the bottom of the list.

I knew the consultant as I had worked on the gynaecology ward as a student, but so far I hadn't seen him. That worried me too. I wanted him to be the one to make the diagnosis, and to decide on the treatment necessary, not those other doctors who had spent no more than a minute considering my case.

However, there was nothing I could do but hope that the best would be done for me.

The porter wheeled me to the operating theatre and the anaesthetist asked me to hold out my arm. He pushed the syringe needle into my vein and slowly injected the drug. Just as I was beginning to drift off, I heard the door open and a voice I recognised as the consultant's exclaimed, 'What's going on?' I struggled against the drug, desperate to talk to him, but I felt the distance between us was increasing, and I floated off into unconsciousness.

The next thing I was aware of was a ghastly drifting, sinking feeling. Desperately I tried to cling to something or someone, but there was nothing and no one there. I was lost: physically, mentally and spiritually. I couldn't locate my body; I was unable to reason what was going on; I didn't even know who or what I was. I seemed not to have an identity – I was terrified.

The pleading and sobbing was coming closer and getting louder. I became aware of my lips and then my throat. I could hear a voice crying out, 'Please help. Where am I? What am I? Please help, please help.'

A voice was shouting in my ear, 'Wake up. It's all over.'

I was struggling to find myself. I became aware that the cries for help were coming from me. My arms became a part of me, and I waved them around in relief. 'Keep your arms still. You'll have your drip over,' the voice shouted. I opened my eyes and choked back my sobs. One arm was free, so I swiftly put my hand under the covers and pulled at a large, padded dressing on my abdomen. What had been done to me? 'Please try and keep still. It's all over,' said the voice.

'What's over?' I asked. 'What's been done? Have I had a hysterectomy?'

'Of course not. You've just had a few fibroids removed, that's all. Now please try and keep still.'

Shaking with fear, I flopped back into my pillow. I didn't believe the nurse. I was convinced that I'd had an extensive operation for cancer.

For the remaining ten days in hospital I was in a state of panic. The nurses seemed to be avoiding me, but whenever I gained their attention, I asked what had been done in the operating theatre. Every time that answer came back, 'You've had three fibroids removed, that's all.'

Several times I crept into the sister's office when it was empty and tried to find the doctor's notes, so that I could read for myself what had been done. Every time someone came before I had found them. I pleaded to be shown the records of the operation, but they refused to let me see them. I was sent away in disgrace.

I kept active in an attempt to ward off my anxiety. The nurses allowed me to help them. I made the empty beds, I took patients' temperatures, pulses and respirations and blood pressures. When there were no more jobs for me to do, I got into bed and tried to concentrate on reading. Somehow I had to escape from the fear that was pursuing me.

I didn't want my parents to visit me because I knew they would be worried to see me in such a nervous state, so I phoned them and told them not to come since the journey would take up to two hours each way and the weather was bad.

Every evening at visiting time I wheeled the telephone to my bedside, and while the rest of the patients were chatting to their visitors I buried myself under the covers and phoned Rita. She was incredibly tolerant and understanding. I poured out my fears that the nurses were hiding something from me. If they had nothing to hide, they would let me read the doctor's notes. I wanted to know the truth so that I could face up to what lay ahead.

Rita listened to my sobs and did her best to console me. I always felt more composed after talking to her.

From time to time during my stay in hospital the doctor did his rounds. On those occasions I wanted to ask him to tell me exactly what had been done during the operation, and whether there was any suggestion of cancer, but his detached manner and his apparent wish to hurry on to the next patient prevented my doing so. Even if, in answer to any questions, he had said that nothing was wrong with me, I wouldn't have believed him.

On the tenth day after my operation the consultant was due to visit the ward. I felt frightened yet hopeful. I believed he would be honest with me and tell me truthfully whether or not I had cancer.

I sat beside my bed and watched the door at the end of

the ward. At last it opened. My heart pounded as the registrar, followed by a group of medical students, walked towards the waiting sister. I looked for the friendly face of the consultant, but I couldn't see him. Perhaps he had been delayed and would arrive in a few moments.

To my dismay the registrar started his round immediately. He was obviously in charge.

I watched him carefully. His one aim, it seemed, was to teach the students. The patients were merely teaching aids. A feeling of intense dislike came over me.

Soon they reached my bed. I heard the registrar explain to the students that I had had a myomectomy. He asked me to lie on the bed. Sister drew the curtains round and he quickly examined me. 'Fine, you can go home tomorrow,' he said, and walked away.

I got right into bed and cried into my pillow. My last chance to find out the truth was gone.

The day for my discharge arrived and Rita came smiling into the ward to take me home. I should have been thrilled but somehow the haunting fear of cancer held me in its icy grip and I couldn't respond. All I could say to Rita was, 'I must get out of here.'

'Have you got a medical certificate?' she asked.

'No, I forgot to get one. I feel too muddled to think about it. Don't let's bother.'

'You must have a certificate,' she said. 'I'll find the sister and sort it out for you.' Rita left me sitting by the bed for what seemed ages. At last she reappeared with the certificate. She picked up my bag and led me to her car. I sat limply in the passenger seat as we drove away.

'When is your next hospital appointment?' Rita asked.

'In six weeks' time, but I won't feel happy until then. I can't get rid of the feeling that the doctors haven't been honest with me. They are hiding something from me.'

'I'm sure the doctors would have told you if it was more than fibroids,' she remarked.

For some time I said nothing. I'd never felt so miserable. Normally I had a happy disposition and made light of any problems that came my way. I thought I should be able to overcome my misery – I expected it of myself, I demanded it of myself – but still I was miserable. 'I feel so tired and moody,' I complained. 'I just want to cry all the time. What's wrong with me?'

'Nothing's wrong with you,' said Rita, 'except that you're being unreasonable with yourself. You're bound to feel tired and moody. Why shouldn't you have a good cry?'

'I ought to be able to overcome these feelings,' I said. 'I mustn't let my parents see me in this state.'

'Why not?' asked Rita.

'It would worry them,' was all I could say.

'You've every right to be moody and to show it. Don't fight against it. Take things easy.'

That seemed strange advice which I couldn't take. My way of coping with feelings and emotions which I didn't approve of, or didn't want to have, was to act as though those feelings and emotions didn't exist, and to absorb myself with something that would bring to the fore the feelings that I could accept in myself. Now my willpower seemed to have gone, I was at a loss to know what to do.

All too soon we arrived home. Rita carried by bag to the front door and rang the bell while I tried to put on a brave face. My mother opened the door and we went inside.

'Margaret will be very tired for a while, so she's to rest as much as she can,' said Rita. 'She's to have a check-up in six weeks' time, and she's not to come back to work until after that.'

Rita stayed for a cup of tea and then left. I put on the record player and lay down on the settee to listen quietly as the sound of Mozart filled the room. For a few moments I imagined myself to be there beside him as he gently played on the keyboard.

Over the next few days I tried really hard to hide my feelings from my parents. I put on a brave face, but my fears remained. I needed to escape.

I remembered Pat. When we had said goodbye to each other at the end of our health visitors' course three months ago, she had asked me to come and stay with her as soon as I could. Perhaps if I spent a few weeks with her, remembering our cycling holiday, I would feel happy again. At least with

Pat I would feel relaxed. She accepted people as they were, and made no demands. That was my answer.

I phoned her that evening and asked if she would let me come to stay with her. 'Come tomorrow morning,' she said. 'I've got a day off, so I'll meet you at the station.'

I was overjoyed. I thanked her and said goodbye. I then rushed upstairs to my bedroom and began packing excitedly.

The train came to a halt and I stepped down onto the platform, clutching my baggage. Passengers were hurrying towards the exit. A whistle blew and the train began slowly easing away from the station. Suddenly with a cry of joy Pat came rushing towards me and together we made our way to her car.

# 2 Suspense: My Life in the Balance

(October 1966 - November 1966)

Pat worked as a nurse, midwife and health visitor combined. Her territory included a number of villages. She had a two-bedroomed flat and a car that went with the job. She had made a few friends among the people in her village, but as they were all potential patients, she couldn't get on a personal level with them. My arrival was a welcome relief for her.

Pat said I could stay for as long as I liked. For the first week I joined her on her visits. I sat in the car when she went into the houses, as I didn't want to get involved with other people.

Pat and the countryside had a calming effect on me. Gradually I felt my willpower return as I became stronger, and by the end of the first week Pat had convinced me that everything was going to be all right. She arranged a week's leave and together we went to stay at her parent's house on the coast. We spent four happy days there, watching the waves and the fishermen with their boats. Soon I began to feel like my old self. We even talked about another cycling holiday in the spring.

One morning we were having breakfast when the post arrived. One letter was for me. It had been sent on by my father. The address was typed, and the envelope bore a London postmark. My hand trembled. I looked desperately at Pat. I tried to speak, but no sound came. I pushed the letter towards her and I stammered, 'You open it.'

Pat tore open the envelope. I held my breath while she

read. The colour drained from her face. 'What does it say?' I whispered.

'I'm sure it's a false alarm, so don't jump to conclusions,' she said. 'The consultant wants you to go to his out-patients' clinic on Monday. He's had the results of a test which he did on your fibroids when he operated, and he wants to see you.'

'You don't really believe it's a false alarm, do you? You've got to be honest with me, Pat.'

She reached across the table and placed her hand on mine. She looked into my eyes. 'No,' she said quietly, 'It sounds serious.' She paused and bit her lip. Then she continued speaking, 'Remember this, Margaret, whatever happens, I'll stand by you. Don't be afraid to lean on me. We've had fun together in the past, and when all this is over, we'll have more happy times.' Her voice broke and tears welled into her eyes.

'Thanks,' I whispered. 'You're a true friend.'

We went out walking for the rest of the day. The wind and rain were in keeping with our feelings. We spoke very little. What was there to say? We could only wait. I tried to absorb myself in our surroundings – the stormy sea, the bleak fields, the cold, the dampness and the lonely cries from the seagulls, as they glided in the grey sky overhead. My emotions became numb as I watched and listened to the ceaseless pounding of the waves. I wanted to be numbed. My fears and anxieties had to be ignored, suppressed, avoided at all costs. I wanted the sea and sky to fold me in its vastness so that I could become a part of nature and forget myself.

Each day until Monday we walked along the beach among the fishing boats. At dusk we returned home and listened to classical music. I had to find a new reality in nature and music. Pat understood and left me in my trance-like state.

On Sunday evening I began to feel nervous and jittery. 'Let's walk to the station and find out the train times,' I said to Pat.

'You don't think I'm going to let you go to the hospital on your own, do you?' she said. 'I've arranged to have the day off tomorrow, and I'm going to drive you there and stay with you to see what happens. If you've got to have treatment straight away, I'll leave you there, otherwise I'll bring you back to my flat.'

'I can't let you drive me all that way,' I protested, but deep down I was relieved. Pat's presence comforted me.

She ignored what I said. 'We'll leave at about 10 o'clock. You've got to be there at 2 o'clock so we should have plenty of time. We'll take sandwiches and flasks of coffee so we can eat when we feel like it.'

'Thanks Pat,' I said quietly, and drifted back into my trance.

Next morning I woke early feeling alert. The day of reckoning had come. In a few hours I would know the worst. Perhaps I'd never see this lovely little house again. I looked at the objects around me and paused. I wanted the atmosphere of the little bedroom to penetrate the wall I had built around myself. I washed, dressed and went downstairs to breakfast. Again I paused, looked out of the window at the garden, then around the room itself. This was my last chance to savour the warmth and affection I felt around me. I sat down to breakfast, and tears poured down my cheeks. 'I might never be able to come here again,' I sobbed. 'I might be dead by Christmas.'

'You'll be back,' Pat said with conviction. 'Once you know what you've got to face, you'll face it and overcome it. You'll win through.'

Her confidence helped to reassure me, but I couldn't manage to eat. I just sat and let the tears flow.

It was time to go. We left the house and walked to Pat's car which was parked a little way down the street. Pat opened the passenger door for me. I hesitated. 'Wait a minute,' I said, and I took some deep breaths of the pure sea air. It was cold but bright and the sun was shining. 'This might be my last chance to enjoy the fresh air, the wind, the call of the seagulls and the sound of the waves.' For a while I stood quietly, looking up at the sky, making the most of those fleeting moments. I wanted to memorise it all, and keep the atmosphere within me . . . .

Reluctantly I pulled myself away and got into the car. We drove off. I stared out of the window and for two hours we remained silent. I was absorbed with the countryside, and Pat concentrated on her driving.

Eventually we reached the outskirts of London. I glanced

at Pat and she looked very tired. 'Let's stop and have some coffee,' I suggested. We pulled into a side street, and drank gratefully from our flasks. For the rest of the drive I directed Pat through the London streets.

At last we arrived. We made our way through the out-patients' department and to the gynaecology section. I showed my letter to the clerk at the desk. 'Wait over there until your name is called,' she said.

As we sat down, I started to tremble. Pat tried to keep up a conversation. After about ten minutes my name was called. I was shown into a small room where the consultant was already waiting. 'Please sit down,' he said. I did so. 'As you know,' he continued, 'when I operated I just removed the fibroids. At the time I considered performing a hysterectomy because the growths were unusual and I was very concerned. But in view of your age I decided to wait until I was more sure of the nature of the growths. I've sent samples of tissue for analysis. The preliminary results make me pessimistic but I've asked for more extensive tests to be done. I should have the results within a week. I'd like you to be ready to come back at a moment's notice so that I can operate immediately if necessary.'

'Is it almost certain that I'll have to have a hysterectomy?' I asked, fighting back my tears.

'It's possible, but I'd like to wait for the results of all our tests. I want to be sure before I take such drastic action.'

'When will I know?'

'I'll send for you in a week to ten days' time.' He stood up.

There was nothing more to say. I got up and walked to the door. I paused in the doorway. 'Please let me know as soon as you can,' I begged. 'I can't bear the suspense.'

I went back to Pat. She looked at me expectantly. 'Let's go to the car. I'll tell you everything then,' I stammered.

We made our way out of the building to the car. With tears streaming down my face, I told her everything.

At first Pat couldn't speak. She stared ahead, her face as white as a sheet. Then she looked at me. 'I'm sorry,' she said quietly. Words weren't necessary. I knew that she felt for me.

She passed me a sandwich and poured some coffee. We ate in silence.

'We'd better be getting back,' she said after a few minutes. 'We've got a long journey ahead of us.'

We set off. We kept our conversation at a superficial level, and concentrated on the road ahead. Once out of London the roads were fairly easy, but it was an exhausting drive back to Pat's home.

We both sighed with relief when we eventually arrived. We had a milky drink and went to bed.

I stayed at Pat's for the rest of the week. There was a nagging anxiety at the back of my mind, but I was able to keep it at bay, and I had a pleasant time sitting in Pat's car enjoying the countryside when she did her visits. When she wasn't working we relived the fun we had had together on our cycling holiday.

At the weekend I decided to go home in case a letter arrived from the hospital. Pat drove me to the station. We had only a few minutes to wait for the train. We waited in silence – a silence that can come between people who understand each other. I had never had such a friendship before, and I deeply appreciated it.

The train drew into the platform. Pat opened the carriage door. 'You'll be all right, Margaret,' she said emphatically. 'You've got determination. I know you'll win through in the end.'

I climbed into the carriage and leaned from the window to say goodbye, but all I could murmur was 'Thanks.' Tears were running down Pat's cheeks but it comforted me. She cared, she understood. She was the sister I had always longed for but had never had. The train moved slowly and through my tears I could see Pat waving to me in the distance.

I sat down, feeling very empty and very alone. With Pat I had been able to share my anxieties and I had felt safe with her. At home with my parents it would be so different. I would try to suppress my sadness and anxiety in order not to worry them. I would have to bear my burden on my own. As the train rattled through the countryside my uneasiness and dread increased.

The next few days were a terrible strain. If I did have cancer, every day of waiting lessened my chance of being cured. I watched anxiously for the postman, while at the same time I pretended to my parents that everything was all right. Most of the time I rested on the settee and listened to music in keeping with my mood, hoping that the music would lift my mind away from myself. But there was no escape. I kept imagining the patients I had nursed with terminal cancer and I saw myself in their place. At night I dreamt of those patients. I couldn't get away from the fear that one day I might be like them.

In desperation I went to my family doctor, told him the state of affairs and asked if I could return to work. He was against the idea, but at last I was able to persuade him that the only way I could cope with the mental strain I was going through was to return to work. Relieved, I went back to work the next day.

The days passed but no letter came from the hospital and I wondered if their letter had been lost in the post, so I phoned the hospital and asked if they had any news. The receptionist told me that the consultant had my records, and that I must be patient.

I couldn't be patient, so from then on I began phoning the hospital every day and pleaded with the receptionist to find out what the results were, but she insisted that she couldn't tell me. I begged her to let me speak to the consultant myself, but she said that he was unavailable.

On the Monday morning four weeks after I had been told by the consultant that he would be in touch with me, Rita asked me if I had had any news.

'No,' I said. 'I've heard nothing.'

'Then you must go to the hospital and demand to see the consultant.'

'I can't do that.'

'Your life is at stake. You can't take any more of this suspense. I'll ask Mrs Bell the clinic nurse to go with you.'

So we had an early lunch and set off on the bus. It took us an hour to get there, and the clinic was in full swing. I went straight to the receptionist. 'I must see the consultant,' I said. 'It's very urgent.'

'I'm sorry,' she said, 'You can't see him without an appointment.'

I was desperate. 'I'm not leaving here until I see him,' I

insisted. 'Please find my records and tell him I'm here.' I wrote my name on a piece of paper and gave it to her, and then I went to the waiting area and sat down with the other women.

'I'm not leaving here until I find out what's going on,' I repeated to Mrs Bell. 'I'll scream the place down if necessary.' The tears started pouring down my face, and she put her arm around me.

I don't know how long we sat there, but after what seemed an age a doctor walked towards me. I looked up. 'The consultant will see you now in his room. Please come this way.' He spoke kindly and gently in a manner I hadn't expected.

I followed him along the corridor and he showed me into an office. The consultant was sitting behind a desk. 'Please come in and sit down.' The doctor left us and I was alone with the consultant. 'I'm glad you've come.' He looked searchingly at me. 'This will be very difficult: you've a hard decision to make.' He paused, letting his words take effect. 'I'm sorry you've been kept in suspense for so long, but the results from the tests were not clear-cut. I have been thinking very carefully about what action should be taken. Only this morning I was discussing you with my colleagues.'

He paused again. To my surprise I was composed. It was as though I had become an onlooker; as though he was talking about someone else who was nothing to do with me. I looked straight at him. 'What conclusions have you come to?' I asked.

'Before I give you my advice I want to know what you feel,' the consultant said. 'I asked for the opinions of our three leading pathologists, and I have their reports here. Please read them.'

He handed me three separate reports. I read them quickly; then again slowly. I immediately understood his dilemma. The first report stated that the growth was a benign tumour, and that there was no reason to expect that the characteristics of the tumour would change – no need to worry there. The second report was vague. It stated that the tumour had unusual characteristics, and although in the opinion of the pathologist, it was harmless at present, at any time it could become malignant, and spread. The third report was alarming. It stated that the tumour probably had malignant tendencies, and was liable to spread rapidly. In the opinion of that pathologist, urgent treatment was necessary.

I handed the reports back to the consultant. 'Thank you for letting me read them,' I said. He was being honest with me, so I knew I could trust him.

'What do you want me to do?' he asked.

I didn't need any time to think. There was only one thing to do. 'Treat me as the third report recommends,' I said, as if in a dream. 'I could't bear to live with the knowledge that at any time cancer could develop.'

'Are you sure?' he asked. 'You know that would mean that you could never have children. Wouldn't you prefer to try to have a child quickly? We would keep a very close eye on you, and then you could have a hysterectomy after that, if it seemed that there was a real risk of cancer.'

'I'm not married or engaged, and I don't want a child, at least not in the near future. It could be years before I might want one. I couldn't live for years with this dread hanging over me. It would be like living with a time bomb inside me. If cancer did develop, could you guarantee that you would be able to diagnose it quickly enough to ensure a cure?'

'No,' he said. 'If the third report is correct, in six months' time I would probably be unable to do anything for you.'

'Please,' I begged, 'don't take risks with my life. Being able to have a child isn't that important to me.'

He sat back slowly in his chair and looked hard at me. 'I'm glad you feel that way,' he said at last. 'I would recommend treating the matter with the utmost urgency.'

'What treatment would you give me?' I asked.

'I would anticipate that a hysterectomy would suffice, but I can't be sure until I operate. It's two months since I saw you and we don't know what might have developed in that time. I don't think you need to worry unduly though. I'm hopeful that we've got you in time.'

'Thank you,' I said. 'I'm grateful that you've been so frank with me.'

'That's settled, then,' he said, and stood up. 'I'll have you in tomorrow morning, and I'll operate on Wednesday.' I walked towards the door, and he followed me. He put his hand on my shoulder. 'I'm very optimistic,' he smiled. I'll see you in the ward tomorrow. Goodbye.'

I walked quickly back to Mrs Bell, who looked very anxious. 'He's told me everything,' I said. 'Let's go.'

I couldn't tell her straight away what had been decided. I had to keep calm until we were on the bus. The last thing I wanted was to give way to my emotions. The decision had been made. Somehow I had to keep control. I could not allow myself to break down now.

At last we were on the bus and I was able to talk. 'It could become cancer,' I said simply, 'I'm to go in tomorrow and have a hysterectomy on Wednesday.'

She put her arm around me, and I let the tears trickle down my cheeks. 'I'm so sorry,' she said.

When we got back to the clinic I told Rita. 'That's a quick decision,' she said. 'Couldn't you have asked for a week to think it over?'

'I don't want to think it over,' I replied. 'I couldn't live with the dread of cancer, so the sooner the operation is done the better.'

It was time to go home, but I wasn't ready to face my parents with the news. 'You all go,' I said to my colleagues. 'I want to be alone. I'll lock up.' Reluctantly they left me.

I sat quietly looking through the window, not really thinking, just sitting there and letting the shock penetrate. I began to feel calm but very weary. Almost too weary to do anything. After a time I found a pen and paper and I wrote to Pat. I narrated the events of the day in considerable detail, and then I poured out to her my inner feelings. I wrote that I was even more worried about my mental state than about my physical condition. I felt that I was losing my grip, and that I was afraid of how the hysterectomy would affect me. I wrote pages. At last I stopped. The letter relieved my anxiety. I got up, walked out of the clinic, locked the door behind me, and caught the bus home.

That evening I told my parents that I had seen the consultant and he had told me I would continue to have fibroids unless I had further treatment, and so it was best for me to have a hysterectomy straight away. I said nothing about the possibility that I might have cancer. There was no point in causing them unnecessary anxiety.

They both looked shocked. At last my mother said, 'Does that mean you won't be able to have children?'

'That's right,' I replied, quietly, and without emotion.

My mother shed a few silent tears. My father put his arm around me and said, 'You are being very brave.'

The subject closed. We talked about unrelated matters for a while and then I went wearily to bed.

# 3 The Hysterectomy and its Aftermath

(November 1966 - January 1967)

My father went with me to the hospital the next morning. It was the end of November 1966. A sympathetic nurse admitted me, and she told my father that he could sit by my bedside for a while. He sat for a few minutes. Then I thanked him and suggested that he left. 'I'm very tired,' I said. 'I'll lie down now and go to sleep.'

Sleep was my only defence against the dreadful fear I was experiencing. Somehow I had to shut my mind to the anxieties that were crowding in. I wanted to go off into a state of oblivion.

I slept through the whole day and the night before my operation, only waking for meals and for the various tests and preparations for the operation that were necessary, but I was in a daze.

Early next morning they came for me and I suddenly found myself being wheeled away from the bedside to the operating theatre. I stared at the walls of the corridor as the trolley moved deliberately towards its destination. I tried not to think, and I avoided contact with the nurses. I wanted to remain detached.

We arrived in the small room leading into the operating theatre. The door swung open and the consultant appeared. He walked up to me and took my hand. 'Hello,' he said. 'Do you still want me to go ahead?'

'Yes please,' I replied. His presence reassured me.

'Good. Let's get on with it then.'

I closed my eyes and drifted off into a peaceful sleep. . . . .

Muffled sounds came to my ears and I felt the sensation of hands holding me, as though I was being lifted up. I opened my eyes and realised that I was back in the ward, and I was being sat up. 'It's all over,' the sister said. 'Let's just make you comfortable.'

'Have I had a hysterectomy?' I asked.

'Yes,' she replied.

'Was anything else removed?'

'No. Everything went according to plan. You'll be all right.'

They left me. I looked anxiously at the blood transfusion equipment hanging over my head. It seemed to be set at a very fast rate. I reached over and adjusted the clip to slow it down. I looked around. There was a patient standing nearby, so I asked her to fetch me some water. It was important to drink plenty after an operation. I wriggled in the bed in an attempt to sit up straighter. I had to breathe deeply to avoid a chest infection. Then I bent my legs up and down, as a preventive measure against thrombosis.

I was very tense and distrustful. I watched for possible signs of complications, and took every precaution against any complications arising. I checked my pulse every five minutes and I kept my eyes on the blood transfusion bottle. I couldn't rest or relax.

Towards evening the ward sister came with a nurse to give me an injection against pain. 'I don't need anything thank you,' I said. 'I haven't any pain.' It was important for me to keep alert, in case I missed a warning sign. A pain killing drug would take me off my guard.

'You soon will have pain,' replied the sister. 'I'm going off duty now, so you'd better have an injection, otherwise you'll have to wait until the night sister does her rounds, and that won't be for a long time.'

'I don't mind. Pain doesn't worry me. I won't call out or bother anyone.'

'You need to have a good sleep,' she insisted. 'This will help you.' Before I knew what was happening the nurse had thrust the syringe needle into my thigh. Then they helped me lie down and I was left alone.

I felt myself drifting and I struggled against it. I had to keep watch on my condition. But I was defenceless against the drug, and the nightmare drifting continued.

Eventually I felt as though I had landed on a solid surface, and I sobbed in relief. Suddenly I was aware that I was being spoken to. 'Are you in pain? We'll soon get rid of that. Nurse will give you an injection.' It was the night sister.

'No,' I gasped. 'Please, I'm not in pain. I've only just had something.'

'That was nearly five hours ago,' she replied. 'We want you to have a really good night's sleep.'

'No, you mustn't give me an injection. I don't want it. It makes me dizzy. I'd rather bear the pain.'

'Nonsense,' she said. 'We don't want you awake in the night crying with pain. You need your sleep.'

I couldn't win. I had to give up my struggle and allow myself to drift.

I soon got wise to the situation. I kept a careful watch for the approach of a sister or staff nurse, and as soon as they came in my direction I pretended to be sound asleep. In that way I avoided being given more drugs.

I was allowed visitors on the day after my operation. I expected my parents to come and I wanted to reassure them as much as possible, so just before six o'clock in the evening I combed my hair, sat up straight and tried to smile. Suddenly the doors to the corridor swung open and visitors began pouring into the ward. I watched the crowd advancing. One woman was pushing people aside in order to get ahead. To my amazement I recognised her. She was Mary, a woman that I had visited regularly when I was a student health visitor. With her permission I had used her family as a case study, and we had grown very fond of each other. She had an eight-year-old son and a one-year-old baby boy. I had written to her the evening before I came into hospital to tell her about my operation.

She rushed towards me. 'Margaret!' she exclaimed, as she reached the bedside. She threw her arms around me and kissed me. Her warmth and spontaneity thrilled me. She stood back and looked at me. 'I suppose you don't look too bad,' she said. 'Your letter worried me stiff. I just had to come and see you as soon as possible. Look,' she fumbled in her bag and brought out a framed photograph of her elder son. She placed it facing me on my bedside table. 'I know how fond you are of Vincent, so I thought his photo would cheer you up.'

'Thanks,' I said. 'Your visit has made me very happy, and I'll enjoy looking at the photo.'

'Here are your Mum and Dad now,' she said. 'I won't stop because they'll want to chat with you.'

'Please stay for a few more minutes,' I begged. I was anxious to keep Mary by the bedside to offset the tension I felt in the company of my parents.

They reached my bedside and Mary stood to one side. 'Hello,' said my mother, in her usual formal manner, and kissed me quickly.

'Hello,' exclaimed my father. 'You don't look as bad as I expected.'

My parents chatted to Mary for a little while and then she said she had to go. 'Write to me, and tell me how you get on,' she whispered, as she squeezed my hand. 'As soon as you're well enough come and see us.'

'Thanks for everything, Mary,' I said and sadly watched her go.

For the rest of the visiting time I managed to keep a conversation going by asking about people we knew. I was relieved when the bell went to indicate that time was up. I said goodbye to my parents as they left.

Alone in bed I thought about the consequences of my recent hysterectomy operation. Now I could never give birth to a child. I began to feel a sense of loss of my womanhood. Even though I had never seriously considered the prospect of having a child of my own, the sudden realisation that I had no longer any choice in the matter anyway came to me like a blast of cold air on a windy day. In addition to this new aspect I also had the sudden feeling that I would be undesirable to men. I reasoned to myself that most men who wished to marry would also want to have children. What man would want me now? I felt as though something vital to my entire personality had been taken away from me and that I was no longer a real woman. I spent many weary hours trying to come to terms with this new situation but all the time I felt as though I had suddenly become a different kind of species to the rest of humanity.

Within a few days other things began to happen which worried me. One day I was sitting up in bed watching the other patients. An old lady walked across to the armchair area and went to sit on a chair. She misjudged her position, and sat hard on the floor and banged her head. Instead of feeling sorry for her, like any normal person would, I found the incident incredibly amusing, and I burst into peals of laughter. Horrified I hid under the bedcovers, but I couldn't control myself. It was some time before I stopped laughing.

There was another lady who never failed to amuse me. She shuffled past my bed at frequent intervals. Her operation had caused her to have a peculiar walk which she found distressing but to me it was hilarious.

Desperately I tried not to let anyone see me when I laughed because they would think I was very cruel and I didn't want to hurt anybody. I couldn't help seeing the funny side of distressing situations, so I put the radio earphones over my head and hoped that people would think I was laughing at an amusing programme.

I could no longer trust myself to behave in an acceptable manner, so I avoided the company of other patients. Whenever anyone tried to speak to me, I would say that I needed to go to the toilet, and so escape from what might have become an embarrassing situation.

At night-time I usually laid back and let the tears roll down my cheeks. I was filled with despair. Sleep would no longer come at will, and my mind couldn't avoid the fears and anxieties which were crowding in. I wasn't unduly concerned about my medical condition. My discomfort would last for only a few more days. I believed that physically it was just a matter of time, and I would be fit again. But I was worried about the state of my mind. In all my nursing experience I couldn't remember seeing a patient behave in the way that I was behaving now. I wouldn't relate to other patients or to the staff. I was highly amused at things which were in no way amusing, and I became anxious and upset over trivialities. My personality seemed to have turned inside out, and I could do nothing about it.

Rita came to visit me one evening. She asked me how I felt. She looked most concerned when I described my moods to her.

The next day my boss from work came to see me. I was in

a very lively frame of mind, and I chatted gaily to her, telling her about the amusing incidents of the day. I knew that I was behaving in a very excited manner over which I had no control. It was almost as if I was slightly tipsy from too much drink.

After a while she put her hand on my arm. 'You must take things slowly,' she said. 'Are you going on convalescence?'

'No,' I giggled. 'I'm going to stay with a friend in the country.'

'I'll see the sister and insist that you have a proper convalescence. I'm worried about you. I think perhaps you should see a psychiatrist. I'll ask the sister if it could be arranged while you are here.'

I dissolved into tears. 'I wish someone could help me. I feel so disturbed and miserable,' I sobbed.

The ward sister walked by at that moment and my visitor spoke to her about my need for a convalescence, and suggested that perhaps I should be referred to a psychiatrist. The sister looked surprised. 'We think she's doing very well,' she said, 'but I'll tell the consultant what you said.'

The day before I was to be discharged, the consultant came to see me. 'Sister has arranged for you to go to a convalescent home for two weeks. Now, how do you feel?'

I assumed he meant physically, so I said, 'I feel quite well, really. My aches and pains have all gone and I'm able to move around all right.'

'I'm pleased to hear it,' he said. 'Now, I've got good news for you. I'm confident that the trouble was contained in the uterus, so you should make a complete and lasting recovery. It might console you to know that you did make the right decision about wanting immediate treatment. More tumours had begun to grow, so it wouldn't have been long before we would have been forced to bring you in, and then things might not have been so straightforward.'

'Thank you,' I said. 'I'm very grateful for all you've done. I don't know how I can thank you enough.'

For the rest of the time in hospital, I felt very depressed. I sat limply by my bedside pretending to read, but I was simply looking into space. I told myself that I should be wildly happy, because the doctor had given me such reassuring news, but in some twisted way it made me feel even worse than before. My reasons for feeling depressed had now gone, yet still I felt more depressed than ever. My concern over this mental state increased, yet I felt too weary, too hopeless to tell anyone. I didn't even have the energy to ask the sister about being referred to a psychiatrist.

The journey to the convalescent home raised my spirits slightly. There were about ten rather sad looking patients in the ambulance. It was strangely reassuring to know that I was not the only person feeling miserable.

Snow was falling heavily as the ambulance bumped its way along winding country roads. The coldness matched my mood, and I felt at one with nature. I wanted to distance myself from people and I hoped that there would be no pressure on me to mix socially during my convalescence.

To my relief I found that so long as I was punctual for meals and bedtimes I had the freedom to do as I chose. I chose to go for short walks on my own in the surrounding countryside. That seemed the easiest way to avoid relating to anyone. The open space of the countryside gave me a sense of freedom so every morning and afternoon I walked along the country lanes and across the fields, paying no heed to the weather. When I was tired I sat on a wooden seat or fence and enjoyed the quietness and solitude. My desire to be alone continued in the evenings when I sat by my bedside in the dormitory. In this way I managed to cut myself off from as many people as possible for as long as I could.

Visiting was allowed at the weekends, so I made the effort to be sociable when my parents came. They noticed how dejected I was, and my father in a magnificent gesture towards me offered to buy me a car. It took a few moments to grasp the significance of what my father was saying to me, but when it did sink in I accepted his offer eagerly. I had been hoping to buy a car to use in my job, and here was my father offering to buy me one just like that. My feelings of depression suddenly became mixed up with feelings of excitement, and I hoped that having the car might help me feel well again.

When I returned home from convalescence, and in response to Pat's invitation, I went to stay with her for two weeks after Christmas.

At Pat's I no longer wished to be alone. I wanted her

company, so when she went on her visits I joined her, but I still remained sad and listless. In the evenings we listened to music, but that didn't dispel my gloom. For most of the time, I just sat and cried.

Pat became increasingly concerned. 'I'll take you to see my doctor and see what he suggests,' she said.

The next day we went to his surgery. 'My friend is very depressed,' Pat told him. He asked me the circumstances of my depression, so I told him briefly.

'I'll prescribe you some Librium tablets. That should tide you over until you go home. See your own doctor as soon as you can, and he'll decide what's best for you.'

For the remaining days I continued going out with Pat on her visits, and occasionally we went for long walks in the countryside. I dreaded the thought of going home. With Pat I felt safe. She was calm and understanding, and I didn't have to hide my sadness. At home I would have to try to appear happy in order not to worry my parents.

On returning home I spent a lot of my time lying on the settee, listening to music. One day my car arrived. I enjoyed sitting in it and I studied all the different controls, but I wasn't able to drive on my own as I hadn't passed my test.

After I'd been home a few days, Pat phoned. 'What did your doctor say?' she asked.

'I haven't been to him yet,' I replied.

'You must go to him. I'm worried stiff about you. Promise me you'll see him tomorrow.'

'All right,' I promised. 'I'll go.'

The next day I went to my doctor's, feeling very apprehensive. I told him I was taking Librium because I felt depressed, and I asked if he thought I should continue with it. Before answering, he asked me some questions.

'Can you describe how you feel?' he asked.

'I feel sad and tired all the time,' I said. 'In the mornings I can just about apply my mind to things, but as the day goes on I feel worse and worse. In the evenings I shut myself in my bedroom and cry. I dread the night-times, and I stay awake as long as I can because I have such dreadful dreams.'

'Do you mean you feel at your best in the mornings?'

'Yes,' I replied.

'That surprises me. Usually people who are suffering from depression feel at their worst in the mornings, because they dread the coming day.'

'I don't dread the day, I dread the night,' I explained.

'Your symptoms aren't typical of a reactive depression,' he said. 'I'm concerned that you shut yourself away in your bedroom in the evenings. Did you mix with people when you were on convalescence?'

'No,' I answered. 'I wanted to be alone and most days I went out walking.'

'Why did you want to be alone?' he asked.

I was beginning to feel distressed by his probing questions. 'I don't really know,' I said. 'I just had an urge to get away from people. I didn't want to be bothered with trying to relate to anyone.'

'Don't you think that was rather abnormal behaviour?' he asked.

'It never occurred to me it was abnormal,' I replied. 'It doesn't worry me that I want to be alone. What does worry me is the way I laughed at things that weren't funny when I was in the hospital, and that I still keep crying and feeling so sad.'

'It isn't good for you to avoid people,' he said. 'You must make the effort to talk to someone about your feelings. You'd better continue taking the Librium for now. Come back in two weeks' time and we'll have another chat.'

I left the surgery, wondering why the doctor was concerned about my desire to be alone. I decided to go for a walk and think the matter through. Soon I became uneasy as I remembered that desiring to be alone was the first sign of my brother's illness. I sat down on a seat by the side of the parish church, and looked back on the tragedy of his life.

My brother Alan was five years older than me. When I was a little girl he was very protective and loving towards me – an ideal brother. I was always happy when he was around because he saw to it that I had my fair share of things and he invented games for me to play. He was sensitive and caring, and it was to Alan that I would turn if I felt upset about anything. In many ways I was closer to him than to my parents.

When I was about 10 years old I noticed that he was

different. We were on holiday. He walked apart from us and he seemed to be in a world of his own. He no longer took an interest in me. He wasn't unkind, just unresponsive, and he seemed somehow anxious and unaware of my presence. I found it very disturbing. I didn't understand what was wrong, but I was worried, and I missed his companionship.

Over the next two years he became increasingly distant and he began to take on a frightened look. When he left school he obtained a clerical job in the city and he seemed to like going to work. Then one morning he decided to stay at home. My mother asked him why he wouldn't go. He said, 'Everyone's against me and they talk about me behind my back. I can't go back to work any more because everything there is against me.' From that day he developed strange eating habits. He ate only small portions of food and he began putting water in his soup to dilute it. When we asked him why he wouldn't eat properly, he replied, 'Because of the starving millions.' Then he began pacing up and down the room, repeating loudly, 'I believe on the Lord Jesus Christ. Do you hear me? I believe on the Lord Jesus Christ.' He looked really scared, and insisted that we listen to him. This became the daily pattern of his life.

It was obvious that there was something seriously wrong with Alan, so my father took him to see a doctor. On their return my father said, 'The doctor thinks Alan is suffering from a very serious mental illness. He advised us to get a second opinion, and he's made an appointment with a Harley Street psychiatrist.'

The next week my father took Alan to Harley Street to see a Christian psychiatrist. When they returned home my father was angry in a way that I had never seen before. My brother went straight upstairs and shut himself in his bedroom.

'What happened?' asked my mother anxiously.

'Don't talk to me about psychiatrists,' shouted my father. 'We were with him for five minutes. That's all. Five minutes. Alan sat there like a dummy and wouldn't say a word. He just stared in front of himself. The psychiatrist asked me a few questions, and then he said, 'There's no hope for the boy unless you get him into hospital. He's very ill with schizophrenia.' Then he stood up, held out his hand and asked for five guineas. Fancy saying there was no hope in front of the boy. These people are insensitive money-grabbers.'

'What's schizophrenia?' asked my mother, as she slumped pale and limp into the armchair.

'It's a split mind,' replied my father. 'It means he can't think straight any more.'

In the remaining days that my brother was at home he sat lifeless in his room. All attempts to get him to respond failed. It was as though life had come to a sudden full stop. He just drank water and ate a little food that my mother took up to him. One day an ambulance arrived to take him to a mental hospital. He wouldn't stand up or move so he had to be carried out of the house.

I ran up to him as he was being carried down the front path. 'Goodbye, Alan,' I called. 'I'll see you soon.' He didn't respond. The ambulance disappeared down the road and I ran to my bedroom, flung myself on the bed and cried. How cruel life was.

Alan was allowed visitors on Wednesdays and Sundays. I begged my parents to let me go with them to see him, but they said that children under 16 weren't allowed to visit. I was only twelve at the time. However, I pestered them so much that after Alan had been in hospital for a month, my parents agreed to take me with them.

I shall never forget the walk through the hospital grounds. There were several patients gardening and it seemed quite peaceful. Then I looked up at the building. At nearly every window was a man's face. They stared in a manner that haunted me for weeks. I read fear in their eyes, and I was very upset. We walked to the door of the ward, and my parents asked if I could see my brother.

'I'm sorry,' was the reply. 'We aren't allowed to let children in. She must wait in the staff room.'

For two long hours I sat and waited, trying to imagine what it was like for Alan to be in a place with people who looked so terrified. It must be a nightmare. At last my parents came back. 'We told Alan you came to see him,' my mother said. 'He's going to stand at the window and wave goodbye.'

That cheered me up. As we walked through the grounds and past the windows of his ward I waved and waved, and he waved back. 'Please come home soon,' I shouted. 'I miss you so much.' We walked on, and I can still picture him waving from the window.

After two months' treatment Alan was allowed home at the weekends. My father was told to stay with him all the time, and to keep sugar lumps with him, because he was having insulin therapy, and if he felt faint he should eat sugar. Also my father was advised to take him for walks as much as possible, because fresh air and exercise were part of the treatment.

I was very excited, and I ran to meet him as he walked up the path on that first weekend home. To my delight he smiled at me, and was willing to follow me around the house, while I showed him the few changes that had occurred during his absence. After dinner we went out for a walk in the countryside. I kept close to him. I wanted to know what he was feeling, whether he liked it at the hospital, and how they treated him.

'What's this insulin therapy like?' I asked him.

'They give you an injection of insulin to make you go into a coma. Then when you come round you feel really faint, and you have to eat a lot.'

'What do they do that for?'

'I don't know. It's supposed to make you think straight,' he said.

'Do they do anything else?'

'I've had shock treatment.'

'What's that?'

'It's a sort of electric shock. It makes you stop worrying.'

'Do you like it there?'

'No I don't. I hate it. They keep talking loudly at me. They are trying to make me think differently. They keep trying to make me believe things I don't believe.'

'What things?'

'I can't explain. I just wish they would stop.'

I took Alan's arm. I wished I could go back with him to the hospital and tell them not to force Alan to believe things he didn't want to believe.

However, despite his dislike of the hospital treatment, it was obvious to me that he was much better. I was talking to him and he was answering me. He was sharing his feelings with me – something that he hadn't done for over two years.

For the next two and a half months Alan came home for the weekends and then, four and a half months after his admission and two days before his eighteenth birthday he was discharged. It was November 1953.

My father told us that the psychiatrist had warned him not to let Alan isolate himself from people. Alan was to get a job without any responsibilities, otherwise he might have a relapse. He was to eat regular, nourishing meals, and we were to encourage him to be more outgoing.

It was wonderful to have him home again. Once more I became very close to him, although it was a different relationship from the one we had experienced as young children. I was the one who wanted to be protective and helpful. I lent him my bicycle that I had recently bought out of pocket money I had been saving, and helped him to ride it. I went out for walks with him and encouraged him to talk about himself. My father had found a job for him in a nursery picking tomatoes. I showed as much interest as I could, and I talked to him about my life at school, and although I was only 13 at the time, I desperately wanted to see my brother leading a happy normal life again.

Within a few months Alan became discontented with his job in the nursery. He was intelligent and he wanted to use his brain. He decided to become a teacher. My father advised him against this because of the strain involved, but Alan insisted that this was what he wanted to do.

He enrolled for an O level course at a local technical college, to add to his R.S.A. certificates. He also began applying to teacher training colleges. He became obsessed with the idea of teaching, but after receiving a number of rejections, he wrote to one of the colleges and asked for an explanation. Their reply was that he must first do his two years' national service. He then became obsessed with doing his national service. My father tried to explain to him that because of his illness, he was exempt. Alan persisted and he wrote to various people. Eventually he received a letter saying that because he had been certified as mentally ill, he was not required to do national service.

From that moment Alan changed dramatically. He blamed my father for having him certified. It became impossible to reason with him, and his fits of temper became increasingly violent. He claimed that everyone was against him. By this time he had finished his O levels, and he found a clerical job in the City of London.

Then his behaviour became more bizarre. At home he would stand in the middle of the room on one leg with his arms outstretched so that no one could get past him. If anyone touched him, he yelled in fury. He said that he was a parrot, and he made animal and bird-like noises. At this time my brother was twenty years old, and this weird behaviour continued for many weary months. In desperation my parents tried to get him to see a doctor again but this only increased his anger and resentment. Alan convinced himself that he was the sane one and that everybody else was ill. He said that if my father brought a doctor to the house he would 'do the doctor in.'

For the next three years he worked in a range of different clerical jobs, and in between jobs he stayed at home for several weeks. During these periods at home he had 'clearing out sessions' when he systematically cut up his belongings with a pair of scissors. Nothing was sacred – books, clothing, photographs all became chopped up into tiny pieces which were then wrapped into neat parcels and placed in the dustbin. When his savings were gone he went out and found another job.

Shortly after his twenty-third birthday he left his latest job because he believed everyone was against him, and from that time onwards he spent his mornings at home in bed. He didn't just lie in bed: he rolled himself in a ball right under the covers. We were amazed that he didn't suffocate himself. Often he went out for walks in the evenings and occasionally it was possible to talk to him. At times he actually showed concern for me and my mother. He would insist on helping with the domestic chores. However, if anyone disagreed with him, or tried to reason with him, he became angry. Often he grabbed my mother by the shoulders and shook her violently, and on a number of occasions he did the same to me. My father was unable to make contact with him at all, partly because of Alan's resentment and distrust and partly because my father was so rarely at home. He was at work in London during the day, and for about four evenings a week and all day Sundays he was out on Church business as a lay preacher. My other brother was away at university so most of the burden of trying to help Alan fell on my mother and myself.

My desperation grew. I loved Alan more than I loved anyone, yet I was seeing him suffer day after day, and he was making me and my mother suffer. As a family we were being destroyed. I had to do something, so I tried praying to God. Every night without fail I knelt down by my bedside and begged God for a miracle to come into our lives. I racked my brain, trying to think of ways of helping my brother, but my attempts were in vain. He read ulterior motives into everything. Any gesture or cough was interpreted by him as evil that I was directing against him. Then I tried to understand the workings of his mind, and to see things from his point of view, and in some ways I succeeded. He accused people of being hypocrites and inconsistent, but I was able to see what he meant, and I agreed with him. 'Don't trust anyone,' he often said to me. 'You've got to watch out for yourself, or they'll get you.' 'Yes, there are lots of wicked people around. I'll be careful,' I would reply. This pleased him, and slowly I came to understand his thinking and we developed a relationship that worked.

At times he showed concern for my wellbeing. If I made a noise he no longer took this as a sign of evil against himself. He became anxious if I was late home from work. He sometimes begged me to leave my job as a bank clerk in London because London was an evil city. As long as I agreed with him there were no problems, but when I tried to reason with him, or to suggest that he might be mistaken, he became angry and violent.

We went for walks together but these were painful experiences which I'll never forget. He made strange gestures, waving his arms in all directions, jumping up and down, shrieking at the top of his voice and pulling grotesque faces. He climbed up at the fences and hedges as we made our way along the road. He invited me to join him in these mad capers, and scolded me for worrying about what people would think of us. Sometimes he broke into a run and I ran after him, terrified of what he might do.

Slowly his life became intolerable. Every evening he sat on the floor in the middle of the sitting room with his head in his hands, crying and groaning like a monstrous child. 'What can I do? There's no hope for me. Whatever can I do?' When we mentioned the word 'doctor' he lashed out at us. It was amazing that nothing in the house was smashed.

The end came suddenly. On 21 January 1958, 2 months after my brother's twenty-third birthday, he sat with his head in his hands, crying that there was no hope left for him. I pleaded with him to trust us and let us help him. I said that I'd find a doctor who would understand. He jumped up in a rage and shouted right in my face, 'You leave me alone. You are as bad as the rest of them.' He shook me and slapped me in the face, then he turned and rushed wildly out of the house. As a rule he would return after about an hour or so, full of apologies. That terrible evening he did not return.

Next morning my father went to the police to report that my brother was missing. The suspense was agonising. For two weeks I continued going to work. Everywhere I looked around myself, wondering if Alan would suddenly appear, although in my heart I felt that I would never see him again. At work my eyes kept brimming with tears, and by the third week I had lost my voice and had to stay at home.

One day, three weeks after Alan's disappearance, the police called at our home. A body answering Alan's description had been recovered from the River Thames by a police launch. The police believed that the body had been in the water for about three weeks. Somebody had to identify the body. We telephoned my father at work and he went immediately.

Later that evening my father came home. He was visibly shaken, pale and drawn. My worst fears were realised as I learnt that my dear brother was dead and gone forever. I felt like rushing out of the house and shouting, 'Is this the way God answers prayers?' But I struggled to hide my feelings. As a Christian I believed it was wrong to question God's actions, and in a fit of stifled anguish I reasoned to myself that this sad loss was of God's choosing, and who was I to argue?

I felt emotionally numb.

At the funeral the church was packed. Alan's coffin stood on two trestles by the pulpit. I stared through tear-filled eyes wondering at the mystery of death. Deep inside me I felt nothing but disgust at the lack of support that had been given Alan by our church. Why did all these people feel the need to attend his funeral now that he was gone? Why didn't they befriend him during his life, when he was in such despair?

At the graveside I overheard people saying how sad it was for my parents to lose their eldest child in such tragic circumstances. No one seemed to think that I should be pitied, and yet I had been closer to my brother than to anyone, he was my nearest and dearest. Watching his coffin being slowly lowered into the ground I suddenly felt desperately alone. It was almost like becoming an orphan. However, I resolved to keep my distress to myself. I held my head high; I felt bitter, yet I refused to admit even to myself that I had such feelings inside me. I had been taught that it was wrong to be bitter. Why had Alan suffered so much? It was sinful to blame God, or the church, or my parents, so I had to blame myself. I should have prayed harder in my brother's cause. I should have had more faith in God's almighty power. Then my prayers might have been answered and Alan might have been cured. I accused myself of being partly responsible for my brother's suffering and death.

I felt very upset as I recalled my brother's illness and death all those years ago. Then I grew uneasy. Could it be that the tendency to isolate myself from other people and the way in which I hid my feelings were leading me down the path to schizophrenia? This was how my brother had begun his illness, and it seemed to me that I too was now at risk. I went through all the arguments about the origin of mental illness, but whatever the cause, environmental or genetic, I began to feel that it could be my turn next. First my brother and now me. As far as I was concerned there was no other illness more dreadful than schizophrenia. It had a devastating effect on the victim and also on the victim's family. I sat motionless, sick with fear.

Gradually I was aware of feeling cold. I realised that I had been sitting thinking about my brother for the past two hours, and it was now growing dusk. I pulled myself together and made my way home, feeling lost, confused and frightened.

Every night for the next week I dreamt about Alan. Sometimes he was just there floating about in my dreams, but at other times he came through much more intensely, pleading with me to help him. In one terrible dream he tried to strangle me, and I woke up lathered in perspiration and gasping for air.

Something had to be done quickly. I believed that my only course of action was to return to work. At work I would be kept busy, I would be kept in a regular routine and I would be kept in contact with lots of people. My colleagues at work were also very understanding and were willing to give me all the help they could.

In a few days I braced myself and went to my doctor to tell him that I felt much better physically and wanted to return to work. He was unhappy about it, and he said that I needed more rest. I appealed to him, and warned him that if I didn't return to work as soon as possible, I might lose the ability to face people. He must have seen by the look of dismay on my face that I really had had enough rest and needed to get involved with the world again.

'All right,' he said, 'but come back to me if you find things are too much for you to cope with.'

# 4 Depression

(January 1967 - February 1967)

I hoped that a return to work would see an end to my fears and anxieties about my mental health. I had an interesting job and helpful colleagues with whom I was able to share my feelings. On the day that I returned to work I felt excited, and confident that I would be able to forget the torment of the past few months. I spent the morning reading through the records to see which families needed an urgent visit, and in the afternoon I made a few calls, but at the end of the day my fears and anxieties still remained; they dominated my mind. My confidence was gone.

In desperation, on my second day I begged Rita to help me relearn the job. She had to go over most of the basic points with me relating to the care of babies, feeding and weaning them. We talked about the common problems that worry mothers, and what they might ask me at the child health clinic that afternoon. We covered sufficient ground to enable me to face my first clinic session. Rita was seeing mothers at the same time in another room, which was reassuring, because I knew that if I did get stuck I could ask her advice. Luckily for me, most of the mothers were more eager to tell me about their babies than to ask my opinion on anything. By listening to the mothers and observing the babies I increased my awareness of some of the problems. Somehow I coped on those busy Tuesday afternoons, although the mental effort was exhausting.

It was also my responsibility to run the relaxation and mothercraft classes on Wednesday mornings. I got by the first week by asking the mothers what they had done previously.

After that I had time to prepare, and Wednesday mornings soon became the highlight of my working week. The rest of the week was a struggle. It was a constant battle between my anxieties and the demands of my job.

By Thursday lunchtime I felt exhausted, and could no longer fight the terror and panic that was coming over me. My first Thursday was typical of many that followed. As I sat alone eating my lunch I felt as though my heart kept missing a beat. I had a sense of foreboding: a sinking feeling inside me. The sensation overwhelmed me like a giant wave on a stormy sea. I jumped up, desperate to escape. I rushed round the clinic, trying to relieve the tension, but my panic increased. Somehow I had to find help, but there was no one around. I saw the phone on my desk, and I seized it with relief. I'd phone Pat.

Luckily she was at home. 'Pat, I feel terrified. I'm so frightened. What can I do?'

'What are you frightened of?' she asked.

'I don't know,' I gasped. 'Everything is crowding in on me. I want to cry all the time,' I sobbed into the phone. Panic held me in its grip.

'Give yourself time,' Pat said. Her voice sounded nervous, as my panic transmitted itself down the telephone lines to her. 'You can't expect to feel better straight away.'

'I know,' I replied, 'but when the panic takes over, I lose control.'

Pat talked about ordinary things and in a while I calmed down. After about ten minutes I said, 'Thanks Pat, I'll be all right now.' We chatted for a few more moments and then said goodbye. I placed the receiver down. The phone call had dispelled the panic but now came a feeling of hopelessness. I sat at my desk with my head on my arms and cried.

On Fridays I managed better. I normally visited elderly people, and in the afternoons I called on mothers with post-natal depression, which involved listening to the mothers' anxieties. This I was readily able to do.

That became the pattern of my week. It was relentless. No matter how hard I tried I failed to control the panics and depressions which swept over me all the time; yet I had to keep working and struggling and fighting because I knew that if I gave in, I would be finished.

The night-times were even worse. Alone in bed I was at the mercy of my dreams, but bad as they were, an even more frightening sensation came to add to my terror. I had gone to sleep when suddenly I began shaking violently and I was choking. Then my whole body became stiff. I tried to move my arms but I couldn't. Then I tried to move my legs, but they were as heavy as lead. I lay there, not knowing whether I was in a dream, or in a trance, or in a fit of some kind, but I knew that something terrible and frightening was happening to me. This was the first of a number of similar attacks.

In desperation I went to the doctor and told him about these terrors in the night. He prescribed sleeping tablets which proved to be a great help. At last I was able to sleep in peace.

I wanted to take driving lessons and I managed to get a few people from the church to sit with me while I drove my car around the streets where I lived. While in the car I felt confident and my worries seemed to fade away, but these moments didn't last because the fears and tensions hung around me like shadows.

In order to avoid causing my parents anxiety, I often shut myself in another room so that they wouldn't see me depressed, and listened to music. The music that I liked most was the sad kind which blended in with my own feelings. The music didn't dispel my sadness, but in a strange way it enabled me to drift outside of myself, so that I became an observer of my own sufferings. On having achieved a degree of detachment from my mental anguish I often progressed from sad music to songs which were in keeping with my mood and which might help me to persevere in my struggle against the onset of mental illness. A song which meant a lot to me at that time was a song in praise of fir trees; even in the depths of winter they retain their foliage. I became inspired by these trees and I hoped that I could persevere through the winter of my depression just as the fir trees persevere throughout theirs.

For three weeks I lived in the hope that I would gradually overcome my feelings of panic. Not only did I hope. I reasoned with myself and kept telling myself that I had no need to worry. There was a very good chance that physically I would make a complete recovery. I had a car which I was learning to drive, I had good friends, a comfortable home, a worthwhile job. The doctor had prescribed pills to tide me over the effects of the shock I had experienced so I could see no reason why I should be haunted by this terrible sense of dread and foreboding. It should be declining.

But it wasn't. On my fourth Monday back at work I felt wretched. I sat at my desk and tried to sort out the visits for the day, but although I sifted through some records, I couldn't take anything in or make a decision about my visits. I must have been flicking uselessly through record cards for some time when Rita came and sat down beside me. 'You feel depressed, don't you?' she said.

'Yes,' I murmured.

'What are you going to do about it?'

'What more can I do?' I asked. 'I'm taking Librium regularly, and I keep telling myself there's no reason why I should be like this, but it doesn't make any difference.'

'You need more help.'

'What else can my doctor do?' I asked. 'I don't want him to send me into hospital. They'd probably give me ECT* which I don't want.'

'I think you need psychotherapy,' she said.

I was stunned. Deep down I knew that I needed help, but I wanted to believe that I could overcome the depression on my own in a few weeks' time. Rita seemed to think otherwise. She was implying that I was mentally ill and, for me, mental illness was synonymous with my brother's condition, which I felt to be the most fearful illness that anyone could have.

'I'm frightened,' I said. 'It's dreadful to have to admit that you're mentally ill and need treatment. I can't imagine anything worse.'

'You are strange,' she commented. 'What's so awful in admitting that you need psychotherapy?'

'I don't trust psychiatrists,' I said. 'I know I need to talk to someone about my anxieties, but I'd rather talk to someone I know. Can't I see your husband a couple of evenings a

*Electro-convulsive therapy.

week? He's a minister, so perhaps he could advise me.'

'Don't be silly,' Rita said. 'My husband isn't a psychiatrist. You need professional psychiatric help. I'm taking you straight to your doctor to ask him for his advice.'

She handed me my coat and led me out of the clinic. I felt too weak to argue so I did as I was told and climbed into her car.

Before long we were in the doctor's surgery. I sat listlessly in the chair and looked to Rita to speak up for me.

'She's deeply depressed,' Rita said to the doctor. 'We are doing all we can to support her at the clinic, but she needs more help than we can give.'

'I know,' replied the doctor, 'but there's nothing more I can do unless she breaks down. Then I can get her into hospital, where she'll be able to have ECT.'

'No,' I whispered, desperately, 'I mustn't break down, and I don't want ECT. I want to have control over what's going on.' I felt really terrified.

'Then you must carry on with the drug therapy, and we'll continue to give you all the support we can.'

My lips trembled, and I began to cry quietly. There seemed no way out. I was trapped in my own prison of despair.

Then Rita spoke. 'Don't you think psychotherapy would help her?'

'Yes, I do,' he replied. 'She needs psychotherapy, but there's no way of getting it through the National Health Service. I used to be able to refer people to the Tavistock Centre, but they are no longer accepting patients from as far afield as this because they've been inundated. In this area there's a two-year waiting list for psychotherapy, so we've no option but to continue with the drugs.'

'What about her having psychotherapy privately?'

'If she's prepared to spend a lot of money, and if she can find a psychotherapist, then all right, but I don't know anyone that I can recommend.'

'I know of an exceptionally good psychoanalyst who accepts patients privately,' Rita said.

The doctor looked both surprised and interested. He leant forward. 'Can you arrange that?'

'I think so,' Rita said.

The doctor stood up. 'Thank you. I hope you're successful. Let me know what the outcome is.'

We left the surgery and got back into Rita's car. 'Well?' she asked. 'Would you like me to arrange a private consultation for you?'

'Yes please.'

'Aren't you going to ask me about the psychiatrist I have in mind?'

'I trust you,' I said, 'and I've nothing to lose.' I sank back in the seat and continued to cry quietly. All my energy and willpower had gone. I was content to put myself in Rita's hands.

It was lunchtime. 'We'll go back to my house and have a snack,' Rita said, 'and while we're there, I'll try to arrange an appointment for you. If you do get an appointment, you'll have to travel to Harley Street.'

'I don't mind where I travel to so long as he can help me,' I whispered through my tears.

We drove to her home and she took me inside and told me to sit down. She then went into the kitchen and returned with a bowl of soup and sandwiches. 'You start,' she said.

She disappeared and I heard her dialling a number. A few seconds passed and she asked for Dr Goldblatt. After a while I heard her voice again. I was able to pick out a few phrases; 'She's extremely depressed . . . I think it's very urgent . . . she had a hysterectomy . . . only 26 . . . .' Soon after, Rita reappeared looking pleased. 'Dr Goldblatt is busy, and he has no free time, but he's agreed to see you in his lunch hour on Wednesday. You're to be there at 12 o'clock. You must realise that he hasn't promised he'll treat you, but at least he'll give you an opinion.'

'Thank you,' I said, and meant it. At last there might be a glimmer of hope. I was curious. 'What's he like? Do you know him personally?' I asked.

'No, I don't know him personally,' she replied, 'but I know a lot about him. A close friend of mine is a psychiatric social worker, and she works with him at the clinic where he does psychotherapy for the NHS. She says he's a marvellous psychiatrist, excellent at his job, kind and caring. He's very well balanced, and happily married. You can think yourself lucky that he's giving up his lunchtime for you.'

'I do appreciate that,' I replied. I felt relieved, and very grateful for all that Rita was doing for me.

After lunch we returned to the clinic and I spent the afternoon planning for Wednesday. I would have to leave the clinic by 10.30 a.m. to ensure being in time for my midday appointment, so I arranged with a colleague that she would finish my morning relaxation class for me. I expected to be back by 2 p.m. so I sorted out which visits would be due for the afternoon.

I wished the time would pass quickly. Dr Goldblatt was my last hope, and I was anxious to meet him.

Pat phoned me that evening. My last letter had worried her so much that she begged me to go to my doctor and ask for more help.

I told her about this new development. 'I have an appointment in Harley Street,' I said, 'with a psychiatrist.'

'Thank God,' she said. 'Tell him he's *got* to treat you. You need to analyse your depression. You must accept his treatment and stick to it, whatever you feel like. Don't give up.'

I didn't tell my parents. They wouldn't have understood. To them, a Harley Street psychiatrist was 'an insensitive money grabber.' I needed approval for this step I was taking. Anyone who might try to discourage me had to be avoided. Deep inside I began to feel guilty about going to Harley Street. I was betraying my brother, because a Harley Street psychiatrist hadn't helped him. Also my Christian upbringing affected my feelings about psychotherapy. I should pray, and have faith in God to make me better. But I had tried all that. Time and again I'd begged for God's help, using every formula in the book. All to no avail. God just wasn't listening and I couldn't wait any longer. Yet I wondered if it were wrong to seek help from a psychiatrist who wasn't even a Christian. There was a real conflict inside me, but right or wrong I would go to him and if he offered to help me, I would accept that help because now there was no other way. I was imprisoned in my mind and this psychiatrist might hold the key to my release.

# 5 My Consultation with Dr Goldblatt

(15 February 1967)

On Wednesday 15 February 1967, two and a half months after my hysterectomy, I set off to keep my appointment with Dr Goldblatt in Harley Street.

At last there seemed to be a chance to escape from the horror of the past few months. It was a cold, bright day as I made my way to the underground station. Waiting on the platform I reflected on the weeks that had now gone by. I struggled to find a word that would adequately describe what I was living through. One word kept recurring in my mind: nightmare.

The train arrived and I snapped back into reality. I slumped into a seat, the doors closed and as the train hissed out of the station, I drifted back into a state of reverie. Had I really been dreaming after all? Were the past months a trick of the mind? What was real and what was the truth? My mind was in a turmoil. I knew I was on a train going somewhere; I could vaguely see the faces of the other passengers all around me. Dark shadows flickered past the windows as the train roared on beneath the London streets. I felt as if I was about to wake up and find that there had been no depression, no operation, no menstrual problems. How wonderful it would be to go back to my carefree days: the days of my cycling holiday to Luxembourg. I smiled to myself, recalling those happy times and the funny incidents that had taken place. I remembered a red-faced Frenchman who had chased us on his motorbike down a motorway. We had cycled onto the motorway by mistake. I remembered the noise of car hooters from passing motorists, who were trying to warn us off. We thought they were hooting at the spectacle of three girls in tight shorts. I also remembered a romantic evening in a youth hostel at Dunkirk. There were young people from all parts of Europe. We had been singing late into the night. We sang Dutch, French, German and British songs. We had been strangers and yet we felt as though we had known one another all our lives. There seemed to be a bond between us. In my mind we were singing away into the night and I began to feel relaxed and happy.

Yet soon my happiness made me anxious. Would Dr Goldblatt believe that I really was depressed? Was I in fact depressed? I was learning to drive, and in a few weeks' time I would be taking my driving test. I had no anxieties about it. I felt quite composed and confident. I also felt confident about talking to Dr Goldblatt. Yet there was this underlying feeling of fear and desperation. Yes, that was it. Moments of confidence and happiness with my memories; then moments of fear and terror.

I arrived at Harley Street in plenty of time so I continued walking around the block until a quarter to twelve.

The time of my appointment had at last arrived. The building in front of me was a large, imposing looking place with a huge front door that was firmly closed. I felt apprehensive. I paused on the step; I looked around me. Everything seemed normal and ordinary, and yet at the same time everything seemed so unreal. What was I doing here? What was happening to me?

I reached out and firmly pressed the bell button. This was it. The moment of truth. The door swung open almost immediately and a young receptionist appeared smiling in the doorway. I said, 'I have an appointment with Dr Goldblatt at 12 o'clock,' and I gave her my name.

'Dr Goldblatt is expecting you,' she said. 'He'll be ready in about ten minutes' time. Please come this way.' I followed her along a short passage way. She pointed to a door in front of us. 'That's the cloakroom,' she said. Then she indicated a door on the right. 'You can wait in there.'

I went into the waiting room and sat down. Slowly I took stock of my surroundings. The room was large – larger than I had imagined. It was almost like a stately home with fitted carpets and comfortable settees. There were mirrors on the walls and at the far end of the room were double doors. The room didn't seem to impose itself on me and I felt strange and alone.

The double doors swung open and the receptionist appeared and said, 'Dr Goldblatt is free now. Please come this way.' I followed her to the foot of a wide staircase. She said, 'Dr Goldblatt's room is at the top of the stairs on the right. Go straight in.'

By the time I reached the landing, Dr Goldblatt was standing in the doorway. He smiled kindly. 'Please come in and sit down.' His voice was quiet, yet distinct. I walked into the room. He followed me and closed the door. I looked around. Behind the door was a couch, and beyond the couch was an armchair. I hesitated. Surely he didn't expect me to lie on that couch. Then I noticed that he was walking across the room towards his desk. There was a chair on either side. He went behind the desk and sat down, and pointed to the chair opposite. Relieved, I sat down.

I searched his face for clues that would tell me something about him. He was still smiling, not just with his mouth but with his eyes. He had kind eyes. His demeanor gave me the feeling that he cared and understood. He was of medium height and slim build with black hair and brown eyes. I imagined he was about 50 years old. He was wearing a neat brown suit. I thought I could trust him but I was cautious. I was so vulnerable. I had to be careful, and make sure that I was fully aware of all that was going on.

He broke the silence. 'Your friend asked me to see you,' he began. 'Can you tell me a little about yourself?'

'I feel so depressed,' I murmured.

'Yes,' he said gently.

I hesitated. I was unable to put my fears and anxieties into words. I wasn't nervous of him, or worried about what he might think of me, but he had given me no lead. How could I explain my moods and fears, my terrors and despair? I looked at him helplessly. If only he would ask a few specific questions that I could answer.

However, it seemed that he had no intention of asking questions, so I had to say something. 'I had a hysterectomy,' I said, 'for suspected cancer, and I feel depressed.'

'What do you mean by depressed?' he queried.

'I want to keep on crying. My moods are up and down like a yo-yo. That worries me, because I never used to be a moody person. I feel frightened, but I can't understand why. I can't pull myself out of it. I try my hardest but it doesn't do any good.'

'Have you ever been depressed before?'

'No,' I replied.

'Are you sure?'

I hesitated. 'I did feel very slightly depressed once, but it was nothing like this. I've always got through on my own.'

'Tell me about it.' He spoke quietly and gently. It was easy to confide in him.

'I had a lung operation when I was nineteen, and for about a month after, I kept wanting to cry, but I soon got back to normal.'

'What's troubling you now?' he asked.

'I don't know, and it's because I don't know that I feel so worried.' I waited for him to speak, but he didn't. I thought hard for something tangible to say. 'I'm afraid I might be frigid.'

'Why do you think you might be frigid?' he asked.

'I can't have children.'

'Why should that make you think you might be frigid?'

'I don't know,' I stammered. I felt confused. I decided to change the subject. 'I have terrible nightmares. Sometimes I'm afraid to go to sleep at night because of them.'

'Tell me about these nightmares.'

'I keep dreaming about my brother who died eight years ago. He had schizophrenia. I can't get him out of my mind. Usually he looks very frightened, and he appeals to me to help, but I can't help him however much I try. I feel helpless, and the fear in his eyes haunts me.'

'When he was alive, did you want to help him, but found you couldn't?'

'Yes,' I replied. 'For years I tried, but it was no good. Sometimes I got cross with him because he wouldn't see reason. I still feel I should have done more to help him.'

'How did you feel when he died?' he asked.

'In some ways I felt that it was a blessing. Life was a torment to him, and it was dreadful for us. Sometimes, though, I feel almost that I killed him, that perhaps deep down I had wished him dead, and he sensed it, and killed himself.' I choked back my tears.

'You said that sometimes you got cross with him. Was he ever cross with you?' he asked.

'Yes, often, but he was always very sorry afterwards.'

'He would only have been aggressive with someone he felt safe with, and with whom there was an intimate link. If he thought you wished him dead, he wouldn't have felt able to express his feelings in front of you. He must have felt close to you, just as you felt close to him.'

His words comforted me. He asked me several more questions about my feelings for Alan, and about our relationship. I imagined he dwelt on the subject in order to comfort me, and I was grateful.

It was easy to talk to him. We seemed to be on the same wavelength, and he didn't use complicated words or phrases. He also gave the impression that he was concerned only for me. He didn't glance at his watch, or try to hurry me. He listened intently to everything I said, and spoke only when it was necessary to clarify my meaning and to bring out information he needed. Most of all I liked his attitude. He treated me with respect and concern, and at the same time as an equal. There was no pomp or affectation or pride in his manner. We were two people sharing a problem, and working together to discover how best to solve it.

There was a pause. I had said all that I was prepared to say. I deliberately didn't tell him that at times I wanted to cut myself off from people, and that I was worried that I might develop schizophrenia. I knew that some psychotherapists believed it was dangerous for people verging on schizophrenia to be treated by analysis, and I was afraid that if Dr Goldblatt knew everything about me he wouldn't risk treating me.

I was desperate for his help. He was the first person to

show me genuine understanding combined with a caring yet confident approach. I believed that if I missed this opportunity I would never recover.

I began to worry in case I had revealed more of my thought processes than I had intended. Perhaps he had detected how confused my mind really was. Perhaps he didn't think I was suitable for his treatment . . . The thought that I might be left alone with my nightmares and mental confusion terrified me. I had to know Dr Goldblatt's views.

'Do you think I need to have psychotherapy?' I asked at last.

'I believe that psychotherapy can help you,' he replied.

'Do you think that psychotherapy would be more suitable for me than any other form of psychiatric treatment?'

'Yes, I do.'

The relief I felt was indescribable. Either Dr Goldblatt was one of those brave psychoanalysts who was prepared to try to help a potential schizophrenic, or he didn't think I was schizophrenic. I wanted to know which was the case, but I was afraid that my worst fears might be confirmed. Instead I asked for a prognosis: 'Do you think my depression will ever go if I don't have psychotherapy?'

He seemed to be considering his answer very carefully. Then he said, 'Provided you talk through your anxieties with people you trust and who can help you understand your problems, you might be able to overcome the depression without the help of an analyst. I understand that you have a few friends whom you confide in.'

'I confide in them up to a point,' I said, 'but I couldn't possibly unburden myself completely. There's so much that's worrying me, and I have so many fears and conflicts that I'd overwhelm my friends if I told them everything. I couldn't use my friends like that. If I did, I wouldn't deserve their friendship, and I value their friendship very much.'

'Then you should have professional help,' he said.

'Please, will you help me?' I begged.

He smiled. 'I'm willing to offer you psychotherapy once a week. I prefer more frequent appointments, but at present I have no time available. To start with I can fit you in where I have a cancellation, and then I shall offer you a regular time as soon as I am able to do so.'

'Thank you,' I said. I heaved a sigh of relief. At last I had found someone who understood how hopeless I felt, who recognised that I needed help, and who was able and willing to lead me out of the darkness and confusion in which I was lost.

Our eyes met. He leant forward, and rested his arms on the desk. 'Let me explain about the treatment I am offering to you,' he said. 'I am a Freudian psychoanalyst and I use the analytic method in my treatment. I shall want you to lie on the couch and free associate. That means that you say whatever comes into your mind, regardless of whether or not you see the relevance of what you are thinking. I shall sit on a chair at the end of the couch out of your sight, and I shall use what you say to discover the nature of your anxieties. By examining those anxieties you will come to have a greater insight into yourself and the workings of your mind. I shall show you why you feel lost and bewildered. When you understand that, you will be in a position to be able to help yourself through your depression. I shall guide you, and equip you with the psychological tools you need, and teach you how to use them.'

'I want that sort of help. I'm desperate to understand what's going on in my mind, but . . .' I hesitated, and looked down at my hands on my lap. How could I face that couch? How could I talk to someone and trust someone I couldn't see? I needed to look into his eyes for reassurance, to check from his expression that he was listening to me. I wanted personal contact with him. The couch seemed isolated, detached. Yet I couldn't express my thoughts. Surely my inability to state my fears and alarms proved that I couldn't free associate. What could I do? How could I be treated if I couldn't carry out his instructions in that way? Somehow I had to force myself to tell him of my doubts.

'I don't think I'll be able to free associate,' I said at last, 'and I think that lying on a couch will make me feel unable to communicate. Can't I sit in a chair, like I am now? I'll be able to talk much more easily if I can see you. It gives me more confidence to look directly at a person. Couldn't you analyse what I say and discover the origins of my problems just as easily face to face?'

'I have found from experience that the analytic method

works more effectively if the analyst remains out of sight,' he replied.

Still I felt uneasy. 'But I'm afraid I'll be no good as a patient if I'm expected to free associate,' I said. 'I'm not a spontaneous person. I don't show my feelings easily. Usually I only say what I choose to say. I know I'll be selective in telling you my thoughts if I have to lie on that couch, just looking into space.' I paused. Our eyes met again. He didn't move or speak. I realised that he wasn't going to change his style to suit me. If I wanted his help, I would have to accept his methods. And I did want his help – desperately. Left to myself I felt that I would not be able to fend off the breakdown which I knew was coming. I shuddered at the thought.

Dr Goldblatt was waiting patiently for my decision.

'I'm sorry,' I said. 'I wasn't trying to be awkward. I'll do my best to cooperate, but I'm afraid that I might work against you unintentionally. I've read quite a lot over the years about mental illness and about Freud, and that could influence what I say and don't say. I'd be tempted to highlight and talk about what I think is significant, rather than say everything that comes to mind. I honestly don't think I'm capable of free associating.'

Dr Goldblatt smiled. 'I don't expect you to free asssociate perfectly right from the start. It takes time.'

'But would my knowledge of mental illness interfere with your analysing?'

'I can make allowances for that. It shouldn't be an insurmountable problem.'

I was relieved that he was taking my doubts and reservations seriously, and I was reassured. 'What is your fee?' I asked.

'Four guineas (£4.20) for a session of 50 minutes, payable at the end of every month,' he replied.

It was less than I'd expected. 'I definitely want to come to you for treatment, if you're still prepared to help me,' I said.

'You must realise that psychotherapy is no quick cure,' he emphasized. 'It could take some time before your symptoms begin to diminish. You need to persevere in working towards understanding your problems, and it can be painful when you are confronted by emotions that you have avoided in the past.

But if you are determined, I can help you through those painful experiences.'

'I know that psychotherapy takes time,' I said, 'I accept that. Once I set out to do something, it's my nature to see it through. I'm desperate to get better, so I'll persevere as long as I believe psychotherapy can help me.'

'Good,' he said, and stood up. 'I can see you next Tuesday at 4 p.m.'

'Thank you, I'll be here.' I followed him to the door. He opened it for me and I walked out on to the landing and down the stairs. When I reached the bottom stair I glanced up. Dr Goldblatt was still standing at the doorway. He seemed deep in thought.

I walked through the waiting room and out into the street. I looked at my watch. It was gone one o'clock. I had been with Dr Goldblatt for over an hour.

I ran all the way to the underground station, not wanting to be late back for work. I managed to squeeze myself through the closing doors of a train, and flopped into the nearest seat. It was some time before I had composed myself, and could breathe normally. The ordeal of the last few months had sapped my strength, and I had lost my physical stamina.

I sat back in the seat in a trance. Dr Goldblatt had encouraged me to talk so freely about my anxieties that I now felt mentally drained as well as physically exhausted. After a while I realised that I was hungry. It hadn't occurred to me that morning to bring a packed lunch to eat on the train. However, there was nothing I could do but wait.

Eventually the train arrived at my station. I could hardly bring myself to move. Slowly I wandered off the train and walked to the bus stop. I leaned against the bus shelter for support.

I arrived back at work at about 2.15 p.m. Just as I sat down the caretaker came in. 'Take it easy for a few minutes,' she said. 'I'll bring you a cup of coffee and some biscuits. The visiting can wait.' I sat quietly and tried to compose myself. The caretaker reappeared. 'Rita told me you had to see a doctor. Is everything all right?'

'Yes thanks. Nothing to worry about. I'll be fine.' I was

touched by the kindness and understanding I was receiving from all the people in my clinic. I didn't think I could survive without them.

After about a quarter of an hour I went visiting. I managed to listen to the problems of the mothers and gave them my advice but I was relieved when it was time to go back to the clinic.

Rita was waiting for me. 'How did you get on?' she asked.

'I was very impressed with Dr Goldblatt,' I replied. 'I'm to go next Tuesday for my first session of psychotherapy, and he'll give me a regular time as soon as he can fit me in.'

Rita was delighted. 'He's extremely busy,' she said, 'so he must feel confident that he can help you, or he wouldn't be seeing you so quickly. You'd better get official permission to have time off.'

I hadn't thought of that. I decided to phone my boss straight away. I soon got through. 'Things have been getting on top of me since my hysterectomy,' I explained, 'so I'm going to have psychotherapy once a week, starting next Tuesday. It will mean having time off, but I don't know yet when my other appointments will be. Will that be all right?'

'I'm so sorry,' she said. 'Of course it will be all right, so long as you let me know when you'll be away, and provided you make sure your work's covered properly. I hope you're soon better.'

To my relief she asked no questions, and I was surprised how helpful and understanding she'd been.

That evening I wrote to Pat, giving her an account of my meeting with Dr Goldblatt. I needed to share my feelings with someone I trusted, and who cared what happened to me, and approved of what I was doing. Pat would also act as a sounding board and as a safety net if I should fall. The treatment might backfire on me. Dr Goldblatt might be too forceful, or try to change my personality. Pat would understand and be able to judge if things were going wrong. I trusted her judgement. With her support I could risk putting myself in the hands of a psychiatrist. As long as she was behind me I would be able to persevere.

Every week while I was undergoing psychotherapy I wrote to her, sharing the experience with her, and she replied to every letter, encouraging me through all the difficulties I encountered.

I decided to keep my own record of the psychotherapy sessions. I believed in Dr Goldblatt's integrity, but I felt vulnerable. There was no reason to suppose that all his Freudian interpretations would be accurate in my case. Lying relaxed on a couch could make me susceptible to persuasion, so that I might blindly accept his views, and not examine them critically. If I wrote down everything, I would be able to look back on it later to see if I agreed with his arguments.

I didn't tell my parents about Dr Goldblatt. I felt that they wouldn't approve and might want to dissuade me from going. I wasn't ready to face opposition. My own doubts and fears were almost overwhelming me, but I knew that I had to cling to Dr Goldblatt or I would sink.

The prospect of help made my life tolerable, but the sinking feelings inside me persisted, and intermittent waves of panic continued. Nightmares plagued me if I didn't take sleeping tablets, and I longed to hide myself away and cry. Yet there was now a glimmer of hope. It was this glimmer of hope that sustained me through the coming months.

During the six days that I had to wait for my first session of psychotherapy I was constantly wondering whether I would be a suitable patient. From one point of view I knew I would be. Once I made up my mind to do something I was determined to put my best into it. I could also tolerate and endure a lot, providing it was not in vain. Not for one moment did I think I'd run away from the treatment, how ever hard it might become. I'd pay what it cost, suffer what had to be suffered, for as long as it took. But from another viewpoint I doubted my suitability. Dr Goldblatt's methods depended on my ability to express my thoughts and feelings – and that I couldn't do. I was in the habit of keeping them to myself. In fact, I was so efficient at concealing my feelings, that often I didn't know myself what my true feelings really were. This habit of a lifetime wouldn't change overnight. I worried a great deal about this.

The financial cost didn't worry me unduly. I would be spending a quarter of my salary on psychotherapy but I reckoned I would be able to cope. I was prepared to make financial sacrifices because I believed that paying for my treatment was a very worthwhile investment. I was investing in my own mental health.

# 6 The First Five Psychotherapy Sessions

(21 February 1967 - 23 March 1967)

### 21 February 1967

As I walked into the Harley Street waiting room, I became less tense. I remembered the room. It seemed passive and unthreatening. I had fifteen minutes to wait. My mind dwelt on the other room upstairs. The room with the couch. How could I lie on that couch and pour out the whole of my life to a total stranger? In the waiting room the atmosphere seemed suddenly to change. The room was now threatening and hostile. I felt as though I were growing smaller. I felt lost, worthless, cold. Suddenly the receptionist called my name. I stood up in a trance and followed her to the foot of the stairs. Dr Goldblatt was standing at the door of his room waiting for me. His movements were slow and his smile was kind. I felt reassured. 'Come in,' he said. Inside the room I noticed that the chair had been taken from his desk; the chair that I'd hoped I would be sitting in for this extraordinary meeting. Dr Goldblatt nodded towards the couch. I hesitated in the middle of the room, uncertain and on my guard in case he said anything or in case I said anything that would bring the whole thing to an end, and leave me running down the stairs in panic.

Dr Goldblatt didn't say a word; he walked briskly to the armchair placed at the head of the couch and sat down comfortably. He produced a packet of cigarettes from his pocket, lit one, and began to smoke. Standing in the middle of the room I felt embarrassed and totally alone. What was I doing? What was happening to me?

The whole thing seemed to be a bizarre game. I looked across at the empty couch. Dr Goldblatt still said nothing, his cigarette burning steadily between his fingers. My mind worked overtime as I recalled the horrors of the past few months, and I suddenly realised that this meeting was probably my last and only chance to get myself back on my feet again. I turned, walked across the room and climbed onto the couch. I lay back and made myself as comfortable as I could and waited. Dr Goldblatt now had the upper hand and I felt that he was waiting for me to say something – anything that would get us out of this impasse.

I drew a deep breath. 'I feel emotionally cold,' I stuttered.

His reply came quickly. 'That's because you didn't receive the warmth you needed as a child.'

There was a long silence. At last I said: 'I often do the opposite from what I really want to do, because I think people expect me to behave that way. Most of the time I try to behave as I think other people expect me to.'

'As a child you didn't feel acceptable if you acted spontaneously,' he said.

'That's true,' I said. 'My mother was pleased I was a girl because she already had two boys, and she expected me to like dolls and pretty things, but I couldn't stand them. I preferred my brothers' toys, and I also wanted to climb trees and fences. She became disappointed in me for not acting as a little girl.'

'You need to learn that it can be perfectly acceptable for you to be yourself and to act spontaneously. When you have learnt that, you will find that emotional warmth will follow naturally.'

For a while we said nothing. His words were comforting and reassuring. I believed that somehow he would teach me what I needed to know.

Abruptly I changed the subject. I was still taking Librium, and I worried in case I became addicted to it.

'I've been taking Librium tablets for quite a few weeks now,' I said, 'and I can't decide whether to stop taking them or not. Do you think I really need them?'

'That's for you to decide,' he said.

'Do you prescribe tranquillisers for your patients?'

'You are here to discuss yourself, not how I treat my other patients.'

'Do you think that tranquillisers are helpful?' I persisted.

'I don't like to generalise. If the anxiety is so acute that it's incapacitating, then tranquillisers might be beneficial for a while. On the other hand, if the tranquillisers suppress the anxiety, it can become impossible to discover the cause of the anxiety, and then psychotherapy becomes ineffective.'

'Shall I try a few days without the Librium tablets?' I asked again. 'I dislike taking them, but I'm afraid that if I don't, I won't be able to cope with my job. On the other hand, they might hinder my psychotherapy.'

'If ever it seems that the Librium is preventing progress I'll tell you,' he said. 'Until then, it's for you to decide, by weighing up the advantages and the disadvantages. Only you can judge how you will feel without the help of tranquillisers.'

'I'd better carry on taking them for a while,' I said, 'otherwise I might not be able to cope with my job, and I daren't stay away from work in case I cut myself off from people. Have I made the right decision?'

'It's your decision, and that's what matters,' he said.

I was glad he wasn't dogmatic about the tranquillisers, and that he treated me as an adult, rational person.

My mind went blank, so I pondered over some of his remarks: 'You need to learn that it can be perfectly acceptable to be yourself.' I wondered how I could learn that . . . . The minutes passed.

'We must finish for today,' he said, and stood up. 'From Thursday of next week I can give you a permanent appointment for 5 p.m.'

I was pleased to know that Dr Goldblatt was now committing himself to giving me treatment. This proved that he believed that he could help me despite my inability to free associate.

For the rest of that week I tried to live up to Dr Goldblatt's advice, but for most of the time it was impossible. At Church on Sunday people said, 'How are you?', and I replied, 'Very well, thank you.' I really wanted to say, 'I feel dreadful,' but

I couldn't. I had to pretend to everyone that I was all right. All through the service I wanted to rush outside. The hymns and prayers meant absolutely nothing to me, and I longed to escape, but I couldn't. It would be quite unacceptable for me to leave in the middle of the service.

At home, when I knew I couldn't hold back my tears any longer, I would go upstairs to my room determined to keep from my parents the despair and fear I felt. I had always hidden my problems from my parents, so it was even more natural to hide my feelings now that I was facing this crisis in my life. It was discouraging for me to see myself as a failure but on the other hand I was encouraged to know that Dr Goldblatt was right. I needed to become myself.

With this new awareness in mind I stepped up my driving lessons just before I took my driving test. The test was scheduled for a Wednesday afternoon. My friend Jill came with me to the test centre. She was very nervous and I actually found myself calming her down. 'Don't worry,' I said, 'I'll pass, there's nothing wrong with my driving.' About half an hour later, I drove the car back to the test centre and the examiner turned to me and said the magic words, 'You've passed.' I sat clutching the wheel with a big smile on my face, and as soon as the examiner had left us I jumped out of the car, untied the L plates with trembling fingers and then skipped around the car, singing, 'I've passed, I've passed, I've passed.'

'Jump in, Jill. I'll drive you home,' I said. We drove off and I was literally jumping up and down in the seat and singing and laughing loudly. I hadn't felt so elated for a long time. My laughter was a tonic. 'I'm better,' I shouted. 'My depression has gone.'

Next morning I awoke feeling very excited. I drove to work and my colleagues came rushing out of the clinic to congratulate me and to admire my car. I was the centre of attention and I was thoroughly enjoying it.

Later that morning I said to Rita, 'I'm going to drive to Harley Street this afternoon.' She gasped in disbelief. 'You can't, think of all the traffic, the one-way streets, the parking meters. How will you find your way?'

'I can read a map,' I replied.

Passing my driving test went to my head and gave me Dutch courage. I decided to confront Dr Goldblatt by refusing to lie on the couch that afternoon. 'I'll demand a chair,' I told myself.

**2 March 1967**

Later that afternoon I drove to Harley Street without mishap. The most difficult part of all was securing a parking space when I arrived. I soon learnt how to nip in quickly as soon as a parking space became available. I couldn't afford to spend time driving round the block, looking for somewhere to park my car.

I ran all the way to Dr Goldblatt's consulting rooms and arrived at the door breathless with half a minute to spare. I was about to sit down when the receptionist announced that Dr Goldblatt was ready to see me. I hurried upstairs and brushed past him as he was standing at the door, waiting to greet me. As he closed the door, I blurted out, 'I'm not going to lie on that couch, I don't like it. I want to sit on a chair.'

He smiled. 'All right,' he said. He walked across the room and moved the armchairs at right angles to each other so that we wouldn't be looking directly at each other when we sat down.

I was taken aback by this, as I had expected some kind of an argument. I was surprised at how easy it was to be myself and how readily he had accepted it.

I sat down thankfully. It was easy to talk with the chairs arranged at right angles. I could choose whether to look at him or not. It helped me to glance at the expression on his face. 'I talked too much about myself last time,' I said. 'Don't you ever get bored, listening to the same old worries and the same old problems over and over again?'

'No,' he replied. 'In fact, it's interesting to see how the same old worries keep showing up in many different guises. By your question you have shown me that you haven't yet learnt that being yourself can be acceptable. You're coming to me in order to talk about yourself. I am your therapist. I asked you to talk about anything that comes into your mind.

Whatever you say is acceptable to me. You are acceptable. We will keep coming back to that until you have learnt it.'

The rest of the hour passed easily. Just looking at him reassured me. He was patient, tolerant and understanding. I imagined my brother would have been like this if he hadn't been ill. I didn't voice these thoughts. Dr Goldblatt might not like to know that he reminded me of someone who had had schizophrenia.

After the session I walked downstairs feeling very discouraged. Dr Goldblatt hadn't praised me for expressing my strong feelings over the couch. Instead, he'd said I hadn't yet learnt that being myself can be acceptable.

On the long drive home I thought over Dr Goldblatt's words. He seemed to be saying to me that I had to drop the habit of concealing my true feelings. From early childhood I had led a secret kind of life due to my mother's preconceived ideas of how a little girl should behave. I knew I had 'tomboy' instincts. I hated 'dollies' and toy prams. I preferred muddy climbs up trees and shouting games. But I paid a high price in guilt for not wanting to be an ideal little girl. Every time I got mud on my clothes or tore my dress in some rough outdoor game I was told that girls shouldn't behave in this fashion. In many more subtle ways, too, I was being constantly reminded that because I was a little girl it was wrong for me to behave like my brothers. At times I felt that anything I did would be wrong. On one occasion I insisted in wanting to cut up bits of wood with a saw at our local church children's club. I joined the boys and finished up with a very tidy looking egg holder made of wood. I didn't get any praise for this. Instead my parents were upset to think I hadn't joined up with the girls' knitting group.

As I grew older I began to lose my sense of identity. I didn't care what girls did. I decided to pursue activities which interested me and which I enjoyed regardless of the social conventions. But deep within me I had developed a sense of guilt over everything. Gradually I came to feel that I was unacceptable as a person. I felt worthless and unwanted.

I arrived home at 7.30 p.m. near to tears. I had to keep trying and learn to make progress. I would 'be myself' now, and tell my parents that I was having psychiatric treatment. It would be difficult and I delayed the moment of truth for as long as I could but eventually I forced myself. They were in the sitting room as I came downstairs. I walked in and spoke right away.

'I've been feeling very depressed, and I can't get over it,' I blurted out, 'so I've managed to get some treatment. I'm going to Harley Street every Thursday straight from work. That's where I've been tonight. I've been three times so far. He's a very good psychiatrist. He thinks he'll be able to help me.'

My parents froze in shock and horror. I stood there trembling; even my teeth chattered. My father spoke first. 'How could you put yourself into the clutches of someone like that? You've got more money than sense. Who put you in touch with him? I suppose it was that Rita who had something to do with it.'

'Yes,' I replied in a strained voice. 'She saw how depressed I was becoming so she arranged everything for me. The psychiatrist is very nice and kind.'

'I'm sure he is,' retorted my father. 'I dare say he's getting a nice lot of money from you in return.'

'Only four guineas a time.'

'You must be crazy,' gasped my father. 'You don't need a psychiatrist. You are just down in the dumps because you are weak after your operations. It's time you pulled yourself together and started looking on the bright side of life. You've got a car, you've passed your driving test, you've got lots of friends. That man will do you nothing but harm. Haven't you any feeling for us? Didn't we suffer enough all those years while Alan was ill? Try and be happy for our sakes.'

'It's because I'm thinking of you that I'm taking this treatment,' I replied, deeply hurt by my father's remarks. 'If I don't go to Dr Goldblatt I probably will be ill like Alan. That's why I'm going. I'm desperate to get over my depression. If I could pull myself together I would, but I can't. I don't care what you say, I've got to carry on with the psychotherapy. It's my only hope.'

'It seems to me Rita has brainwashed you into thinking you are depressed,' my father said. 'It's her influence. Stand on your own feet and pull yourself out of it.' The atmosphere in the room grew tense.

There was no point in arguing. I walked out of the room

and ran upstairs into my bedroom and sat on the bed. How tired I felt and yet I dreaded sleep. I might dream, I might have more dreadful shaking sensations in my sleep.

For two whole hours I sat there, staring at the carpet. What could I do? Dr Goldblatt was so far away. If only I could talk to him right now. But even if he were here, he wouldn't give me any different advice. He would tell me to be myself and accept myself for what I was. That seemed impossible. I couldn't do that any more than I could follow my father's advice to 'pull myself together'. Wearily I got into bed. I hadn't taken any sleeping tablets, but I felt myself dozing off into sleep. I struggled to keep awake, but I couldn't. My arms were like lead. I tried to move my legs, but they were fixed, too. I was breathing in but unable to breathe out. I struggled to breathe out and to wake up. Then I thought, 'I'm dreaming, stop struggling, just wait patiently for the dream to end.' And that's what I did. The sensation felt ghastly, but I kept saying to myself, 'It's only a dream, be patient.' Gradually the spasm left me and I found that I was lying quietly, and gently breathing. When I realised what had happened, I sat up. I seemed to have found the secret of coping with my night time physical terrors. The feelings might come again, but the fear could never be as bad for I had learnt how to ride out these storms.

I had several more of those 'attacks' that night, and by morning I was exhausted. Yet I felt I had made progress. I decided I wouldn't take any more sleeping tablets. I would now cope with each night as it came. I had to overcome my symptoms, and I felt that the sooner I started, the better.

Next day at work I decided to stop taking my Librium. Maybe I could break the habit and do with out it altogether. But as the day wore on my sadness turned to anxiety, and by evening when I had returned home, I was in a state of sheer panic. I was desperate. I had to get help. I must phone Rita. The phone at home would be no use. My parents would overhear everything I said.

It was pouring with rain and pitch dark, but that didn't worry me. I had to escape from the house and from myself. I slipped on a raincoat and went quickly out of the front door. I ran down the road as fast as I could. Someone was in the phone box so I paced up and down the street until the phone box was empty. I dialled Rita. Her voice seemed far away.

'I'm desperate,' I said. What can I do? Please help me.'

'What's happened?' she asked in alarm.

'Nothing has happened. I just feel so frightened, I can't bear it any more. What can I do? Is the psychotherapy making me worse?'

'You'll probably feel worse before you feel better,' Rita said. 'Be brave and keep going, and then talk it over with Dr Goldblatt next week.'

'I did without Librium today,' I said.

'You fool. No wonder you feel bad. Go back home and take your tablets immediately, then take a sleeping tablet and get straight into bed.'

I left the phone box and walked home in the pouring rain. I did as Rita had told me and went to bed.

I didn't remember a thing until my alarm clock rang next morning. I woke up and my mind flashed back to the day before. For only one day I had stopped taking my tablets and the panic and fear which came over me as a result had been so intense that I had had to give in and start taking them again. It began to dawn on me that recovery would take more than just willpower on my part. It seemed that I needed the help of tranquillisers to get through each day, and if I was to recover completely I needed the help of Dr Goldblatt.

It was a sobering thought, and ran contrary to my need to be independent and to help myself. I became confused. 'If I try very hard to help myself, I end up in a state of panic, and if I don't try to help myself I'll probably break off all social contact and develop schizophrenia. How can I measure the amount of effort needed to regain my equilibrium?' I asked myself.

I didn't know the answer, and for the next few days I wandered around in a state of resigned despair, just managing to cope with the basic essentials of my life and my job.

**9 March 1967**

I arrived for my third session with Dr Goldblatt in a strange state of mind. For the first time I was nervous, almost afraid, of facing him, but I didn't know why. As I perched on the edge of the large settee in the waiting room my hands were shaking and I was nervously rubbing my feet backwards and forwards on the carpet.

I felt as though I was a failure. Over the past week I'd tried my hardest to cope with my life and my despair, but I only felt worse. I blamed Dr Goldblatt. Why hadn't he given me more advice last week? Why did he leave me to flounder? Why did he allow me to suffer in this way? The waiting room was closing in on me. I stood up and then sat where I could look through one of the mirrors into another, so as to imagine that the room was bigger. The illusion gave me space: room to move, room to breathe, room to think. But what to think: failure? the future? blackness? . . .

'Dr Goldblatt will see you now.' The receptionist's voice startled me. I had forgotten where I was. Like a robot I walked through the doorway and up the stairs. Dr Goldblatt was smiling at me in a supercilious way, or so I thought. I walked past him into the room: there was no chair for me to sit on – only the bare, unfriendly couch. How thoughtless of him; how uncaring.

I said nothing but climbed onto the couch, feeling that I was just another number on his list. For some time I couldn't bring myself to speak. I just stared at the rosette patterns on the wall, feeling that they were placed there deliberately to taunt me.

At last I began speaking. I told him about the day when I hadn't taken Librium, and how panic-stricken I'd felt. 'I think it was unwise of you to try to do without them,' he said. 'You need to be patient.'

'Supposing I get addicted to them,' I asked.

'There is little danger of that,' he said. 'You will have no difficulty in doing without them once we have dealt with the experiences that are most painful to you.'

We paused. 'For how long will I be in need of tablets?' I asked.

'It's impossible to say.' We paused again.

'When will my life become less of a problem?' I asked.

'When you let me get to the root of your problem,' he answered. I felt annoyed. I hadn't driven all this way at four guineas a time just to be given evasive answers to questions that were worrying me so much.

'Why don't you tell me what you think about me?' I suggested.

'That isn't my purpose,' he replied. 'My job is to help you to think constructively for yourself.'

'I can't think constructively lying here like this,' I protested. 'I want you to comment more, and to help me. I want to get better, not just lie here passively doing nothing.'

'In lying passively you are not doing nothing,' he said. 'You have never learnt how to be passive or how to depend on others. You must learn that life is not all action. There are times to be quiet and times to be still. Think of a baby feeding at his mother's breast. How do you advise mothers who are breast feeding?'

'I tell them that the most important aspect of breast feeding is the pleasure it gives to both mother and baby,' I said.

'Do you advise mothers to keep their babies drinking throughout the whole of their feeds?'

'No, I suggest that babies should feed at their own speed and pause when they want to, and I encourage mothers to let the babies nestle against the breast and to experience the comfort of closeness as well as the comfort of feeding.'

'Then try to apply this advice to yourself,' he said slowly. 'Don't hurry yourself. Relive the experience of breast feeding. Experience total dependence while you are here. We are in no hurry. When you need to express your anxieties, do so. When you feel like pausing and 'playing at the breast' as it were, do just that. It's all part of the relationship of dependence. You can't physically go back to being a dependent baby at the breast, but emotionally while you are here you can go back. Depend on me. Express your needs to me as a baby does to its mother. Let me decide what you need from the cues you give me. Trust me.'

He spoke quietly. I felt calmed and comforted. I wanted to trust him. For a while I lay quietly thinking about what 'trusting him' would mean. Did I dare? Where would it lead? Would I lose control of the situation? Were his motives pure? Could he possibly know what was best for me?

'You must go now,' he said suddenly. 'We'll continue again next week.'

I drove home deep in thought. 'Experience total dependence while you are here.' That sentence kept echoing in my mind. How could I trust him like a baby trusts its mother? A baby is unaware of its vulnerability. Was Dr Goldblatt naive, or did he think I was? How could one hour a week cure my depression, even if I were able to achieve emotional dependence on him?

When I arrived home I wrote to Pat telling her of Dr Goldblatt's ideas. I expressed doubts about the outcome of the treatment. What was the good of being told that I had to depend on him like a baby?

The day after Dr Goldblatt's 'baby session' I was alone at work during the lunch break when panic gripped me. I felt suddenly afraid of being alone, but I hadn't the courage to go outside because I was also terrified of being with people. I looked around the room in desperation. I saw the telephone. It seemed a stupid thing to do but I had reached desperation point. I needed to hear someone's voice urgently. I dialled Pat's number, and to my relief she answered.

I cried into the phone, 'I'm frightened, but I don't know why. I've always enjoyed my own company; now I'm even frightened of myself. When will this dreadful nightmare end Pat? I can't stand it much longer.'

'You'll be all right,' Pat insisted. 'You've got a first class psychiatrist, understanding colleagues, and more determination than anyone I know. You will get better even if it doesn't seem that way now. Come and stay with me at Easter. That's only two weeks away. Drive down if you can, and I'll be able to see your new car.'

'Yes I'll do that Pat,' I said, 'if I can survive that long.' I put the receiver down, grateful that I'd been able to talk with my dear Pat. She had a way of calming me down. My terror had gone but I still felt in despair. It was impossible to do any visiting, so I busied myself with clerical work as best I could.

On the Sunday afternoon Rita phoned to ask me if I would like to join her and her family on a walk. Eagerly I drove to her home, but the walk was disappointing. I wanted to talk about myself, but in the presence of her family I was unable to say anything. I was relieved when it was time to leave.

Driving home I decided that being dependent on others was hopeless. I had to wait two weeks before I could see Pat, and Rita had her own family and was unable to give me her full attention. Dr Goldblatt was only available for one hour a week, and I could no longer cope with my job. I seemed to be hemmed in by brick walls. It was as though I was running around in circles getting nowhere fast. Should I cut myself off from everyone and become completely independent? Dependence on others seemed to be causing me nothing but anguish. I felt like a tiger pacing up and down inside a cage of my own making with a distant hostile world beyond the bars. No escape from without and no escape from within. These feelings dominated my life until my next meeting with Dr Goldblatt.

**16 March 1967**

Dr Goldblatt was standing in his usual place at the doorway of his consulting room. I walked in. That couch again. I wished he would realise how difficult it was for me to relax on the couch; how much easier it was to talk to him when I could see his face and watch his movements. However, I didn't have the confidence to protest.

After fidgeting on the couch for a while, I told him I felt like ending my friendship with Rita, and giving up my job. I also felt like never seeing him again.

'Why do you feel like that?' he asked.

'I'm becoming more and more dependent on people,' I replied. 'At work I'm watching all the time for an opportunity to tell Rita about my anxieties, and I want her to talk to me and give me lots of attention. The more I depend on her, the more I want to, but there are limits on how far I can go with anyone. I used to be very independent emotionally, and in many ways it was easier then, because I didn't get hurt.'

'When you were a child you didn't learn to depend fully on anyone emotionally,' he said. 'You never had that deep need satisfied.'

'Why didn't I learn to depend on anyone?' I asked.

'We'll discover that as we talk more about your childhood.

However, for the time being we'll leave that aside. What I want you to think about during the coming week is the nature of relationships. A sound relationship doesn't consist merely of dependence or of independence. A good sound relationship is one of interdependence.'

'What do you mean by interdependence?' I asked.

'I mean mutual dependence; a relationship in which both parties have needs which are satisfied within the relationship. Each one gives to the other, and each receives from the other. In giving, you receive, and in receiving you give. Think about these things.'

I closed my eyes and relaxed. He spoke gently and quietly, pausing between each sentence so that I could think about his words. *Inter*dependence: that was a two-way process. In the past I had tried to give affection to people but I had been afraid to receive it in return. Now I felt I had nothing to give, but I was desperate to receive affection from others. I had gone from one extreme to the other. Somehow I had to find a balance between the two. *Inter*dependence . . . .

'We must stop now,' he said, gently. As I was getting off the couch he said, 'In the coming week you can make progress by looking for examples of interdependence in relationships. Examine the relationships within the families you visit, and among your colleagues. See how satisfying their relationships are.'

He sounded concerned, as though he really cared about my predicament. 'Thank you,' I said. 'I'll try my best.'

He smiled. I went to the door and he opened it for me. I walked out, grateful for his courtesy.

That week I thought a lot about relationships. There were many examples for me to observe when I visited mothers. On the Monday morning I visited two mothers with six-week-old babies. The first, a Mrs Ball, was finding her child rather trying. 'He seems to want my attention all the time,' she said. 'I change him and feed him and hold him for a few minutes, and he's quite contented. Then as soon as I put him down, he cries. I can't be at his beck and call all day long.' It was clear to me that Mrs Ball was under pressure because of the baby's dependence on her. The baby needed her attention between feeds, but she had other things to do. Dr Goldblatt had said that in a good relationship 'each gives to the other'. Mrs Ball was giving to her baby, but receiving nothing in return. I had to find a way of helping her to receive pleasure from her baby.

'May I see him?' I asked. We went to the baby's bedroom. He was crying. I bent down close to him and spoke quietly. He stopped crying and watched me. 'Look,' I said to his mother, 'He's watching my face and listening to my voice. See how much he's progressed since he was born.' I stood aside so that she could be near him. She picked him up and looked closely at his face. Then she spoke quietly to him. He watched her intently, and then he gave a tiny smile. She was thrilled.

'Why don't you put him in a baby-relax chair and have him where you can see him?' I suggested. 'You can talk to him while you are working, and watch his response. It's fun to watch a baby develop. You'll miss a lot if you keep him in the bedroom.'

She followed my advice. I dared to hope that as a result, her relationship with her baby would become one of interdependence, in which both mother and baby were getting satisfaction out of their contact with each other.

The next mother, Mrs Wright, needed no advice from me. She made me welcome and gave me a cup of coffee. She was breast feeding her baby and enjoying the experience. The baby was always in her sight. She kept him in a carry cot while he slept, so that she could carry him around the house with her as she did the housework. When he was awake, he was in his baby-relax chair, placed where they could see each other. She was excited over everything the baby did. She loved cuddling him, and his occasional cry wasn't a burden to her. Instead, it was an excuse for more cuddles. Their relationship was a beautiful example of interdependence. She was giving her baby all the care he needed, and he was giving her a great deal of emotional satisfaction.

On my way back to the clinic I thought about these two mothers. Their different relationships with their babies was a revelation to me. For the first time in my life I realised that the prerequisite for a sound relationship was a solid foundation of interdependence.

My mind remained on this subject at lunchtime, but to my dismay I found that instead of feeling happy over my discovery, I was feeling increasingly despondent. I had glimpsed the ideal, but I was not a part of it. My own mother hadn't enjoyed me as a child, as Mrs Wright was enjoying her baby now. I had been a burden to my mother. I felt a sudden pang of sorrow that the love and affection which comes from interdependence had been denied to me as a child. I sat at my desk, I put my head on my arms and cried.

Until I was due to go to Harley Street again, I lived in a daze. I couldn't bear to think about interdependent relationships. It was too painful, because it showed how much I had missed as a child. There seemed no way of making that up, so I tried to dismiss the matter from my mind in order to keep going.

## 23 March 1967

I arrived early for my fifth appointment, so I had plenty of time to prepare myself. My mind drifted back to the previous week, to Dr Goldblatt's kind, soothing voice, and his gentle smile. I felt lonely and I longed for his presence. If only the couch wasn't there. If only I could sit and watch him. Somehow I had to learn to accept the couch and not let it bother me. I decided to plan my opening sentence.

It seemed reasonable to tell him about my early childhood, since it was on my mind, and as a Freudian he would want to know about such things. So far he hadn't asked anything about my early life, but maybe it was important.

'Dr Goldblatt is ready for you now.' The receptionist was standing at the door. I walked past her and went upstairs.

Dr Goldblatt greeted me with a smile. I smiled back and tried to keep my eyes on his face as I walked into the room. I climbed on the couch and began speaking even before I was lying down.

'I thought you might need to know something about my childhood,' I blurted out. 'I've often asked my mother what I was like as a baby, but she can't remember. It was during the war. She already had two boys, and she believed it was wrong to bring another child into "this wicked world". She says her life was a nightmare. She expected that at any time a bomb would fall on the house and kill her children. She remembers my birth – it was quite easy. I was born during a lull in the Battle of Britain. My mother was glad I was a girl, but she doesn't remember looking after me as a tiny baby. She assumes I fed easily. I looked like my brother Brian, who is two and a half years older than me, so my mother assumes I must have been like him in many ways, but she doesn't know. She can't even remember my attempts at talking. She thinks the first word I ever said was "scissors". Apparently I used to hold a pair of scissors for hours on end, and they became my favourite toy. My mother was disappointed in me because I wasn't interested in girl's things. I was always either sticky or dirty or muddy.

'I asked my aunts about my babyhood. They said my mother kept me in a clothes basket most of the time, and hid me under the stairs or under the table, in case a bomb fell on the house. She was in a terrible state. My great-aunt sat me on her lap when she visited us, and she talked to me and tried to make me respond, but I only stared solemnly at her. I don't remember any of that of course, but I've always felt very attached to my great-aunt, and to me she's the most wonderful person I've ever known.

'I remember that all through my childhood my mother was harrassed and caring for us was a strain. She did her best as she saw it. She didn't smack us, she always had our meals ready for us, and made sure we had clean clothes to wear. She never went out and left us on our own. We were her responsibility and she believed it was her duty to be at home. For her, motherhood was a duty, not a pleasure.' I stopped talking and waited.

'You didn't experience the mutual joy that interdependence brings, because your mother didn't enjoy you. You caused her anxiety. That's why you feel the way you do now. If you depend on someone now, you feel you will cause them anxiety and you feel you'll be a burden. You want to be dependent, and you need to be dependent, but you are frightened because you feel you'll become a burden to others.'

'How can I overcome this fear?'

'First of all you must realise that subconsciously you are projecting your childhood experience into all your relationships. If you recognise that, you'll be able to help yourself. Learn from your experiences now. What do you say in your mothercraft classes, when you talk about relationships?'

'I tell the mothers to enjoy their babies,' I replied. 'Those early weeks and months in a baby's life are precious. I tell them it's wonderful to hold their babies in their arms, and to feel the thrill of giving their love to them.'

'Do you think the mothers get something out of their child's dependence?'

'Yes, of course. I've seen it in mothers I visit. It must be one of the most emotionally satisfying experiences a person can have.'

'So by depending on the mother, the child is giving as well as receiving.'

'Yes,' I agreed.

'You have been afraid of depending on people because you have failed to realise that depending on others is giving.' We both fell silent.

I thought about Pat's last letter to me in which she told me that my psychotherapy was helping her as well. I believed at the time she was only trying to cheer me up. Now I realised she'd meant it. By sharing my experiences with her we were both receiving benefit. Maybe with Pat I could maintain a relationship of interdependence.

I rested quietly on the couch and pictured a mother with her baby. I tried to imagine the dependence of the baby and the joy of the mother. It was very comforting. Dr Goldblatt sat quietly. He let me linger over the experience. I was glad he was so patient. Something of his personality seemed to come over me. I felt less anxious. The minutes ticked by . . .

'It's time to go now,' he said quietly. As I was getting down from the couch he said, 'I'm taking a week's holiday, so I shall see you again in two weeks' time.'

I felt as though a bucket of cold water had suddenly been thrown over me. I looked at him in alarm. 'That's a long time to wait,' I stammered.

'Yes, it is,' he agreed, 'but I've given you plenty to think over and to work on. Think about dependence and interdependence in the relationships you see around you. Analyse your own relationships with people. Remember that in depending on someone you are giving as well as receiving. Work towards interdependence in your relationships.'

'I'll try,' I murmured. As I made my way to the door, he said, 'It is important for you to grasp these concepts both intellectually and in your own experience.'

# 7 I Stay with Friends and Deliver a Baby

(23 March 1967 - 5 April 1967)

I drove home, feeling very anxious. How could I survive the next two weeks without Dr Goldblatt's help? I would have to depend even more on my friends, but there must be limits to their endurance. Whenever I could I talked to Rita about my anxieties, and asked her advice. Any satisfaction she might derive from our relationship was probably outweighed by the strain of being pursued by me. If I wasn't careful, I would drive my friends away.

My anxiety turned to panic. I felt an involuntary tightening of my grip, a sinking sensation, an intense dread. Suddenly I was afraid of being alone, and I had a strong urge to run. I knew I couldn't keep driving. My panic was increasing so rapidly that I could no longer concentrate on the traffic ahead. I swerved into the kerb and screeched to a halt. I sat back in the driving seat and began to breathe deeply and slowly, trying to relax. I was illegally parked on double yellow lines in the middle of the rush hour, with lorries thundering past the car. Somehow I had to regain my composure . . . .

It was useless. My eyes misted over and I could no longer focus properly. As if possessed, I grabbed my handbag, pulled the keys from the ignition, opened the door and scrambled out. A car screeched past, hooting loudly. I leapt onto the pavement and ran along the street, gasping and sobbing. Soon I was out of breath. I leant against a shop window to recover. The panic was still inside me. I looked desperately up and down the street. I spotted a telephone.

Relieved, I ran forward as fast as I could. I had to phone Rita. She would listen to me and calm me down. I stumbled into the call-box and dialled her number. 'Please be in, please be in,' I gasped in desperation.

Rita's voice suddenly came to me.

'Rita?' I sobbed. 'I'm desperate. Dr Goldblatt is having a holiday, so I can't see him for two weeks. What can I do? How can I cope?'

'Why don't you go and stay with your friend in the country? Have you any leave to come?'

'Yes, I've got a few weeks' holiday owing me, but I wasn't going to take it because I've been away so much already.'

'You must take it. Don't worry about work. I'll see to everything for you. As soon as you get home, phone your friend and ask if you can stay with her from tomorrow. Dr Goldblatt's holiday has come at an unfortunate time for you. You must be with people who can help you through this crisis.'

I leant against the side of the phone kiosk and took a couple of deep breaths. Rita was right. I had to get away . . . I began to feel weak and dizzy. . . 'Are you still there, Margaret?' Rita sounded anxious. 'Are you fit to drive yourself home?'

Her concern touched me. I burst into tears and for some minutes I cried uncontrollably.

'A good cry will do you good,' Rita said gently. 'You'll feel better soon.'

For some time I leant against the side of the kiosk, crying. Luckily I had a good supply of coins. Gradually I began to feel more composed . . .

'I'll be all right now,' I said at last. 'I'll do what you suggest and stay with one of my friends. Thanks for being so patient and understanding.'

'That's all right, Rita replied. 'Now, drive home carefully. I'll look forward to seeing you again in two weeks.'

My panic was over. I walked back to my car and drove home.

That evening I phoned Sue. She was another friend from my student health visitor days. She worked as a health visitor in the same part of the country as Pat. Her home was by the sea.

I told her how I felt and asked if I could stay with her. 'Yes, I'd love to see you,' she exclaimed. 'Come on Saturday morning and stay till Thursday. Then you can go on to Pat's for a long weekend.'

'I must warn you Sue, I think I'm going crazy,' I said. 'I'm terribly moody and ready to burst into tears at any time, for no reason. You'll need a lot of patience. If I say anything out of place, don't take me seriously. Honestly, I've never known anyone behave like this. I'm so changeable.'

Sue laughed. 'You'll forget your moodiness once you are down here. You can take my dog Tess for long walks across the cliffs and along the sea front. That will soon straighten you out.'

'If only it were that simple,' I replied. 'It's going to be a long job. Anyway, enough of that for now. See you on Saturday.'

My father was delighted I was going away for a few days. 'You'll be out of that Rita's clutches at last. Sue is a level-headed, sensible Christian woman, so perhaps she can talk some sense into you, and Pat is one of the nicest people I've ever met. Let's hope you come back your old happy self.'

Would my father ever understand?

On Saturday morning I set out early. The long drive was difficult. The first part of the journey was a mass of Z bends. There was a lot of traffic, and many drivers overtook me dangerously. My tension mounted and the tears in my eyes made driving difficult. Just as I was about to stop for a good cry, I noticed a sign ahead showing that I was in the county where Sue and Pat lived. My mood changed to excitement. I bounced up and down in my seat as I drove, shouting out, 'I'm on holiday, I'm free, I'm free.'

How I got to Sue's home I'll never know, but eventually I arrived. I pulled up outside her pretty little cottage and slumped forward over the steering wheel, exhausted and unable to move. At last I managed to press the hooter, to announce my arrival.

Sue came running out. 'Stop that noise, you've frightened the dog. Let me help you with your luggage. It's really nice to see you. Come in.'

This was the first time I'd been to Sue's cottage. It was

clean, tidy and homely. It was double fronted, with a sitting room on one side and a dining room on the other. The kitchen was at the rear. Upstairs were four bedrooms, a toilet and bathroom. Sue was very well organised and practical, and the cottage reflected her personality. I envied her and her adjustment to life. I couldn't imagine anything getting her down.

She led me into the sitting room and sat me in an armchair. Tess was crouching terrified under a coffee table in a corner of the room. While Sue was in the kitchen Tess and I looked at each other. 'Silly dog,' I whispered. She whined. Sue brought in the coffee. She told me about her job. I was still nervous and shaky from the long drive, but somehow I managed to concentrate on what Sue was telling me. Apparently she used her home as her office. She had an extraordinarily detailed timetable of work she had set herself; not a minute was wasted. She ran her life like a well-oiled machine.

'I'll be able to tell the time by what you are doing,' I teased.

'Yes,' she replied. 'That's how I like it.'

'What about meals?' I asked. 'Shall I cater for myself?'

'Certainly not.' she replied. 'You'll fit in with me. I'll prepare the meals. It won't be much extra work for me. If you want to help, you can wash up and take Tess for walks. It will be good for both of you.'

'What happens if you don't feel like keeping your routine, or supposing you don't want to visit one day? Do you force yourself to keep going?'

'What a strange question,' she said. 'I work this way because I like to be systematic. I always feel like visiting.'

'Do you ever wonder if there is any point in visiting? Do you ever think the mothers may not want to see you? Do you ever think your advice may not be much use anyway?'

'No, I've been professionally trained and I know my job. I wouldn't be a health visitor if I wasn't sure I was doing a worthwhile job and helping people.'

'I wish I had your confidence, Sue,' I said.

'Perhaps you're in the wrong job. You'll be able to think about it when you take Tess for walks along the cliffs. Now, excuse me, I must see to the dinner. Have a browse through some of the books.'

She disappeared. I sat glaring at Tess for a while and she

whined back at me. Then I got up and went into the kitchen to talk to Sue. 'I'm taking Librium,' I said, 'three times a day.'

'Do you think it's helping you?' she asked.

'I don't know. I suppose I'm reasonably calm for a couple of hours after each dose, but my moods change so much, it's difficult to say.'

'Perhaps you're on the wrong dosage,' she said, 'or perhaps it's nothing to do with that. Perhaps you're not at peace with God.'

'You're right there. God and I have fallen out.'

Sue was shocked. 'You're only hurting yourself by adopting that attitude,' she said.

'What attitude?' I retorted. 'I'm merely stating a fact which I can't alter. Just because you enjoy going to Church, and just because you find it easy to keep your Christian faith, it doesn't make it easy for everyone else.'

'Life isn't easy for anyone,' she said quietly.

I knew I'd hurt her and I was sorry, but I couldn't bring myself to say so. I stamped back into the sitting room, and shouted at Tess, 'You stupid creature.' Poor Tess fled. I was suddenly appalled at my behaviour – it was so uncharacteristic of me. Sue's confidence annoyed and unnerved me. Maybe I was jealous. In comparison to hers, my life was useless and pointless.

'Dinner's on the table, Margaret,' she called. I walked slowly into the dining room and sat down. I ate in silence while Sue tried to keep a conversation going despite the chill atmosphere. After our meal, she said, 'I'll wash up while you unpack.'

'I suppose you're frightened I'll smash your precious crockery,' I snapped, unkindly. I stamped upstairs in a fit of shame and horror at the way I was behaving.

After a while Sue called to me. 'I'm taking Tess out for a walk along the cliffs. Do you want to come?'

'Yes please,' I called. Ashamed and humiliated I came down, and forced myself into a relationship with Tess. Kneeling, I said, 'Good Tess, dear old Tess,' and fondled her ears. She wagged her tail; all was forgiven.

It was a pleasant walk through pretty countryside. A sea breeze came across the fields, and then we saw the sea itself;

calm, with waves hissing majestically across the sand. What beauty, what peace, what tranquillity, I thought. What therapy for the disturbed mind.

'It's wonderful, Sue. I must stand still and absorb the atmosphere. You go on with Tess. I'll catch you up.'

I stood there on the cliff-edge, enchanted, wanting to hold on to that magic moment for ever. No cares, no worries, just a cool breeze, and the seabirds gliding freely in the sunny sky. The waves followed each other in a timeless pattern, to and fro, to and fro. There was no conflict, no chaos, only the fusion of order and freedom and harmony. It was sheer bliss to my troubled mind.

I lingered, reluctant to break the spell. If only I could enter into the spirit of the seabirds, soaring and gliding, in their element, carried along by the wind and using the air currents for their own benefit. Not mastering the elements but using them for their own pleasure.

I don't know how long I stood there meditating, but at last I looked around and there was no sign of Sue and Tess, so I made my own way down to the beach. It was so unspoilt and deserted. The gentle waves refreshed and soothed me. I looked out to the horizon. It was full of hope, full of promise, offering me a better future. Standing with my feet pressed into the sand, I saw my dream. It was a dream filled with hope, a dream of opportunity, a dream of self-realisation. I knew that some day I would overcome my problems, and I would be at peace with myself and with the world.

Reluctantly I turned my back on the sea and walked home to Sue's cottage. I was deep in thought. The sea had made me feel very calm.

When I arrived, tea was ready and Sue greeted me with a smile. 'Did you enjoy your walk?'

'It was wonderful, marvellous, uplifting.'

My peace of mind stayed with me all evening, and that night I slept soundly.

Next morning I went to Church with Sue. After the service Sue's mother arrived for lunch. She was fun. She spoke her mind and laughed at Sue's ordered style of life. Sue was embarrassed by her mother's outspoken manner, but to me it was refreshing.

We went to Church again that evening, and afterwards Sue invited the vicar home for coffee. He was a very pleasant man. He obviously respected Sue, and she had a high regard for him. I wondered whether a romance was in progress, but I didn't dare ask.

Sue showed us her colour slides from Africa. She had worked as a midwife there for two years. That evening was typical of Sue. She was the perfect hostess, entertaining us throughout. I went to bed feeling calm.

Next morning, after Sue had gone to work, I took Tess for a walk. I felt low, so I decided to go back to the cliffs, to try to recapture the magic of Saturday, but Tess wanted to walk the streets. I tugged at her lead, but she whined and resisted, sniffing at every tree and lamp-post.

'You wretched dog,' I shouted. 'Come on.' She wouldn't budge. In despair I gave in to her and she turned and ran towards home, pulling me behind her.

When we arrived at the cottage, I told Tess what I thought of her. 'You're a nasty dog, spoiling my morning like that. Stop whining. Go away and shut up.' Unknown to me, Sue was in the kitchen – it was her coffee time – and she overheard everything I said.

'Don't talk to Tess like that,' she called. 'You're not being very kind to her. She doesn't know where she is with you.'

I sat down listlessly, the tears ran down my cheeks. Sue placed a cup of coffee in front of me. 'I can't help myself,' I said. 'I don't mean to be unkind. I feel so depressed.'

'You behaved perfectly all day yesterday, so why can't you behave like it today?'

'How do I know?' I cried. 'If I could be different, I would. You don't really understand, do you?'

'Yes I do,' she said, 'But you must try to help yourself.'

This remark proved that she didn't really understand. We both fell silent.

For the rest of the day I felt wretched. My dream of Saturday had been blotted out. An impenetrable gloom now engulfed me. The more I tried to fathom the reasons for this anticlimax, the more imprisoned I felt. My dream was gone, and my hopes had vanished with it. There was nothing left.

That night I slept fitfully, tossing and turning and searching in my mind for a sign of hope, but no sign came. Instead my fears intensified and my body began to shake in terror. How long, I wondered, could I carry on living like this without becoming suicidal? Inches away from me stood a bottle of Librium and a bottle of sleeping tablets. What if an uncontrollable force took hold of me, and made me swallow those tablets? I climbed out of bed and slowly opened the bedside drawer. I stared at the tablets for some time. Then I lifted the bottles out of the drawer. 'In a little while I might decide to put an end to my misery,' I whispered, 'but how can I be sure that the end of this life will be the end of everything? Perhaps an existence after this life may be even worse than anything I've known so far. I'm afraid to die; I don't want to die.' I stared at the bottles in my hand. My moods were so unpredictable that in a few moments I might unscrew the bottle tops and swallow all the contents. What could I do? Sue must help me.

'Sue, Sue,' I screamed. I rushed into her bedroom and switched on the light. 'Help me, help me.' I was trembling and sobbing.

Sue had been sound asleep. She sat bolt upright in bed in alarm. 'What on earth's happened?'

'Take these tablets and hide them away from me,' I screamed. 'I'm afraid I'll swallow the lot. Keep them until morning, or I might suddenly kill myself.' Sue became very annoyed. 'Fancy waking me up with that nonsense,' she shouted. 'You haven't taken the tablets so you are not suicidal. Go back to bed and stop making all this fuss.'

'I ll go back to bed when you've taken these tablets from me,' I screeched. 'I may not be suicidal now, but I might be in a few minutes. Take them, take them, take them away from me.'

Sue realised she wouldn't get any more sleep that night unless she took the tablets. She held out her hand and I gave the bottles to her, then I rushed back to bed. I tossed and turned and sobbed until morning.

When daylight came through the curtains I got up and tiptoed onto the landing. Sue was there, looking tired. 'I'm going to the cliffs, but I won't take Tess. We don't get on.' I said.

After breakfast I left the house. I dawdled along the road until I came to the path that led up to the cliffs. It was very windy, and within a few minutes it began to rain. I carried on walking and by the time I reached the cliffs, it was raining so heavily I could scarcely see the sea. There were no birds to be seen and the horizon was just a blur. My dream was gone. There was no hope for me, no opportunity, no way to overcome my problems. I sat down on the grass in case the wind blew me over the cliffs. I peered through the rain, hoping to see a clearing in the sky, but there was none, and, blinded by my tears, I found that the sea had disappeared into the mist. I sat there in the soaking grass, a forlorn, dejected little lump of humanity.

What could I do? Suicide was too fearful and struggling was too painful. I could only wait. Wait for a clearing in the sky, wait for the rain to stop, wait for the birds to reappear, wait until the horizon became visible. I sat there for hours, waiting and watching. I knew I was behaving like an idiot. I began to feel colder and colder. I was soaked to the skin, covered with mud. I was hungry, thirsty. Yet I was transfixed. I couldn't move until a clearing in the sky gave me a ray of hope, something to believe in.

Gradually the rain began to ease. My eyes scanned the sky. Was that a light patch where the sun should be? I waited, watching and hoping.

At last it came: a sudden burst of sunlight through the clouds. The sun seemed to be laughing at me, so I laughed back. I looked towards the sea: it was still there, rougher than Saturday, but still ebbing to and fro. Then the horizon appeared.

'There is hope, there will be opportunity, I shall win through,' I shouted. 'I'll overcome the darkness, the sun is there even when I can't see it, the horizon is there even when the mist and the rain obscure it.' I jumped up and began running up and down the cliff path, waving my hands and shouting and laughing, not a care in the world. Then the rain stopped. I fell, breathless, against a tree. Suddenly I thought about Sue. She'd be worried, even to the extent of thinking I had killed myself. I had to get back to the cottage.

The way back led down a hill, and I was able to run

quickly. Within a quarter of an hour I was banging loudly on Sue's door. 'Sue, Sue, I'm back, I'm back.'

The look on Sue's face when she came to the door was indescribable. She was horrified. There I was, soaked to the skin and plastered in mud. I laughed crazily. She became very angry.

'I'm sorry,' I gasped. 'I got carried away on the cliff and I forgot the time. I didn't mean to worry you.'

'Look at the disgusting mess you are in. Drenched to the skin and covered in mud. There's even mud in your hair.'

'It can be washed off,' I chuckled. 'I'll go straight to the bathroom and clean myself up. I'll put my muddy clothes in a plastic bag.' I ran upstairs, and Sue followed me with a bag for my clothes.

My hot bath was fun. I sang at the top of my voice while I scrubbed the mud off my body. Then I dried myself, dressed and skipped downstairs. Sue placed a bowl of soup in front of me.

'You're so good,' I said. 'I don't deserve it. My walk on the cliffs had blown my cares away. I'm over the moon with happiness.'

Sue wasn't pleased to know that I was 'over the moon with happiness'. 'I'd rather you were just content and normal,' she said.

'So would I, but I'd rather be happy as I am now than in the depths of despair. Let's enjoy my happiness while it lasts.'

'Well, I'm not happy,' she said. 'I've been worried sick all day long about you.'

'I bet you've had enough of me, haven't you?' I said, provocatively. 'Would you like me to go tomorrow instead of Thursday? I'll go and plague Pat.'

Sue was exasperated. She said no more, but brought my dinner from the kitchen.

'You're a marvellous cook,' I said after dinner. 'Now let's have a party.'

'No thanks,' said Sue glumly.

I tried to control myself. I felt really happy and carefree, but I could tell my behaviour was beginning to get on her nerves, so I decided to quieten down and browse through some of her books. That way, I could have a good chuckle when I wanted to without annoying her.

My elation lasted all evening and into the night. When bedtime came, I crept upstairs and slept like a baby.

Next morning I worried about the effect of my behaviour on our friendship. I decided it was best for me to go, or we might not part as friends.

'Sue,' I said over breakfast. 'I'll leave today and go to Pat's a day earlier than I'd planned. She won't mind. You've had to put up with so much from me. I don't want to ruin our friendship.'

Sue didn't argue. She said, 'I hope you get yourself straightened out soon. Give my love to Pat when you see her.'

I packed my things quickly and put them in the boot of the car. Sue stood by the door of her cottage, looking sad and perplexed. I hugged her tightly, but she didn't seem to respond. Tess seemed to know that I was leaving, and she wagged her tail as if to say, 'Good riddance.'

I got quickly into the car and drove away. In my rear view mirror I could see Sue standing there. She gave a slight wave of her hand, and then she was gone.

I didn't need to phone Pat to tell her I was arriving a day earlier than expected. She wouldn't mind.

**29 March 1967**

The drive was very pleasant, through lovely countryside all the way. Spring, with its promise of renewal, was everywhere. There was hope in the air and hope in my heart.

It was mid-morning by the time I arrived at Pat's home. I let myself in. There was a note on the coffee table. It read: 'Pleased you've come. I'm asleep in bed. Been up all night on a delivery. Don't wake me. Make yourself a drink.'

I guessed Sue had phoned Pat to let her know I was coming. I worried in case Sue had spoken badly of me. I looked around. The flat was a mess; magazines littered the room, empty coffee mugs were standing on the table; cushions were scattered all over the floor. I picked up the dirty mugs and took them into the kitchen. The kitchen was an even bigger mess. Obviously Pat had been extremely busy recently. I looked in the pantry. There was very little food but to my amazement there were dozens of empty milk bottles. I counted them: there were eighty-four in all. I giggled: eighty-four empty milk bottles, a few slices of bread, a piece of cheese and an empty shopping basket in the food cupboard. My giggles changed to hysterical laughter. What a joke. What a mess.

'Don't stand there laughing,' said Pat suddenly. I turned. She was standing in the doorway yawning.

'I was laughing at the eighty-four empty milk bottles. What are you collecting them for?'

'I'm not collecting them. I'm just too lazy to put them on the doorstep.'

'I'll put them out for you,' I said, anxious to help.

'Not all at once,' Pat murmured. 'The milkman won't take that many.'

'The food cupboard is empty,' I said.

'I know. I've eaten everything. I've been out on deliveries for the last four nights, and I've had no time to go shopping. You can go to the shops for us if you like. That will be more useful than keeping me awake with your giggling.'

'What shall I buy?' I asked.

'Whatever the shop's selling. There's no choice in this village. If the shop's selling liver, you buy liver, if they're selling sausages you buy sausages. You don't have to make any decisions. When you come back, if you must laugh, stuff a hanky in your mouth. I need more sleep.'

Pat went back to bed, yawning, and I tiptoed out of the house, still chuckling at the chaos and the lack of routine. Pat's 'take me as you find me' attitude was such a pleasant contrast to Sue's strict routine. Here with Pat I felt relaxed and at home.

When I returned from the shops I tidied the flat and made myself a cup of coffee. I then sat quietly in an armchair, looking out of the window. I felt quite happy. Outside there was an enormous garden. It was overgrown, but it must have been a haven for many little creatures. A haven for them, just like the flat was a haven for me.

Pat appeared a couple of hours later. 'I've got a lot of nursings this afternoon,' she said. 'Can you pack some food and make a flask of coffee while I get ready? There's a lovely little village green near my first visit, so we could have our snack there. Then I could do the rest of my nursings. Later we can go down to the river. By then it will be about six o'clock, just in time for a meal at a quaint old inn overlooking the water.'

Soon we were on our way, carefree and happy. Pat was infected by my light-heartedness, and she giggled with me. 'Make hay while the sun shines,' she laughed. 'Tomorrow who knows what life will bring.'

We enjoyed ourselves that evening at the inn. At last it was time to go. 'We must get back,' said Pat. 'There's a baby due any time now in my village. I might be called up again to-night, so I'll try to get some sleep this evening.'

We arrived home at eight o'clock and chatted over a cup of coffee.

'How did you know I was coming this morning?' I asked. 'Did Sue phone you to tell you I was on the way?'

'Yes,' said Pat, 'and she warned me you're very unpredictable.'

'I feel ashamed at the way I behaved at Sue's. I don't understand why I was like it.'

'You probably felt let down by Dr Goldblatt,' Pat suggested.

'What do you mean?'

'Well, according to your letters, Dr Goldblatt has been encouraging you to depend on him, and just as you were beginning to do that, he suddenly told you he was going on holiday. You were left high and dry, so you were still feeling let down when you arrived at Sue's. Without meaning to, you probably took it out on her.'

'I feel really bad about it,' I said.

'There's no harm done. Forget it.'

We talked ourselves into a sleepy state and then went to bed.

That night the phone rang and I heard Pat leave the flat. I tossed and turned in bed and a sense of fear came over me. Why did I feel so frightened? Only a few hours ago I was laughing and joking with Pat.

Later that night Pat returned. I called out to her. She came into my bedroom and sat on the end of the bed. 'She's in her early stages of labour,' Pat said, 'so I've come home to get a bit more sleep. I'll go back and see what's happening first thing in the morning.'

'Pat,' I whispered, 'I'm crazy, aren't I?'

Pat laughed. 'No more than I am,' she said. 'Now, get to sleep, and you'll feel better in the morning.' She left me.

I cried on my pillow until it was saturated. No one could have a more understanding friend than I had in Pat, yet still this terrible depression was engulfing me.

Next morning I felt wretched. I just wanted to hide myself away. 'No you don't,' said Pat. 'You can help me. This mother in labour needs someone to sit with her this morning. I've got some visits to do, so I'll take you to her, and you can keep her company until I get back. I can't be in two places at once.'

I agreed. Pat took me to the woman's house and introduced me. Then as she left us she called, 'Back in two hours.'

The grandmother was also in the house. I decided to make the best of the situation. 'Let me make you more comfortable,' I said. I rearranged the mother's pillows, and wiped the perspiration from her forehead. I looked at her closely. This didn't look like early labour to me. 'How often are your contractions?' I asked. I was concerned.

'Ever so often,' she replied. 'In fact, I think I want to bear down.'

I quickly pulled on a mask and white gown, and pulled the bed covers back. The mother was right. The tip of the baby's head was just visible. I ran to the kitchen, washed my hands thoroughly and tugged on a pair of sterile gloves. I called out to granny, 'Baby will be here in a minute. Could you warm the cot please, and the baby's nightie?'

Luckily Pat had set everything in readiness. The important thing for me was to keep the mother calm. 'Don't worry,' I said. 'I'm a midwife from London. I've delivered hundreds of babies.'

The mother was delighted. 'Just wait till I tell my neighbours that a special midwife came all the way from London to deliver my baby,' she said proudly.

Gently I eased the baby's head out of the birth canal and within seconds he cried. Then I eased his shoulders and body up from the mother and laid him down and cut the cord. I checked him quickly and saw that he was perfect. 'You've got a lovely little boy,' I said.

She held her arms out and I gave him to her to cuddle. It was a model delivery. The mother was very calm and co-operative, and there were no problems. 'Enjoy your first contact with him,' I said. 'It's a unique experience. Rest his cheek on your breast, ' I waited a while and let the mother handle her baby. She soothed and suckled him. Then she handed him back to me. 'Thank you,' she said. I wrapped the baby in a warm towel and handed him to the grandmother. Then I attended to the mother.

I had just finished washing the mother, when Pat arrived, grinning from ear to ear. 'Baby O.K.?' she asked. Then she spoke to the mother, and checked her over. 'All perfect,' she said. 'I knew it would be.'

On our way home I said to Pat, 'Was that intentional? Did you know I would have to deliver that baby?'

Pat laughed but refused to say. 'I knew you'd handle whatever might arise. Who can predict the exact moment a baby will be born?'

I was proud of my day's work. The incident proved that however bad I felt I could rise to the occasion when necessity demanded action.

# 8 My Feelings of Inadequacy are Brought to the Surface

(6 April 1967 - 15 May 1967)

My first five treatment sessions with Dr Goldblatt dealt with one theme: 'dependence and interdependence'. My traumatic holiday with Sue and Pat gave me first-hand experience. With Sue I experienced an unsatisfactory form of dependence. I needed her help, but because I could give her nothing in return, she felt as though I was using her. I felt frustrated and guilty. With Pat, on the other hand, our relationship differed. There was a real state of interdependence between us. She entered into my feelings of elation and she enjoyed having a good laugh with me. She was indeed lonely herself in her tiny village. My company was good for her. When I became depressed she sympathized with me, she understood what was going on in my mind and she understood the nature of Dr Goldblatt's treatment. I had written to her every week, sharing my thoughts, my hopes, and my fears. I had quoted as accurately as I could many of Dr Goldblatt's comments, and as a result Pat was confident in the way she comforted me when I fell into despair. She derived great satisfaction in being able to help me through those dangerous times.

Dr Goldblatt's concept of interdependence had developed from being an intellectual acknowledgement on my part into a personal emotional experience.

There was still a long way for me to go, but at least I believed I was making progress in being able to apply Dr Goldblatt's theory to a real life situation.

## 6 April 1967

My first meeting with Dr Goldblatt after my 'holiday' was the sixth session of treatment. I felt tense. There was so much to say in so short a time. I began by telling him about the way I had behaved on my 'holiday'. I was afraid I might become suicidal. I talked about my brother Alan, and how resentful I felt towards the doctors who had treated him.

Dr Goldblatt didn't say a word. I was annoyed. I might as well have been talking to myself. He could be asleep, or reading a book, for all I knew. Eventually I sat up. 'I hate this couch,' I said. 'Why can't I sit watching you? How do I know you're listening when you won't say anything?'

'You distrust me,' he said.

'Yes I do. I need to see you, otherwise I can't trust you.' I turned around, and sat on the edge of the couch, so that I could see him. I remained in that position for the rest of the session.

Then I told him about my interdependence with Pat. He looked pleased.

'But there's something that's worrying me,' I said.

'Tell me about it,' he said gently.

I hesitated. This would be difficult. He might not understand. 'I'm in a state of conflict all the time,' I blurted out. 'I've had a very strong religious upbringing, and some of those beliefs don't seem to hold water any more. My religion has taught me that it's wrong to seek self-satisfaction, but this idea doesn't seem logical to me. If I follow my reason and accept the idea of self-satisfaction I feel guilty because I am going against my religion. I feel bewildered and imprisoned in a maze of contradictory arguments going on inside my head.'

'Growing up involves reassessing the beliefs and standards your parents have given you,' he said.

'But how do I know my reason is more reliable than what I've been taught?' I asked.

'Your ego isn't fully developed,' he replied. 'Be patient, and you will know.'

How could I be patient when I was feeling more and more tense and anxious by the minute? My mind flitted desperately from one topic to another. I couldn't concentrate.

I struggled to find something to say that would convey to Dr Goldblatt how desperate and confused I felt. I could see from his expression that he cared; I could see he wanted to understand, but I felt a distance between us that words couldn't bridge. I felt he couldn't possibly understand the hold my religious upbringing had on me. Had I been brainwashed? Was I addicted to it like a drug? Or was Dr Goldblatt brainwashing me? Was I becoming addicted to him? How could I assess my position when I couldn't think straight? Whom could I trust? Whom could I rely on?

At last I managed to say, 'I'm frightened of depending too much on tranquillisers . . . and on you.'

Dr Goldblatt said nothing. He seemed to be waiting . . . waiting for me to tell him about my real worries . . . waiting for me to put my confusion into words . . . but I couldn't. I was afraid to admit to myself that my Christian Faith, around which my life had revolved, now meant nothing to me. Without it I would have no purpose in life; no standards; no morals. I wanted to retain my Faith . . . I *would* retain my Faith . . . .

I felt dizzy and sick, swinging between feelings of satisfaction at my resolve to stand firm in my Christian beliefs, and feelings of unease at the incompatibility of many of those beliefs.

I wanted to jump off the couch, stamp my foot, shout at Dr Goldblatt for not rescuing me from my dilemma, and rush from the room. I pictured the drama, but I couldn't act it out.

Eventually I said, 'The way I oscillate between excitement and despair worries me more than anything.'

'It's a symptom of the conflict you are experiencing between your own reason and your own conscience,' he explained.

'If I resolve the conflict, shall I overcome my unstable moods?'

'It would seem so,' he replied.

After the session I walked slowly back to my car and got in. I didn't drive away immediately. I had to think carefully about the implications of what had been brought home to me in that eventful hour. I had discovered that my mood changes were a symptom of the conflicting ideas, hopes and fears that were dominating my mind. To cure the symptom I had to sort out those conflicting thoughts. Yet how could I? I was afraid of the consequences of doing that. My only defence against my confusion was to stop questioning my religion. I must accept what I had been taught and trust in God.

I realised that I needed and wanted Dr Goldblatt's help, but it would have to be on my terms, not his. I wanted him to cure my symptoms without driving me to question the whole basis of my life.

I drove home, determined to keep hold of my religion with one hand, and Dr Goldblatt with the other. I would just have to try to ignore the conflicting thoughts and feelings these seemingly opposing forces were causing.

However, my daily life still had to be lived. On Friday morning the thought of visiting filled me with dread. I felt I had nothing to offer the mothers. Why should my advice be of any use to them?

Determined not to give in, however, I made up a list of families needing routine visits, and off I went. At the first house I hesitated before knocking on the door. What was the point, I thought. What do I say when the mother comes to the door? My uneasiness increased. The more I tried to force myself to knock the more convinced I became that I had nothing to say. I turned and fled. This fiasco happened three more times until I realised it was useless to keep on trying. I drove back to the clinic in a state of embarrassment and abject disgust.

At the clinic I told myself that I was useless and I had better find another job. But I couldn't think of any job I would be capable of. I squeezed my hands together and stared out of the window, desperate for inspiration; but none came. My eyes filled with tears as I sat at my desk, a sad and lonely human being.

'What's the matter?' a voice called. Rita had returned from her visits. She came and sat beside me. 'I told you psychotherapy would be difficult,' she said.

'It isn't that,' I sobbed. 'I'm no longer fit to do this job. What can I do?'

'What on earth are you talking about?' she said. 'The mothers love your Wednesday classes.'

'But it's the visits,' I replied. 'I feel totally inadequate. I should have called on four mothers this morning and each time I ran away. My father keeps saying psychotherapy is doing me more harm than good. But if I stop going, where else will I get help?'

'It seems to me you're craving for approval all the time. Just do what you know is right; give the advice you think is appropriate, and be content with that. You can't run the whole of your life according to what other people think.'

'You sound like Dr Goldblatt only more positive and forceful,' I said. 'He thinks my ego isn't developed.'

'How right he is,' said Rita. She made me a cup of coffee and we chatted for a while.

'How do I know if I'm giving mothers the right advice?' I said. 'Supposing I've got everything all wrong: back to front?'

'You've done enough analysing for the time being, save it up for Dr Goldblatt,' said Rita. 'Let's have some lunch.' She talked about unrelated matters while we were eating our sandwiches and I tried to join in, but it was difficult. After lunch I made a second attempt and visited mothers with postnatal depression. Luckily I found those visits relatively easy, but afterwards I worried that I hadn't really said anything constructive to them. I felt angry on their behalf that they were seeing a psychiatrist for only ten minutes each month. The NHS seemed to be totally inadequate in its provision for depression cases.

By the end of the day I was exhausted. I decided to go home and try to think things over. Why did I suffer from having such a nagging conscience?

I spent the evening alone in my bedroom. I realised I would have to think constructively about the conflict in my mind if I were to regain my equilibrium. In practically everything I thought about or did, my conscience pulled me one way, while my reason pulled in the opposite direction. My conscience and my reason were most noticeably opposed over the way I was dealing with my mental illness. I felt I ought to accept the illness as being 'God's Will' and trust him with the outcome. If I could do that, my conscience would be clear. However, I wasn't prepared to trust God with the outcome, in case he allowed me to develop schizophrenia like my brother. I wanted to fight and overcome my problems by whatever means offered a chance of success, even it if meant turning away from God.

I had to admit that my mental health was more important to me than my Christian Faith. If put to the test on matters of real importance, I would follow my reason in preference to my conscience and my faith.

I felt sick and dizzy with anxiety. Who was I to question my conscience? How could I question my faith? By definition, faith was something one accepted. Once questioned, it ceased to be faith.

I felt stranded. I had no faith. My ego (or self) was underdeveloped. I was left with the worst of both worlds. Christianity with no faith was hypocrisy, and therefore useless. Life with an underdeveloped ego was hell.

I had to escape from the hell my life had become. But how? Dr Goldblatt had implied that I should develop my ego, but to do that I would have to think about myself; I would have to remind myself of what I wanted and what I needed, and what I was capable of. Yet my conscience would only leave me in peace when I thought about my failings and inadequacies. However, when I did that, I felt so useless I couldn't cope with life.

It was a catch 22 situation of the worse kind. I saw no way of escape from my debilitating conscience, but if I gave way to the dictates of my conscience it would destroy me.

These thoughts occupied my mind for days but I didn't make any progress. At the weekend I felt totally confused and bewildered. I had an increasing desire to be on my own. My awareness of my lack of ego intensified when I came into contact with people. I felt inferior, inadequate and useless. I tried to think my way through the stalemate when I was on my own at home but, after a wasted weekend of self-analysis, I went back to work on the Monday feeling even more discouraged. What use were my sessions with Dr Goldblatt? I couldn't even solve one simple problem on my own.

Suddenly my thoughts cleared. Dr Goldblatt! Of course! He was helping me. I was not on my own. I counted the days to when we would meet again. I realised I trusted him and respected him. I believed in his integrity. This trust was not a blind faith, but it was an acceptance of the evidence I'd had from my dealings with him. I would try to depend on him from now on, because he had shown himself to be dependable.

It was strange. All weekend I had worried and worried, then, just one thought had suddenly released me from the dreadful cage into which I had trapped myself.

Straight away I felt more confident and able to cope.

**13 April 1967**

The waiting room at Harley Street was becoming familiar to me like my own room at home. I felt relaxed and full of anticipation. Even the couch no longer filled me with dread. I trusted Dr Goldblatt and I believed he was really helping me. I looked forward to seeing him because I felt he could bring me a step nearer to sanity.

The receptionist told me to go upstairs. Dr Goldblatt was waiting on the landing as usual. To my surprise he showed me to an armchair; he then sat at right angles to me in a second armchair. I felt more ready and able to talk: more human. On the couch I really felt like a patient.

I began talking. 'It was terrible at work at the end of last week,' I said. 'I couldn't visit my mothers. I felt so inadequate I wanted to change my job.'

'Why do you think you felt inadequate?'

'I think it was because I wasn't sure my advice was the best advice to give,' I said. 'I had no confidence in my judgement, or in my ability to judge the difference between right and wrong. I'm still confused now, but from Monday I felt much better.'

'What made you feel better?' he asked.

'I felt better when I realised I could trust you, and I believed you would help me.'

'You seem to be learning to depend on me,' he said. I couldn't tell whether he was pleased. His expression betrayed nothing.

'My parents don't understand why I'm having psychotherapy. They believe it will do me harm.'

'What your parents think doesn't matter,' he stated categorically, 'as long as you are confident you've made the right decision.'

'But I'm still confused about right and wrong,' I replied. 'I'm not confident about anything. What's my prognosis? Will I ever overcome my depression? How long must I suffer like this?'

'It's impossible for me to say, but this week has been encouraging for both of us. You now seem able to resolve some of your inadequate feelings by applying the ideas we have been working on. You have learnt to depend on me to some extent, and that is progress. I have a month's holiday at the end of August, but judging by your progress so far, maybe you will not miss me too much.'

'I'm still confused about right and wrong,' I said. 'I'm torn all the time between my reason and my conscience. Sometimes I don't know which way to turn.'

'Let me give you a tip,' he said. 'Question your conscience every time doubt arises. If you think you ought not to do something, ask yourself 'why not'. If you can't find a satisfactory answer to that question, then go ahead and do what seems reasonable.'

I left the consulting room more confident in Dr Goldblatt than ever. He had compromised by allowing me to sit in an armchair where I could watch him. He had given me straightforward advice. This new approach showed me that he understood my needs and was ready to meet them in a way that I found acceptable.

That evening I felt confident that my state of mind was improving, so I decided to stop taking my Librium and sleeping tablets. There was no adverse effect the next day, but on the second night I had a most unpleasant dream about my brother Alan. He was trying to strangle me, and I woke up at the point where his grip around my neck had tightened so fiercely I could hardly breathe. I sat bolt upright in bed, my heart pounding. The dream terrified me. I wanted to have pleasant memories of Alan. He was loving, kind and gentle, but the dream left me shattered. That weekend I couldn't get the horror from my mind. I could actually feel my brother's hands gripping into the sides of my neck.

On the Monday I had a hospital appointment. It was a routine check, following my hysterectomy. Throughout the weekend I had a slight abdominal pain and diarrhoea. I told myself that these symptoms were of psychological origin.

On the Monday morning I was very nervous so I took a Librium tablet, hoping it would calm me down. I didn't really want to keep the appointment.

The out-patients' department was like a cattle market. There were dozens of women sitting huddled together, waiting for their turn, and most of them looked very miserable. The woman sitting next to me began talking.

'I had a hysterectomy two years ago,' she said, 'and I had a nervous breakdown afterwards.'

'Did you have any treatment?' I asked.

'I had ECT.'

'Did it help you?'

'It did for a while. But then I got depressed again, and I had to go back into hospital for more ECT. The trouble is I've now become forgetful.'

I was glad I was having psychotherapy and not ECT. From what this woman told me, her treatment seemed to have nasty side-effects.

At last my name was called. The nurse showed me into a tiny cubicle, where a young doctor was waiting. 'Any problems?' he asked, as I was climbing on to the couch.

'I'm having psychotherapy for depression,' I answered, 'and I have a few pains, but I think it's psychological.'

He examined me. 'Fine,' he said. He paused. 'Er – are you thinking of getting married?'

'No,' I replied. 'I haven't got a boyfriend.'

'Well,' he said. 'Don't let this operation affect you. If you do get married and want to adopt children, we would be happy to give you a medical certificate clearing you as medically fit.'

'Oh, thank you,' I said. It was a great relief to know that one part of me at least was all right.

After the check up my diarrhoea stopped; but a feeling of despair came over me. That evening I sat alone in my bedroom, staring at the floor. I was drained of energy. I crept into bed.

The next thing I remember was seeing my brother Alan staring at me. I couldn't escape. I tried to tell him I loved him and meant him no harm, but I couldn't speak. I stood rooted to the spot. Alan came towards me; nearer and nearer. I was about to scream when his hands shot forward and seized me by the throat. I began kicking him, but his grip tightened. Then a violent trembling sensation passed through my body. I was suddenly alone, but I was shaking from head to toe. I tried to struggle, to scream, to fight against it, but it was hopeless. Exhausted, I abandoned myself to the dream, and gradually the trembling died down.

I woke up sobbing and gasping. I was bathed in perspiration. I looked at my watch. It was still the early hours of the morning, so I took a sleeping tablet. I must sleep or I'd be unfit for work in the morning.

That morning I woke up early. Alan's face was etched on my mind. The feel of his hands still seemed to be around my neck. The bedroom was cold and silent and yet only a few hours ago I had fought a terrible battle with my own dear brother. We had been locked in deadly combat. I shuddered and went to the bathroom. Somehow I dressed and made myself ready for work.

## 20 April 1967

In Dr Goldblatt's waiting room that Thursday the atmosphere had changed. There was more activity; there were more people than usual. A man was sitting in an armchair at the far end, but he made no attempt to look at me. A receptionist I had never seen before was bustling about. Somewhere a buzzer sounded, but it was ignored. After a few moments I heard Dr Goldblatt's voice, 'Will you come up please?' He was standing at the exit door waiting for me. I rose and walked towards him. He stood to one side to let me pass up the stairs first, then he followed me. I walked into his room, expecting the two armchairs to be arranged at right angles, but they weren't. Instead I had to lie on the couch. I felt humiliated. 'He thinks I'm not good enough to sit in his armchair,' I thought. I climbed reluctantly on to the couch. I lay there quietly for a few minutes, then I said, 'I haven't taken any Librium this week except when I had to go to the hospital on Monday.'

'If you are going to mess about with your tablets,' he said, 'it's probably as well not to take them any more. You must do one thing or the other: either take them regularly or not at all.'

He seemed to be irritated, but without seeing his face I couldn't be sure. I wanted to cry, but I managed to control myself. My thoughts went to Alan. 'I've had terrible dreams about my brother trying to strangle me,' I said.

'Did he ever really do that?' Dr Goldblatt asked.

'He did grab me around the neck sometimes. It was very frightening, but I don't think he was actually trying to harm me.'

'Nevertheless, you would have been frightened,' he said, 'and your human nature would have sought self-preservation. You would have wanted to fight back, but the thought of fighting back would have made you feel guilty because in your subconscious mind you would have really wanted to kill him.'

'I don't believe I ever wanted to kill him, not even subconsciously. I loved him.' The idea that I wanted to kill my brother was offensive.

'Wanting your brother dead,' persisted Dr Goldblatt ruthlessly, 'would have made you feel desperately guilty. You need to understand that you are feeling guilty about something which is a part of your essential make-up, your drive for self-preservation. Without this, you would be dead.'

He spoke loudly, emphatically, determined to pursue me with his interpretation of my dream, despite the pain it was causing me. His whole approach and manner were different; more aggressive. He was driving me into accepting his point of view. It was a point of view I didn't want to accept.

The following week was full of struggle and conflict. Although I disliked Dr Goldblatt's new method, I knew I needed him. Memories of Alan haunted me day and night. On my own I couldn't escape. Dr Goldblatt was my only hope. I wished the week away until my next session.

## 27 April 1967

That next session as I lay on the couch I tried to recall my problems of the previous week.

'I feel resentful towards my parents,' I said. 'They should have understood Alan better, and they should have done more to help him. I blame them for much of his suffering.'

'Your resentment towards your parents is a form of misplaced guilt. You feel guilty because you didn't fully understand Alan and because you were unable to help him. You are projecting your guilt on to your parents.'

'I can't see that,' I said. 'I don't feel guilty about Alan any more because at the time I did what I could, and I was too young anyway to know how to help him. My parents were the guilty ones. They didn't bring him the help he needed. They allowed him to suffer for years.'

'Perhaps you don't feel guilty about Alan; but you do feel guilty about condemning your parents.'

'It's wrong to cast judgement on people,' I said.

'Why?' he queried.

'It's what I've been taught.' I thought of a verse in the Bible which begins, 'Judge not.'

Dr Goldblatt continued: 'Question your conscience. Is it wrong to judge others? Is it wrong to disapprove of people's actions? You seem to feel you must either approve of others or run the risk of being rejected by them.'

'I want approval,' I said. 'I want my parents to approve of what I'm doing. I feel guilty that they don't approve of my psychotherapy treatment.'

'You are in a position where whatever you do is wrong to your way of thinking. You even feel it's wrong to think for yourself.'

There was a long pause. What could I say? He had trapped me. I looked at the clock. I was wasting money, lying on the couch and saying nothing.

'I'm stuck,' I said. 'Please say something.'

'Tell me what you advise mothers in your mothercraft classes when you discuss their relationship with their babies.'

'I tell them to enjoy their children and to adapt to their needs. I don't give any rigid advice, but I encourage them to be fairly permissive and understanding.'

'You don't have this permissive attitude to yourself,' he remarked. 'Do you feel guilty about giving this advice? Are you doing the right thing?'

'I wouldn't be happy giving any other kind of advice,' I said.

'I must say I approve of the advice you give to your mothers,' he said. 'Apply this to yourself. Don't be so severe with yourself.'

I was silent again, but this time I didn't feel uncomfortable. Time was passing. I began to realise the implications of what Dr Goldblatt was telling me. My whole attitude to myself needed revising.

'You must go now,' Dr Goldblatt said. Slowly I got up from the couch and wandered out of the room and down the stairs. I didn't want to hurry away, so I went into the cloakroom. For a while I leant against the wall, thinking of nothing in particular; just allowing my mind to take in some of Dr Goldblatt's words: 'You feel guilty' . . . 'Question your conscience' . . . 'Don't be so severe with yourself.' It was easy to say these things, but far less easy to apply them to myself.

There was no let-up in my feelings of inadequacy at work. My clinics and my mothercraft classes were highlights of each week, but they failed to compensate for my failings during the rest of the week. Rightly or wrongly, the advice I gave to people on my visits seemed to me to be worthless. There was no feedback.

In addition, another problem came along. I dreaded going into shops. Although I lived with my parents, I was independent in the sense that I prepared my own meals and did my own washing. This involved regular shopping trips. The shops that I dreaded most were those with an assistant behind the counter. My mind would go blank and I was unable to think of what to ask for. Even the supermarkets caused me anxiety as I was afraid I might accidentally drop something into my bag and be accused of shoplifting. What a disgrace it would be if the local paper carried headlines:

HEALTH VISITOR CAUGHT SHOPLIFTING.

I decided not to take my own shopping bag into shops; I would buy only what I could carry out in my arms. This practice eased my anxiety but it increased the number of shopping trips I had to make. The difficulty of thinking what to buy still remained. I solved that problem by eating the same meals every day.

This method didn't solve my shopping problems, but at least it enabled me to cope with life a little better.

I never discussed my shopping phobia with Dr Goldblatt because it didn't come to my mind when I was with him. It worried me only when I needed to go shopping; but shopping was only one of many bits and pieces of my life that were difficult. Most of the time I felt tired and unable to enjoy anything. Often I wanted to hide myself away and blot out my feelings. But I realised that to recover I had to keep on facing the world each day as best I could and not try to run away from myself. It was as if I was being made to walk about lugging a pair of giant suitcases, loaded with my fears and anxieties.

## 4 May 1967

On the couch again I presented Dr Goldblatt with my most worrying problem, my feeling of inadequacy at work.

'You need approval for everything you do,' he said; 'If you are not shown approval you are discouraged. You must learn to identify the signs of approval in other people, so that you can recognise approval when you are in need of encouragement.'

There was a long pause.

'I don't know what to say to you,' I complained. 'I keep harping back to the same old theme. You must get bored. I wish I could think of something interesting to say.'

There was another pause.

'Please ask me some questions,' I said. 'It's such a waste of time, just lying here saying nothing to you.'

'It is true that you keep harping back to the same theme, and you will continue to do so until you have worked right through it.'

'Then help me by asking me questions,' I persisted.

'I won't ask you questions,' he said. 'You are reluctant to

keep talking about what's on your mind because you think you are not as I want you to be. You think you will bore me, and you think I don't want to be bored.'

'Isn't that true?' I asked.

'It is misrepresentation of me,' he replied. 'You bring this misrepresentation into all your relationships, and that is why you want to please me and to be approved of by me.'

'But I can't help wanting to please you,' I said.

'I simply want you to be yourself,' he replied.

'But I can't,' I groaned.

'I'm satisfied with the way you are. All that you have said today has given me what I want: an insight into your feelings.'

'It's difficult to believe that people will accept me as I am,' I said, 'because I can't accept myself as I am. I feel insignificant because I can't have children. Every man has the right to expect his wife to give him children. If ever I married I would deny my husband that right. That's why I feel so badly about myself.'

'Think again about the implications of having a hysterectomy. There are disadvantages in not being able to have children, but you have the wrong idea of those disadvantages.'

'Maybe there are disadvantages I haven't considered,' I replied. 'But the biggest disadvantage is that I would not be able to fulfil my responsibilities as a wife.'

'You had those fears and anxieties before your operation,' he said. 'They are not the result of the operation.'

I thought about his last remark. He implied that I was using my hysterectomy as an excuse for my depression. I felt defenceless. Dr Goldblatt wouldn't let me hide behind my operation. If my problem was not caused by some external factor then there must be something more fundamental wrong with me.

I felt very confused, but I could find no words to express that confusion. I lay quietly until it was time to go.

My struggle continued, but since my stay with Pat I hadn't had any moments of elation. Life was becoming increasingly difficult to bear. Doubts about the wisdom of continuing with psychotherapy plagued me. I wondered whether Dr Goldblatt would like me to end the treatment. Maybe he realised that I was unsuitable but he was too kind to say so.

During the occasions when I was able to cope, I wondered if I needed treatment at all. After all, my father believed I could overcome the depression on my own. Doubts engulfed me at every turn.

In the hope of finding some distraction, I bought an old TV to use in my bedroom. Most of the time I was brought to tears because I knew I lacked the confidence of the people I was watching on the screen.

Dreams were a problem, but I didn't want to start taking sleeping tablets again. I began drinking – just a small glass of sherry at bedtimes. I kept the sherry by my bed, and every time I woke up in the night I reached out for the bottle. Some nights I drank half a bottle or more. The sherry seemed to take the edge off my depression. My conscience told me it was wrong to try to drown my sorrows in drink, but my reason told me that without drink my depression could overwhelm me.

I was comforted by the thought that I was now beginning to follow my reason and argue against my conscience. Trying out Dr Goldblatt's advice in this way meant that at last I was acting more positively.

The week passed by and at last Thursday came when I would see Dr Goldblatt; he was still my only hope.

## 11 May 1967

I drove to Harley Street. It was difficult to find a parking space. I was in a panic. If I missed my treatment I would not survive another week. I drove around until eventually at some distance from Harley Street I found a parking space. Sobbing with relief I parked the car and hurried to Dr Goldblatt's, arriving just in time.

As usual Dr Goldblatt was standing on the landing outside his room; he smiled kindly and followed me in. I was envious of his composure. I wondered how such a calm, mature man could understand such an insignificant, pathetic creature like me. If he did understand me then he really was an incredible person.

I climbed onto the couch and stared at the ceiling. My mind was a blank.

'I don't know what to say,' I said, then the room fell silent. The sound of Dr Goldblatt striking a match to light his cigarette broke the silence. I wanted to scream. Psychotherapy seemed totally useless at that moment.

'There's still a lot of conflict in my mind,' I said at last. 'There were times last week when I felt I was getting worse, and I thought if you knew I was deteriorating you wouldn't want to continue treating me. Then when I felt better I thought I might be wasting your time, bothering you with trivialities.'

'You are constantly trying to work out what other people want of you. You don't consider what you yourself want,' he said firmly.

I became very tense. Together we seemed to have reached a dead end. I fidgeted, not knowing what to do or say.

'You are very tense,' he said. 'That's because you don't know what I want of you. You feel you have nothing to give.'

There was a long uncomfortable pause.

'My mind is a blank,' I said. 'I prefer you to do the talking, so that I have something to think about.'

'I have already said plenty for you to think about.'

'Then why do I feel so inadequate and uncertain of myself?' I asked.

'As a child you experienced a disparity between your natural inclinations and what was expected of you. You felt that if you behaved naturally, you would displease your mother. You wanted to please her but she was unable to show approval or pleasure, so you were confused about what would please her. You didn't know what to do to please her. Now you are bringing those same feelings into our relationship. You are hoping to please me, but you are confused about what I really want of you. Even though I tell you I approve of you, you are unable to feel it to be so.'

'Then what can I do?' I asked in despair.

'You must recognise your feelings for what they are,' he replied. 'Your feelings are not related to reality; they don't convey to you what you really are. You are of value and you are of worth. You have got to learn not to act entirely on your feelings. You have to act on what you know to be true.'

'But you also say I should accept my feelings,' I protested.

'Yes, I agree,' he said. 'You should accept your feelings, but you have to learn to discriminate between those feelings which are based on misconceptions and those feelings which are a normal part of you. It's my task to help you do that.'

'But how can I lead a life feeling inadequate, yet knowing I'm not?'

'Given time your feelings will gradually change, and come into line with what you know to be true. It will be a painful process, but you must be patient and brave.'

Intellectually I understood what Dr Goldblatt meant. In many ways my feelings were incompatible with my reason. Somehow I had to discriminate between my feelings which were based on misconceptions, and my feelings which were normal; but in my confusion I doubted my ability to discriminate.

As I was about to leave, Dr Goldblatt asked if he could change my appointment to Wednesdays at 5 p.m. I was glad. It meant that I had only six days to wait until the next session, when he could once more help me to sort out the muddle in my mind.

The next day I visited a midwife I had known during my training. She had recently come home after an extensive operation for cancer. Two years previously she had had a hysterectomy, and had been told she was cured. We sat and chatted for a while. She asked me how I was feeling and I told her about my depression.

'Your trouble is,' she said, 'you don't explode. You've had an awful thing done to you. You are young, and you've been denied the chance of having children of your own. Yet you speak as though you shouldn't be depressed. You should be. Show your feelings, shout and rave at people a bit. I do.'

'I couldn't be like that,' I said. 'When I go to Church on Sundays I often feel like walking out, but I force myself to stay through the service.'

'Why?' she asked. 'After I had my hysterectomy I often got up and walked out in the middle of the service. Why shouldn't I? Why shouldn't you? Your feelings are as important as anyone else's. A church service shouldn't be an endurance test. When you've had enough, walk out.'

I smiled. Sound advice or not, I could never follow it.

'Don't brood,' she said. 'Join a club; meet new people.'

'But how?' I asked. 'I don't like dancing. How else can I meet people?'

'There are some tennis courts at the back of the Methodist Church. The tennis club meets there every Saturday afternoon. Do you play tennis?'

'I did when I was a teenager.'

'Then join the tennis club,' she said. 'Turn up at 2 p.m. on Saturday and ask for Muriel. Tell her I sent you.'

That Saturday, feeling extremely nervous and self-conscious, I went to the tennis courts with my racket and some money. There were about ten people sitting in deckchairs. On each court a doubles match was taking place. I stood around for a few minutes, but no one took any notice of me. Eventually someone looked in my direction, so I asked for Muriel. I was directed to the changing rooms.

Muriel was about ten years older than me. She was quite pleasant, but she had little to say. Then she called out to the people sitting on the deckchairs that I was a new club member. A few heads turned and smiled. I sat down on a spare deckchair and watched the games in silence.

Eventually it was my turn to play. All at once I had a strong urge to run. I hadn't played much tennis. Feelings of inferiority swamped me, and I played really badly. I thought the other players were exasperated, so I said I wasn't feeling well, and someone else took my place. For the rest of the afternoon I sat silently in a deck chair. No one spoke to me.

When I arrived home I wondered about whether to go again; but if I didn't go, I'd feel defeated. My feelings of worthlessness had to be overcome, so I resolved to continue, however much I might dread Saturday afternoons.

I went to Church as usual on Sunday, but I felt no enthusiasm for what was going on. In fact the service seemed meaningless. I didn't belong anywhere any more. I shuddered. The thought that even my religion held no hope for me left me feeling cold and empty. The hymns brought tears to my eyes, and the prayers hit out at me and condemned me.

# 9 Facing My Central Problem

(16 May 1967 - 31 May 1967)

I remained in a state of deep depression. Everything I did was a great effort, and required all my willpower. On the evening of Tuesday 16 May 1967 I sat in my bedroom and watched television, hoping it would distract me. My mind wandered. I felt worse than I could ever remember. Despite my psychotherapy treatment my symptoms increased and intensified. Was this because of the psychotherapy I wondered? Yet if I hadn't gone to Dr Goldblatt I believed I would have deteriorated anyway. I might have ended up in the hands of doctors I didn't trust. At least with the present situation, I had some degree of control over my treatment, but I wished I had more. I wanted Dr Goldblatt to be less analytical and more supportive. I had gone to him originally because my symptoms had become intolerable. I had asked him to help me. I hadn't realised he would pull me to pieces. Now he was taking his time to put me back together again. I was hoping he would be able to reduce my symptoms so that I could lead a more normal life. Why couldn't he do that? Why couldn't he postpone dealing with my personality defects until later when I hoped to be stronger in my mind?

Supposing his analysing went too far? Supposing he pushed me beyond the point of no return? How could he know what he was really doing to me? I saw him for only one hour a week; in that time I couldn't tell him everything I was going through, and I tended to keep some things to myself. I felt that the extreme anguish I was experiencing was not being revealed. Dr Goldblatt was hearing only a part of my story.

I felt trapped. Dr Goldblatt was my only life-line. I had to hang on to him or I'd sink. Yet that very life-line seemed to be dragging me down. Was there no way out of my hell? If I died there might be an even worse hell in store for me.

There was no alternative but for me to endure life. I had to believe that Dr Goldblatt really had my welfare at heart. I had to believe that my few friends would remain loyal to me and pick up the pieces if I disintegrated. How pathetic I was: completely dependent on three people – Dr Goldblatt, Rita and Pat; unable to help myself in my desperate plight.

Wearily I switched off the television and got ready for bed. I took my sherry bottle from the cupboard; I climbed into bed and sat resting against my pillows and began drinking.

My mothercraft class on the Wednesday morning was like an oasis of happiness. The mothers were happy and their friendliness was a tonic to me. I was slightly light-headed from the sherry of the night before, and their laughter was infectious. We were discussing permissiveness in child-rearing in relation to the feeding of babies. I always enjoyed that topic because it gave me an insight into the mothers' attitudes, and it helped me to give appropriate advice when I visited them after their babies were born. After the discussion we did relaxation training together, and then the mothers dozed for a short time while I had a cup of tea before the next class came.

I had two classes on Wednesday because of the demand. The first class was from 9.15 a.m. until 10.30 a.m., and the second class was from 10.45 a.m. until 12 noon.

It was a hectic morning, but I liked it that way. If I kept going I could cope. By working hard and by concentrating hard I could almost forget my despair. It was as though I could actually put it to one side. Right up until the last mother left at 12 o'clock I was outwardly lively and happy, and entering into the mothers' experiences.

But once the clinic door was closed, I rushed to my desk and dissolved into tears. The effort of the morning's work was so great that it took me at least half an hour before I was able to recover enough to eat my lunch.

My colleagues were baffled at the strange contrast in my behaviour.

'You are funny, Margaret,' one of them said. 'On Tuesday afternoons you are all right when the mothers come to see you, and on Wednesday mornings the clinic is alive with happy expectant mothers enjoying themselves. Yet as soon as they are gone you suddenly become downhearted. What is the real you like?'

'I don't know,' I said and burst into tears again. 'I'm so mixed up. I don't know what to think any more. You're all so understanding and tolerant, but I feel absolutely useless.'

That afternoon I managed to compose myself sufficiently to visit a few expectant mothers, and invite them to the next mothercraft class. Then it was time for me to drive to Harley Street.

Wearily I got in my car and headed for London. A feeling of gloom and foreboding engulfed me, and I could no longer ignore it. There was no need to concentrate on my driving, since I knew the way by heart; every bump in the road was familiar to me. My mind wandered.

The prospect of seeing Dr Goldblatt didn't uplift me. I didn't expect to feel any better after the session. I just hung desperately to the hope that, despite how I felt, Dr Goldblatt would help me through.

## 17 May 1967

I found a parking space without too much trouble, and walked slowly along the familiar roads to Harley Street. I soon arrived and wandered through into the cloakroom. My eyes were puffed from too much crying and I looked a picture of abject misery. Maybe Dr Goldblatt would take pity on me. I walked into the waiting room, sat on the first settee I came to, and stared listlessly into space.

'Please come this way.' The receptionist's voice startled me. Feeling dazed, I picked up my bag and went through the door to the stairs. Dr Goldblatt was standing at the door of his room as usual. I looked up at him, but I was unable to judge what lay behind his kindly expression. Was he really kind, or was his expression a professional mask?

I longed to ask to be allowed to sit on a chair, but I was uncertain how he would react, and I couldn't face a confrontation. I wanted him to be kind.

I climbed onto the couch and lay down. I waited a few seconds, then I said, 'I've felt very depressed since Sunday. I've felt lonely and isolated; outside of everything that's going on. I've never felt so depressed before.' I waited for him to say something.

After a pause he said, 'What right have you to feel anything other than depressed?' I detected no kindness in his voice. He sounded harsh.

I was startled, shocked. What was he trying to do to me? 'I don't understand what you mean,' I murmured.

'What right have you to feel anything other than depressed?' he repeated. 'Who has made you feel you have a right to happiness?'

Stunned, I simply replied, 'No one.'

'You seem to think you have no rights,' he said. His words stung me. I wanted to run away or shout at him to stop, but I couldn't speak.

'You feel you have no right to be happy, no right to be miserable, no right to be what you are,' he persisted.

Why was he being so cruel? I couldn't understand what had provoked this outburst.

'Have you no rights at all?' he continued.

I cringed. Why was he persisting? Why wouldn't he stop? Somehow I had to escape from the torture he was inflicting on me. Desperately I tried to change the subject. 'I've been feeling muddled this week. When I feel depressed I can't see straight.'

'You are right. Mentally you do not see straight, and that's why you're depressed.' His bluntness hurt. I felt as though he was deliberately twisting a knife into my wounds in order to inflict the maximum amount of pain. He had cornered me. I could not escape. I waited for the next blow.

'I've been writing your name incorrectly on the bill I give you every month,' he continued. 'I wasn't aware of my mistake until I looked at your cheque last week. Had you noticed it?'

'Yes, I had,' I said.

'Why didn't you correct me?'

'I didn't think it mattered,' I answered. By now I was frightened of what else he might say to me. 'I don't mind. It's of no consequence to me. I didn't think it would be important to you.'

'Of course it's important to me. Don't you think I want to write your name correctly?'

'I knew the bill was meant for me. What difference does it make?' I wished he would leave me alone, but he showed me no mercy.

'Do you have no sense of pride in your name? Don't you realise your name is your identity?' He spoke firmly.

'I don't feel my name is my identity. It doesn't matter to me how it's spelt. Please let's forget the matter.'

'It's necessary that we deal properly with this subject,' he insisted. 'Why is your name so unimportant to you?'

'It's just a word. It doesn't mean anything. I don't feel I'm a part of my family, so it doesn't matter whether I have their name or not. Quibbling over the spelling of a name is pointless. What does it matter? I don't care what you call me or how you spell my name.'

He would not let me go. 'It is important that you have pride in your name, pride in your identity.'

'Please,' I begged, 'don't keep on about it.'

'It's necessary for you to understand that you have the right to have your name spelt correctly, and you need to stand up for that right.'

I felt shattered. For the first time I wanted the session to end, but there was still another five minutes to endure. I turned my face to the wall, wishing I could hide from him.

'What do you think my attitude to you really is?' he asked.

'I don't know. I'm confused. Terribly confused,' I replied.

'What impressions are you getting?'

'I told you. I'm confused. I get conflicting impressions. I don't know what I should think any more.' If only he'd leave me alone.

'I'm interested in you as an individual; as a person in your own right. Your identity and your individuality are important to me. He paused. I could not respond, so he continued, more slowly, more quietly. 'Obviously you didn't appreciate how important your identity is to me, otherwise you would have corrected my mistake.'

For the remaining minutes I lay motionless. Neither of us spoke. I felt like a dog that had been whipped, and I needed to lick my wounds. I closed my eyes and waited for the pain to die away.

Dr Goldblatt let me lie there for five minutes beyond my scheduled time. At last he said, very gently, 'I'm sorry, you must go now.'

Slowly I sat up. I couldn't look at him. He had shattered me, humiliated and confused me.

I felt too dazed to go into the street, so I went to the cloakroom and locked myself in. I leant against the door and waited until I felt steadier. After a while I realised that I must make my way home, so I washed my face in cold water in an attempt to revive myself. Then I walked out into the street.

Once outside I looked in each direction and tried to recall where I had parked my car. I couldn't remember. There were so many streets and so many parking meters. Over the months I had parked north, south, east and west of Harley Street and occasionally in Harley Street itself. Sometimes I had been around the corner, sometimes ten minutes' walk away. I could picture a dozen different places where I had parked my car on previous occasions, but I couldn't even recall my journey that afternoon, nor my walk to Harley Street. I could vaguely remember parking the car, and putting some money in a parking meter, but I had paid no attention to its' location.

I wondered what to do. There was no point in going back to Dr Goldblatt. He probably had another patient with him and, anyway, he was hardly likely to help me search for my car. There seemed nothing else for it. I had to do my own systematic search.

I felt too weary to panic. I looked carefully in both directions, but I could see no sign of my car. I decided to walk in the direction of the streets where I had most often parked. That was northeast from where I stood. I walked slowly. Many of the cars had gone, so that made my search easier. From the top of some of the streets I could see all the cars that were parked there.

It was like a nasty dream and I began to wonder if I would soon wake up. Still I walked on, up one road and down another, and then, just as I felt ready to sit on the kerb and cry, I turned a corner, and there in front of me was my car.

I was too depressed to feel excitement or pleasure. I just walked to the car, unlocked it, and got in. For a few minutes I sat there, shaking. Gradually I became aware I had a long drive ahead of me, so I put on my seat belt and drove away.

The drive home was a nightmare. I thought back to the session with Dr Goldblatt and my eyes brimmed with tears. How could he have been so cruel? He had taken no notice of my plea to forget the matter. He must have known the distress I was in, yet he had persisted. My feeling of isolation was increasing. No one, not even Dr Goldblatt understood or cared how wretched I felt.

My thoughts turned to Pat. In her last letter she had written that I was very lucky to have a psychiatrist like Dr Goldblatt. Little did she know; little did she care. She had been so set on encouraging me, that she hadn't noticed from my letters that I was deteriorating. She had let me down. I hated her . . . Yet how could I feel like that about my most loyal friend? What was wrong with me? Alan had turned against the people who had loved him most. Was I developing Alan's illness? Was I developing schizophrenia?

My thoughts were muddled and confused. Dr Goldblatt's words, 'Mentally you do not see straight' were ringing in my ears. I couldn't get away from his voice, taunting me.

Escape. How could I escape from that voice?

I was driving parallel to a lorry along a one way street. 'If I get ahead and then swerve in front of the lorry, perhaps my misery will be over forever,' I thought. But I couldn't do it. Depressed as I was, I was not divorced from reality. I was aware that an accident would involve other traffic, and cause serious injury to other people. There was nothing for it but to endure my agony.

When I got home I rushed into the kitchen and shut myself in. I had trained myself to eat regularly but my appetite was like my moods – unreliable and changeable. When I was depressed, I wanted nothing to eat, but when I was elated I became ravenous. That evening I had no appetite, but I forced myself to cook a dinner of liver, carrots and greens.

Tears were still streaming down my face as I washed up the dishes. My parents remained in the sitting room and I was glad. I didn't want them to know how dreadful I felt. I would remind them of Alan. They had suffered enough, and I didn't want to bring more suffering to them.

I was desperate. I had to find someone somewhere who would care about me, or I wouldn't be able to carry on. In panic I ran from the house to the local phone box. I would talk to Rita.

Trembling, I dialled the number. After what seemed an age, Rita's husband answered.

'Please may I speak to Rita?' I gasped.

'I'm sorry,' he replied. 'She's out, and I'm not expecting her back until late.'

I put the phone down. I didn't believe she was out. She had told her husband to say that because she was fed up with me, and didn't want to hear any more of my troubles. She was avoiding me.

My isolation was now complete. I felt devastated.

I wandered the streets. I didn't want to go back home in case I saw my parents. They mustn't know how bad I was. I struggled mentally to think through my despair, but my mind was now beyond my control.

'Alan used to wander the streets like this,' I thought. 'I am becoming like him. I must be developing schizophrenia.'

'Don't keep wandering the streets,' I argued to myself. 'Break the pattern. Do something different. Don't let your mind take you where you don't want to go. Don't allow schizophrenia to get a hold on you.'

Suddenly something my father had said, years ago, when Alan's illness was first diagnosed, came into my mind. 'The doctor said schizophrenia can occur in anyone. It just comes.' Then he had looked at me and said, 'It could happen to you.' That sentence now haunted me. How could I avoid something that 'just comes'?

'Do something,' I said to myself. 'Do something, or you'll go crazy.'

'You are crazy.' Those words flashed into my mind as though someone else had said them.

'Only one more step, and the thoughts will become voices in your head, telling you what to do,' I said out loud.

I panicked. I was actually going crazy. I broke into a run. There was nothing else to do. My footsteps echoed down the empty street. I had to run away from this terrible situation. I could no longer cope.

I don't remember how long I kept running but by the time I reached home I was gasping with exhaustion. I rushed upstairs and flung myself on the bed.

Still my mind would give me no peace. 'Alan used to break into a run for no apparent reason,' it thought.

I decided to have a bath, hoping it would cleanse my mind as well as my body.

I went into the bathroom and turned on the taps. I stood motionless, watching the bath fill. As the water level rose, I thought to myself, 'How easy it would be to lean over the side of the bath, put my head under the water, and start breathing in and out as fast as I could . . .'.

Suddenly I realised what I was imagining. Horrified, I turned off the taps and wrenched out the plug. The water gurgled out of the bath. 'What a wicked thing to do to Mum and Dad,' I told myself. 'Imagine what it would be like for them to find their only daughter drowned in the bath.'

I replaced the plug just before the last inches of water ran out, then I climbed into the bath and dabbed water over myself. It was the worst bath I had ever had, but at least I wouldn't drown.

For some months afterwards I didn't run more than a couple of inches of water in the bath just in case my reason left me.

After my bath I went to my room, still feeling desperate. My only means of escape now was the sherry bottle. I took it from the cupboard and climbed into bed. Without further thought, I tipped up the bottle and guzzled sherry till it ran down my chin and onto the bed clothes. That night I slept soundly.

Next morning I woke with the sound of trains running through my head. I had a hangover. I took some aspirins to help me get to work. At work I tried to keep out of everyone's way. I thought my hangover might show. My eyes certainly felt 'bleary'.

At coffee time, one of my colleagues gave me a very hard stare. 'You look really depressed and unwell today,' she said. 'This psychotherapy is doing you more harm than good. Why don't you give it up? If that psychiatrist was going to help you, he would have done so by now. After all, you've been going to him for three months. You are wasting your time and your money, and you are not getting better. Go back to your family doctor and ask him for antidepressant tablets.'

I looked appealingly at Rita, hoping she would come to the defence of psychotherapy, but she said nothing.

Eventually I said, 'It takes time. I'll give it a few more weeks.'

After lunch a terrible feeling of panic came over me. In desperation I phoned Pat. She sounded happy and relaxed, just the opposite to how I felt. How could I ruin her day by plaguing her with my misery? I decided to cover up.

'I just phoned for a chat,' I said, as light-heartedly as I could.

'Do you want to come down this weekend?' she asked. 'My sister will be here, and she'd love to meet you.'

'No, I can't come,' I said. How could I go in this state? I'd ruin their weekend.

'Well, come as soon as you can,' she insisted. 'There's so much I want to ask you about psychotherapy. You write super letters, but there's a lot you don't say. I'd love to meet Dr Goldblatt. He sounds smashing.'

'I'll let you know when I can come,' I said. ' 'Bye for now.'

For the rest of the afternoon I sat in a small unused room at the clinic and cried my heart out. Pat had no idea. She didn't, she couldn't understand. She'd be enjoying her weekend with her sister while I'd be swamped in misery.

The depression did not lift. All that weekend I suffered. On Monday morning Rita had a chat with me. 'What's wrong?' she said, sympathetically.

'Dr Goldblatt doesn't understand, I said. 'He kept on and on about something, even when I asked him not to. I don't think I can take any more.'

'With psychotherapy you do feel worse before you feel better,' she explained. 'Looking into your mind is very painful. Psychotherapy opens up wounds that have been covered over but not properly healed. Those wounds have to be opened. It's part of the treatment.'

'But he's so brutal,' I cried. 'He doesn't care how I feel.'

'Of course he cares. Perhaps he doesn't know just how bad you are. You should tell him.'

'Wednesday is so far away,' I said.

'Then phone him today and tell him,' she persisted.

'He'd be annoyed. It wouldn't be fair to disturb him. It must be bad enough for him to put up with me on Wednesdays.'

'He's your therapist. Use him. Tell him how you feel, and what you think of him.'

'I might go too far,' I said nervously.

'That's his problem, not yours. It's his job to control matters if they get out of hand. He'll tell you if you overstep the mark. You're not his first patient. He's very experienced and highly trained.'

'I think it would help me if I could speak to him,' I said. 'But it's an awful cheek. He wouldn't like it.'

'You don't know that,' she said. 'I should think he'd be pleased to hear from you. Tell him what you feel like.'

That lunchtime I phoned Harley Street. A woman answered the phone. 'I've got to speak to Dr Goldblatt,' I stammered.

'Who's speaking, please?'

I gave my name.

'Just a moment, please.'

'Hello, what can I do for you?' It was Dr Goldblatt's calm, gentle voice.

'I feel really depressed,' I said, shakily. 'I've never felt so bad. What's happening to me?'

'What's happening is this. We've reached a point in your treatment where we are dealing with the central part of the problem. You have been suffering under a misconception about yourself. You believe you are worthless. You are now feeling up to that. What we have got to do together is to rebuild the foundation of your thinking and get you away from this idea of being worthless. You feel afraid because what I'm asking you to do is to demolish the foundation of your personal philosophy and to rebuild it with a set of new ideas.

I'm trying to get you to challenge the way you think. This can be very frightening and it will be a traumatic experience for you to go through.'

'What can I do?' I asked nervously. 'How can I last out until Wednesday? I just can't carry on any more.' I hoped desperately he would offer to see me that evening. 'You'll find a way,' he replied firmly. 'I'll see you on Wednesday. Goodbye.'

The line went dead. I felt numb and dizzy. He knew how bad I felt. He had known all along, yet he left me alone to my fate.

For the thousandth time I experienced an overwhelming sense of confusion. I felt as though I was living in a ghastly dream. Life tormented me. On the one hand I respected Dr Goldblatt for his composure, but on the other hand I hated him for being so detached from my anguish and for leaving me alone with my fears. He was putting the onus on me to find my way out of my own nightmare. My confidence was gone. At the moment he put the phone down I didn't believe I would still be alive on Wednesday.

Somehow I managed to survive, but my life was hell. I had no appetite and what little food I ate made me feel sick. I slept fitfully each night, my bedroom walls closing in around me. The sleep I had was filled with horrid dreams and shaking sensations. In one ghastly dream I was sitting on the edge of a gigantic couch. The couch was blazing and I had to escape. Below me was a drop of several hundred feet into a dark swirling sea. I jumped and I felt I was falling for ever. When I woke up I was waving my arms about, not knowing where I was.

**25 May 1967**

As I walked into Dr Goldblatt's consulting room I felt embarrassed because of my phone call. I felt I had gone too far by bothering him with my worries. I climbed onto the couch and my embarrassment increased. I had to say something about the matter, but I was afraid to show my anxiety directly, in case he cornered me. I carefully formulated my sentence so that his searchlight would be directed away from me.

'Did you mind my phone call on Monday?' I asked at last.

'No, I didn't mind, but you must realise I can't talk for very long on the telephone.'

'I didn't expect you to talk for long,' I said quickly. 'In fact, I didn't expect you to talk to me at all.'

'Why didn't you expect me to talk to you? You had a perfect right to phone me: if you were a psychiatrist, surely you would consider that a patient had the right to phone you.'

'Yes, of course I would,' I replied.

'Then why don't you give yourself the same rights you give to others?'

'I don't know,' I said desperately. I couldn't bear to hear him talking about 'rights'. The idea of fighting for my rights was something I didn't want to face. I didn't like protesting about anything, yet he made me want to protest at him. I felt decidedly uncomfortable.

'Let me suggest a reason why you don't give yourself rights. I think it's because you believe you are worthless – you are not worthy of rights.'

'I am worthless,' I said. 'I hated you for keeping on about rights last week. You shattered me. Then on Monday last, after my phone call, I hated you even more, because you left me alone with my fears. I shouldn't hate you, I know, but I do. It isn't your fault I feel so terrible, but I blame you for it.'

'Hating me doesn't mean you are worthless,' he said. 'Hate is a natural emotion and you must learn to accept your emotions and stop trying to deny you have them.'

'I must be very ill,' I said weakly.

'You are ill,' he said seriously.

'How ill am I?'

'You know that as well as I do,' he replied.

I was anxious about my illness, and I wanted him to tell me exactly what was wrong. I decided to be more direct. 'I've been worrying about whether I'm schizophrenic,' I said.

He didn't speak. It was as though he hadn't heard me. I tried again.

'Why am I ill? What's wrong with me?' I asked.

'You are not well because you haven't grasped the basic

principle of rights. You have to build a new foundation for yourself based on that principle, and until you do that, your ego will remain underdeveloped. At the moment we are dealing with your central problem and that's why it's so difficult for you. Unconsciously you are resisting the treatment. You struggle against yourself. You cringe, you go silent, you try to change the subject, you refuse even to look at the problem because you're afraid of the trauma.'

'What are you going to do then?' I asked.

'I shall persist,' he said. 'You want my help, even though you're afraid of that help.'

'Have I got schizophrenia?' I interrupted. 'It would help me to cope with life if you'd tell me.'

'I'm not going to classify your illness,' he replied. 'I've explained it clearly to you. If you want to know whether or not you have schizophrenia, you must work it out for yourself.'

'But I'm filled with dread. I'm terrified of schizophrenia. I can't bear to live with the anxiety. What am I to do?'

'If you really can't cope,' he said, 'you must take Librium. Not just one tablet, but a proper course of tablets. That means taking Librium continuously until your crisis is over.'

'Are you advising me to take Librium?' I asked.

'I would prefer you to manage without it if you possibly can,' he said. 'You can't bypass this crisis. You have to come to terms with it sooner or later, and you'll probably get through sooner without the tablets. But if you feel you can't contain your fears alone, you must get Librium tablets from your doctor.'

'How long will it be before I begin to feel better?'

'I don't know.'

'I might not survive the struggle,' I said. 'I keep imagining I'm committing suicide, and it's only my conscience that's stopping me. If my confusion and despair and isolation continue much longer, my conscience may not be strong enough to stop me. I might come to believe I have a right to put an end to my misery.'

'I agree you're on a razor's edge,' he said, 'but at the moment I don't think you really want to die. It's only one of your alternatives, but it isn't your main alternative. In fact, it frightens you when you find yourself thinking about suicide.'

'If I thought I really had got schizophrenia I would want to die.' I said. 'I saw how my brother suffered, and I saw how we as a family suffered throughout his illness. I wouldn't allow that to happen again. I'm more frightened of living with schizophrenia than I am of dying.'

'Well, maybe you are afraid of being ill,' he said slowly, 'but it seems to me you are also afraid of being well. Unconsciously you are resisting me in my efforts to make you well again. How many times today have you steered away from thinking about your rights? First you try to prove to me you are worthless; then you digress to the question of how your illness may be classified, then you talk about feelings of suicide. So far today you've found it easier to talk about illness and death than to talk about being healthy.'

'But I do want to be well,' I protested. 'Why am I so afraid of thinking about being healthy?'

'Being well will be a new experience for you,' he explained. 'You must cast off your old ways of thinking. That will make you feel very insecure. You will be venturing into the unknown, and that's a frightening prospect for you.'

'I'm confused,' I said. 'I don't know which way to turn. I'm in a terrible dilemma.'

'That's true,' he agreed. 'You are at a crossroads. You can no longer follow the road between illness and health. The contradictory feelings which have resulted have become too much for you. They are overwhelming you. You can't delay indefinitely or you'll put an end to your misery. What other alternatives have you? You can follow the road that leads away from your natural feelings and your rights, but you know that road will lead to mental illness. On the other hand, you can follow the path to mental health. That will involve coming to terms with your natural feelings and rights. I think you realise the path to health will be long and difficult. The prospect of going along that road frightens you.'

I lay still, feeling as though my strength had gone. It was true: I was at a crossroads in my life; but my dilemma was not a choice between which path to follow. I had made a choice months before when I first thought I might have schizophrenia. I had decided then I wanted to be well, however much it cost, and I would never go back on that decision. No, my dilemma now was how to overcome the urge to kill myself. I wanted to be well but it seemed the treatment was destroying me. I feared that my despair would drive me into a state of imbalance.

I wanted comfort; I wanted pity; but all that Dr Goldblatt offered me was the hard and stony prospect of a battle against my unconscious mind. He wouldn't tell me how long the struggle might last, or whether I could survive the ordeal. All he would tell me was that I had to battle it out for myself. At that moment I saw him as a cruel and callous spectator to my suffering. I felt annihilated.

His voice broke into my reverie.

'It's time to go now.' He stood up and went to the door.

I got off the couch, feeling utterly miserable. I looked at him, appealing for a few words of comfort or sympathy.

'Goodbye, we'll continue next week,' was all he said.

I glared at my tormentor as I crept towards the door. How I hated him and how I wanted him to see I hated him. He smiled but I wouldn't smile back. I stalked past him and hurried down the stairs. How dare he take such a risk with my life.

I stamped along the road to my car, wishing I could get even with Dr Goldblatt for his cruelty. If only I could rush back and shout obscenities at him, and call him a cruel beast to his face.

Driving home, I imagined I was shouting abuse at Dr Goldblatt while he lay on the couch. I tried to picture what he would look like – a failed psychiatrist cringing on his own couch. . . . Yet try as I might I couldn't picture him like that. I realised if I did attack him verbally he would react by saying, 'I'm glad you are learning to express your feelings.'

It was as though a penny had dropped in my mind; I was making progress. My imaginary outburst would please Dr Goldblatt, especially if he knew I didn't feel any guilt about my anger. No, I didn't feel guilty now as I would have done last week. I felt relieved. I had enjoyed my anger. This was probably the first time in my life I actually enjoyed being angry.

The knowledge that I now seemed to be making progress

helped me to face my mental anguish. Even though I seemed worse and my symptoms were increasing, I suddenly felt a new spark of progress.

The next day Rita had lunch with me in the clinic. 'How did you get on with Dr Goldblatt?' she asked.

'He was no help at all,' I said. 'When I told him I was afraid of suicide he said I was on a razor edge and I must get on with it.'

Rita looked at me in disbelief. I wanted to shock her; I wanted to show her how callous Dr Goldblatt could be.

'I asked him if I had schizophrenia but he wouldn't tell me. When I pleaded with him, he said I must work it out for myself. Now I've got to live with the anxiety.'

'Of course you haven't got schizophrenia,' said Rita. 'I don't understand why he didn't tell you that himself, but I suppose he had a good reason.'

'You really think highly of him, don't you Rita?' I said scornfully.

'Yes,' she replied. 'My friend has worked with him for years, and she believes he is an exceptionally good psychiatrist. You are lucky to get treatment from him.'

'I know that,' I replied. 'It's just that he's too persistent, and I feel in such a state all the time, it's practically impossible to do my job.'

'You must see your doctor and take sick leave until you feel better,' she suggested.

'No, I daren't stay away from work,' I said. 'I might not be able to face coming back.'

'I think you should have a week off at least,' she said. 'Ask Dr Goldblatt what he thinks next time you see him.'

**31 May 1967**

By the time I saw Dr Goldblatt my anger had gone. 'Over the past week I've had mixed feelings about you,' I told him. 'Last Wednesday I felt upset and angry at the way you refused to say if I had schizophrenia. You seemed cruel.'

'From your point of view I was cruel,' he said, 'but the fact is, I couldn't tell you.'

'Surely after all these months you must know,' I exclaimed in disbelief.

'Well, it isn't that simple,' he replied. 'Did you work it out for yourself?'

'Not really,' I said nervously, 'but one of my colleagues at work tells me I don't have schizophrenia, and I'm ready to believe her.'

He ignored my reply. 'Let's take it a step further,' he said. 'Do you believe you have the same illness as your brother?'

'I don't know,' I said, 'but there is a great deal of similarity between the way he behaved and the way I'm behaving now.'

'Let me help you,' he said slowly. 'Think about your brother's anger: was it rational, or, did he become angry for irrational reasons?'

'His anger often seemed irrational to me,' I said. 'If I coughed he would get angry, because he believed my cough directed evil towards him.'

'Have you ever been angry for a similar reason?' he queried.

'No, I haven't.'

'Tell me, on the occasions you have felt angry, were there rational reasons for your anger?'

'Yes.'

'Now do you think you have the same illness as your brother?'

'No,' I replied.

'You believe your brother killed himself. Do you think you will kill yourself?'

'No, I don't think I will,' I said slowly. 'As long as I believe I'll recover, I shall fight against my suicidal urges.'

There was a long pause. I let my mind wander.

Then I said. 'Lots of thoughts go through my mind, but I can't always bring myself to speak. . . but I am beginning to feel I want to argue with you.'

'Yes, you are beginning to argue,' he said. 'It's a healthy sign.'

'I feel I've made some progress this week, but my depression hasn't gone. Will I be depressed for much longer?'

'Yes,' he replied. 'You have a long way to go before you can overcome your illness. You will also have to adjust to the effects of your hysterectomy, and you will have to cope with being well, because new demands will be made on you.'

'By illness, I suppose you mean my inability to react normally,' I said, 'my inability to show anger.'

'Yes,' he replied, 'but you are learning.'

My mind wandered back to when I had tried to get Dr Goldblatt to tell me whether I had schizophrenia. I realised he still hadn't expressed an opinion: I was still uncertain. Perhaps he really thought I might have schizophrenia, and perhaps that explained why he had never challenged my fears. Perhaps he really believed my fears were justified.

Gradually I began to realise it was no longer important to me how my mental condition was classified. I was receiving treatment from Dr Goldblatt who had every intention of continuing with that treatment and believed he could help me recover. Even if I might be suffering from the illness that my brother had, there was no reason to expect that the outcome of my illness would be the same. Alan had not received the kind of help I was receiving now. Dr Goldblatt was an expert who had my interests at heart. He wanted me to recover and he believed I would recover.

I felt encouraged and I felt hopeful. Hope would enable me to persevere.

It was time to go. I got off the couch and walked to the door. I paused and turned to Dr Goldblatt. 'Thank you,' I said, and hurried away.

# 10 Learning to Accept Normal Emotions

(31 May 1967 - 28th June 1967)

That evening, the last day of May, I sat in my bedroom and thought back over the last few weeks. It seemed to me that my life would be less traumatic if only I could trust Dr Goldblatt. Perhaps I should let him do the worrying: I was balancing on a tightrope stretched across an abyss of despair and suicide. Dr Goldblatt was beckoning me to safety. It was for him to worry about the dangers. He was my guide; he knew the way. All I had to do was to keep my balance and keep moving forward. If I struggled against him, it would make his task more difficult, and I would be more likely to fall. I resolved there and then to trust him.

I realised it wouldn't be a matter of passive trust. It was also necessary for me to help myself, and to go in the direction he was indicating. Constantly I asked myself what that direction was. It seemed I had to accept myself and my emotions for what they were. I resolved to make a careful note of my feelings during the coming week. I had been in the habit of telling myself I did not have certain emotions. Now I would watch for them, and talk about them to Dr Goldblatt.

At lunchtime on the Friday the daughter of a clinic nurse called to see us at our clinic. She was a lovely person; happy and full of life, and looking forward to the future. I liked her but I also felt jealous of her. There was such a contrast between her life and mine. She was so full of life while I was so full of despair.

I also felt jealous when Rita talked to me about her son. I had formed a close relationship with Rita, and I felt the need to confide in her and to ask her advice on many matters. To some extent she was like a mother to me. However, I couldn't confide in her as frequently as I would have liked. When she talked to me about her son, it brought home to me the closeness I had missed as a child. I felt jealous.

Suddenly that week I began to feel physical discomfort, abdominal pain and cramp. I was alarmed and went to my doctor. After examining me he assured me there was nothing wrong, and my symptoms were probably psychological. I readily accepted his diagnosis. Then he asked me how I was getting on with psychotherapy. I was anxious not to go into detail because I felt vulnerable, so I said it was difficult. but in the long run it would be worthwhile. He then asked if I was aware that fibroids sometimes originated through emotional stress. I said I was not aware of it, and I walked out of his surgery feeling very cross. How dare he make such a statement to me concerning something which was not proved.

I reflected on my angry reaction, and I realised that a few weeks ago I wouldn't have been angry at all. I would have accepted what he said, and blamed myself for my own misfortunes.

At last I was beginning to see where Dr Goldblatt was leading me. He was telling me to give vent to my feelings. That was the way to mental health.

## 7 June 1967

At my next psychotherapy session I found it easier to discuss the feelings of anger and jealousy which I had experienced. I wanted to talk about these emotions instead of hiding them.

'I've been having emotions I don't like,' I said to Dr Goldblatt. I told him about my colleague's daughter. 'I feel jealous of her because she's so happy and well adjusted. I'd like to be like that myself, but it's beyond my reach.'

'It's natural you should feel like that,' he said. 'It's a step forward when you admit you have that kind of emotion.'

'I've also been feeling jealous of Rita's son. I hate it when she talks to me about him. I've never felt so jealous.'

'It's a normal reaction. Why don't you tell her how you feel?'

'I couldn't,' I said. 'She's so good to me. I don't want to spoil our friendship.'

'It would help the relationship if you told her how you feel.' he said. 'You have acknowledged the feeling to yourself and to me. Your next step is to accept it as normal. When you have fully accepted it, there will be no place for guilt. You will then be able to share your feelings with her – not in the form of a confession, but as one friend sharing feelings with another.'

'I can follow your reasoning,' I said, 'but I'm not sure I could talk naturally about it.'

'That's because you haven't accepted jealousy as a natural emotion,' he said.

'I suppose I haven't.' There was a pause. Then I told him about my visit to my doctor. 'My doctor said that fibroids could be brought about by the state of a person's mind. What do you think?'

'I don't agree,' he said. 'I see no justification in saying that. It's only a theory.'

'I was angry with my doctor for saying that to me.'

'Did you express your anger?'

'I suppose I did in a way; I didn't say anything, but by the way I walked out of the surgery, it must have shown.'

'Your anger was a normal reaction and it was healthy to express it,' he reassured me.

As I lay on Dr Goldblatt's couch, my thoughts turned to the tennis club. 'Not all my reactions are normal,' I said. 'I still have a strong urge to run away from people. I go to a tennis club on Saturday afternoons. The people are pleasant enough, but all the time I'm at the club I really want to be on my own. The feeling is particularly strong when they are all laughing and joking. I can't bring myself to join in with them.'

The urge to run away is really an urge to get away from what's painful,' said Dr Goldblatt. 'When you see other people being natural and showing their feelings and emotions, it hurts you because it brings home to you that you are not like that.'

'No, I'm not like that,' I repeated. 'Most of the time I have to make a definite decision and a positive effort to show my feelings. I'm not spontaneous in my reactions. I weigh up everything before I decide what I should do.'

'It's important for you to concentrate on what you think and feel. Don't concentrate on what you 'should' think and feel. Leave the 'should' out of it.'

'That's what you are working on with me now,' I commented.

'Yes,' he replied.

'I suppose I find it difficult to show my feelings because of my upbringing. My mother disapproves of anyone who shows their feelings. She says it's an indication of weakness. She rarely expresses herself clearly. Most of the time it's impossible to know what she wants. When I was a little girl, I deliberately copied my father and not my mother, but some of her ways must have affected me.'

He said nothing.

'Of course, I used to copy my brother Alan, because I looked up to him. He never showed any signs of jealousy or nastiness as a child. He was always kind and gentle.'

Still Dr Goldblatt didn't comment. I wanted him to say something to encourage me. I thought he might respond if I showed him I was making progress.

'Although it's difficult for me to show my feelings,' I said, 'at least I'm aware of them now. At one time I tried to hide my feelings even from myself, because I thought it was wrong to be jealous or angry, but now I'm able to accept myself more readily.'

'You are still very self-critical,' he remarked, 'although you are not as malicious with yourself as you used to be.'

I wasn't sure what to feel by his comments. He may have been giving me a little encouragement.

'I am thinking straighter on the whole,' I ventured.

'Yes, you are,' he replied. 'I'm pleased with the way you now think through your conflicts.'

I wondered if he realised I had deliberately made my last two comments in order to receive encouragement from him.

I did feel encouraged when I left Dr Goldblatt that evening. I felt the session had gone well. I seemed to be working with him instead of working against him as I had done over the past few weeks.

But I was growing impatient. It was now four months since I first went to Dr Goldblatt and, apart from showing my anger on one or two occasions, there was no noticeable change in my condition. I still had terrible dreams at night; I still felt a sense of dread and foreboding; and I still lacked confidence. Each day was a struggle for me, and each day I felt like giving up.

Strangely enough, however, it was my feelings of anger and jealousy which led me to believe that somehow some kind of change was taking place within me. Would it be change for better or for worse?

It was now June, but the sunny days had no effect on me. It could have been winter for all I cared.

For several weeks Pat had been writing to me about a cycling holiday. She and Kathy were hoping I would join them but, much as I enjoyed cycling, I didn't feel enthusiastic. I didn't have the physical stamina of the previous year. Constant tiredness had become a part of my life, and I knew I could never cycle for six to eight hours a day. Pat responded to my excuses by offering to let me decide how much cycling we should do each day. She also suggested that my tiredness was probably due to psychological stress. I agreed with her but I didn't think my tiredness would go away. The problem was solved eventually when Pat wrote telling me she couldn't have her holiday during the same weeks I was due for my 'holiday' from Dr Goldblatt. I was in such a state of nerves that every move I made had to coincide with my visits to Harley Street.

On the Friday Pat phoned me. 'Please come with us,' she begged. 'We had such a lot of fun together when we cycled to Luxembourg last year. You need a break. You need to enjoy yourself with us. Forget about your depression.'

'I'm sorry, Pat, my depression will stay with me wherever I go,' I moaned. 'I can't run away from it.'

'So what?' she said. 'We don't mind how you are. If you are still depressed we can share it with you; then it won't seem so bad.'

'I can't, Pat. I've got the feeling I'm on the edge of a breakthrough with Dr Goldblatt. I've got to stick with it. If I miss even one session, I might lose ground and slip back.'

'O.K.' she said reluctantly. 'You know best where that's concerned. Don't overdo it, though. I think you drive yourself far too hard.'

We chatted for a while longer, then said goodbye. That evening I thought about my decision. It seemed incredible I should be giving up a chance to be with Pat just so that I could continue my weekly psychotherapy sessions. I had become far more dependent on Dr Goldblatt than I had realised. I felt suddenly afraid I might even lose my friend. This illness was driving me mad.

On the Monday evening there was a programme on the television about schizophrenia. People with the illness were shown being assessed by doctors. I was very upset by the programme. The people with schizophrenia were made to look comical, and their feelings were ignored. The doctors spoke of their patients as though they were interesting cases with weird patterns of behaviour. There was no indication that the doctors had any idea of the feelings of their patients. It was as though the patients were guinea pigs.

I worried about that programme. Were doctors really like that? If so I hated them all. Was Dr Goldblatt like that? Was I just another interesting case: an intellectual challenge to his professional ego? He certainly tried to help me, but was it just because I was unusual and challenging? He probably had no idea how I felt. On my visits to Harley Street he sat in his detached way out of sight at the head of the couch, while I lay there in a state of mental distress. I hated him. I wanted to escape from him, but I couldn't; I was in his clutches. I felt he had abused my trust. He had got me into a state of mind where I was now addicted to him. All I could think of was 'Goldblatt' . . . 'Goldblatt' . . . 'Goldblatt' . . . .

I could no longer bear the torment that was building up inside me. I got ready for bed and took my sherry bottle from the cupboard. I got into bed and drank slowly, until my mind became cloudy and I drifted off into another night of haunted dreams.

## 14 June 1967

As I walked into Dr Goldblatt's consulting room, I was aware of strange, conflicting emotions inside me. He was standing there with his usual smile, and I wondered if he had any emotions of his own. He was always in the same mood. Why didn't he scowl occasionally, or tell me he was fed up with my complexes? Why didn't he let me see what he was really like? Why did he have to be so professional?

I watched him sit down. He was waiting patiently for me to lie on the couch. I wondered how I would react if he suddenly yawned, or showed that he was an ordinary human being. I was beginning to think of him as a robot: no feelings; no emotions; no compassion.

I gave him a hard stare as he was about to light his cigarette. There was no suggestion of tension or irritation, or any emotion about him. I had an urge to snatch the cigarette away from his mouth, just to see how he would react, but I'd only make a fool of myself, and he would probably throw me out.

He looked at me, but said nothing. I then realised I wanted him to behave as he always did. I felt safer. If I had to contend with his moods as well as my moods, psychotherapy would be impossible.

Relieved, I climbed onto the couch. 'Free association' I thought. 'If I freely associate I will have to put all my thoughts about Dr Goldblatt into words'. I just couldn't bring myself to do that. My thoughts embarrassed me and I shifted uneasily on the couch.

I had to say something. I hadn't driven all this way just to keep my thoughts to myself. I had a psychiatrist at my disposal, so I'd better start using him. I decided to challenge him by talking about the programme I had seen on television.

'There was a programme on the TV about schizophrenia. It showed an incredible lack of understanding for the feelings of the sufferers.'

He didn't speak.

'I hated the psychiatrists because of that. I hated all psychiatrists, especially you,' I burst out.

'You hated me because you are projecting your feelings

about psychiatrists in general on to me,' he said quietly. 'You are afraid I might not be a good person, or I might give you bad treatment. You feel at my mercy, just as those patients seemed to be at the mercy of their psychiatrists.'

'Yes, I do feel that,' I agreed.

We were quiet for a while. I was struggling to tell him what I had been thinking before I got onto the couch. 'I had all kinds of thoughts when I first came in here,' I said. 'Were you aware of that?'

'Yes,' he replied calmly.

'I can't bring myself to tell you what I was thinking. You might not like it.'

'You can't tell me because you are afraid I might not approve. You are afraid you are not good enough, and I might not want to treat you any more.'

It was uncanny. I wondered if he could read my thoughts. I changed the subject quickly.

'My friends are going on a cycling holiday to Cornwall in July. They want me to go with them, but I told them I can't.'

'Why can't you go with them?'

'It would mean missing psychotherapy. Even though you sometimes make me feel worse, I've become dependent on you.'

'Working through your central problems is painful.' he explained, 'and it is necessary for you to depend on me.'

I couldn't think of anything more to say on that topic, so I began to think about him again.

I tried to imagine him outside his consulting room. I knew he'd be kind and understanding, but would he be spontaneous? Surely this analysing and introspection he was practising all day would inhibit him. Instead of accepting people as they were he would analyse their every move. I wondered what his faults were. Was he always tolerant and patient, or did he get irritable with people? I had no way of telling. After all these months I couldn't detect a single flaw in his character. What were his hobbies or his interests . . .?

I wondered if I would like him if I met him socially. Would I be attracted to him, and want to be in his company? I tried hard to imagine him in a social context, but I couldn't. Perhaps it was just as well. I didn't object to sometimes hating him, but I couldn't bear the thought of feeling love for him.

Nothing had been said for a long time. I glanced up at the clock, and saw it was ten to six – time to go. Dr Goldblatt was silent. Maybe he had gone to sleep. If so, I'd better wake him up.

I cleared my throat to attract his attention. 'I've been dreaming today,' I said, 'but I don't want to tell you about my day dreams.' I got up from the couch.

'That's because you feel your thoughts are bad or abnormal, but in fact they are normal,' he remarked as he stood up.

I looked at him triumphantly. You are wrong, I thought. I know my thoughts are perfectly normal and proper. I just don't want you to know them. I'm entitled to some privacy of my own.

I smiled smugly and said goodbye.

As I drove home I felt pleased with myself, more pleased than I had been at any time during my illness. I had caught Dr Goldblatt out. He had guessed wrongly about my daydreams. I felt I had scored a point over him. He no longer had the upper hand. I now knew enough about his methods and the way he applied his Freudian theories to be able to run rings around him. I could have great fun, I thought. I could say things which would lead him off down any path I chose. It would be like playing chess. With practice, I might even beat him at his own game. The thought amused me. Psychotherapy could be fun.

I arrived home feeling lighthearted. Instead of eating my evening meal alone in the kitchen as I normally did, I went into the dining room to join my parents. I wanted them to see I was happy. After I had eaten, I went upstairs to watch television, but as soon as I closed my bedroom door I felt sad and lonely. The pendulum that controlled my moods had swung across to sadness.

I thought about my fir tree song: it might uplift me, so I picked up the record and read the words on the cover. Once more the words 'hope' and 'perseverance' stood out. I struggled to get inspiration from them, but it would not come.

'Hope' – was it just a word? Was there any hope left for me? I had enjoyed myself outwitting Dr Goldblatt but how foolish it was of me to try playing games with the only person who was helping me. Even if I could really outwit him, where would that leave me? I would be even more stranded, without any hope of a cure. I was not going to Harley Street in order to prove I could be as clever as my psychiatrist. I was going there to get help. If I tried to outwit him, to play games with him, to deceive him, how could he possibly help me? I would become untreatable . . . was I untreatable?

In my first consultation with Dr Goldblatt he had said, 'I shall want you to free associate.' Yet, looking back over the months, I realised I had never free associated once. My thoughts would not transfer automatically into words. I always selected my words. Some things I chose to say, and other things I chose not to say. I had always been like that, and there was no way I would change. I reasoned that if I couldn't free associate, then I couldn't be treated. Perhaps I had better face facts, and finish with Dr Goldblatt once and for all. What was the point of wasting my money on psychotherapy, when I was unable to cooperate in my own treatment? Psychotherapy depended on the patient's cooperation. I decided to be realistic and write to Dr Goldblatt explaining that I no longer wished to carry on with the treatment.

I found my writing paper and stared at the blank sheet in front of me. I began shaking. Suddenly I couldn't bear the thought of giving up. Dr Goldblatt was like a drug to me. I needed him; I wanted him. My mind was in a turmoil. If he couldn't treat me, it was best to make the break now.

I felt desperate. I was torn between letting him go and clinging to him. I didn't know what to do. If only someone could help me. I felt dizzy, as though I was falling into a giant whirlpool. I thought of Rita – she must advise me.

I ran out of the house to a phone box. Nervously I dialled, and to my relief, Rita answered. I poured out my problem to her. I must have sounded very agitated and confused, but Rita understood.

'Persevere,' she said. 'Persevere. Dr Goldblatt has told you that you are making progress, so you must be making progress. He has been able to treat you so far, so why shouldn't he be able to carry on treating you? If he thought he was unable to help you any more, he would say so. I'm sure of it. He would never take your money under false pretences.'

These were comforting words. I said goodbye and hung up the receiver.

As I walked home I wondered why I hadn't been able to reason things out for myself.

When I got back to my room, I re-read the words of my German song. Even when all hope was gone, there was still perseverance left. I wrote the word 'Perseverance' on a piece of paper and then I wrote the word 'hope' on another piece, and placed both words in my top drawer. I hoped that if one of the words could not see me through, then the other one would. I was desperate beyond belief.

The next day, Thursday, I was incapable of doing any work. I sorted out a number of names and addresses of people who were due for visits, and I set out, determined not to allow my depression to get the better of me. But each time I arrived at someone's gate, I stopped and began shaking. I couldn't even think why I was doing the visit. I went to several houses on my list, but each time I was unable to even knock on the door. Finally I conceded defeat, and returned to the clinic in a state of utter despair.

At lunchtime I went to a nearby supermarket. I walked between the shelves in a trance, up one aisle and down the other, clutching an empty basket. The more I tried to work out what I wanted to buy, the more muddled I became. A shop assistant gave me a hard stare, and I realised I was becoming conspicuous, so I replaced the basket in a rack and fled out of the store. All hope was gone. That afternoon I said the lines of my German song over and over again, 'Perseverance gives fortitude and strength at all times.'

On Monday evening, my brother Brian telephoned to say his wife had given birth to a second son. I couldn't join in my parents' happiness when they told me the news. Instead, I was overwhelmed by feelings of jealousy and hate. I managed to force myself to say, 'That's good; I hope the baby gets on all right.' Then I rushed upstairs to my room.

As a child my relationship with Brian had been different from my relationship with Alan. Throughout our childhood, Brian and I had fought and quarrelled. We had never been sensitive to each other's feelings, and now as adults we were far apart. I recalled bitterly my brother's response last

November when I told him I was going to have a hysterectomy operation. Reluctantly I had telephoned him and told him I would be going into hospital. His reply was, 'Are you? By the way, we are expecting another baby. We're delighted.' That was all he had said.

I had never forgotten nor forgiven him. Now the baby was born, hurt and bitterness welled up in me. Why had my brother Alan, whom I had loved so much, been taken ill and died? It should have been Brian . . . . I shook myself for nurturing such dark thoughts. But if Alan were alive, he would have cared; he would have stood by me and tried to help me. If he hadn't been ill, he would be alive now.

If Alan hadn't been ill! For the first time I realised how bitter I felt at Alan's illness. A bitterness that for years I had kept inside me. I had been afraid to admit I felt bitter. I had believed it was wrong to question God's will. God in his wisdom allowed tragedies to happen. Now I had to admit I was bitter. I hated God; I hated Providence; I hated my parents; I hated those who had caused my brother to be cruelly ill, and to die. I wanted Alan; I needed Alan. I threw myself on my bed and burst into tears.

That night I slept fully dressed. The longing for my brother was so strong inside me that nothing else was important. I drifted between sleep and wakefulness, dreaming and sobbing until the cold grey light of morning brought another day of torment.

## 21 June 1967

Wednesday came, and it was time to go to Harley Street. By the time I arrived I felt like a robot. I remembered to take careful note of where I parked my car, then I walked slowly and mechanically to the house. I had been coming to this place for four months, yet I felt more wretched than ever. I looked around me. The waiting room was just as it had been on that very first occasion in February: the mirrors, the settees, the carpet and the empty space. Emptiness – the room reflected my empty life, and my empty future. Could Dr Goldblatt really help me, or was he just experimenting?

Every flicker of hope he gave me was countered by despair. Why did he let it happen? Why wouldn't he ease my suffering?

The receptionist called my name. Slowly and lethargically I stood up and walked through the waiting room to the stairs. I hadn't even the energy to look at Dr Goldblatt. I entered his room and with a sigh I got on to the couch.

I wondered where I should start. Perhaps I'd better tell him I doubted my suitability for his method of treatment.

'I've felt really awful this past week. There's been no let up. I thought seriously about not coming to see you any more. I was going to write and tell you.'

'Why? What's wrong?'

'I can't free associate the way you expect me to. I just can't say what comes into my mind. I have to choose what to say before I speak.'

'You set yourself too high a standard,' he said. 'If you are not perfect, or if you don't succeed entirely in what you set out to do, you feel you are a failure. Don't measure yourself against what you think you ought to be. Measure yourself against what you were like when you first came to see me. Then you will see progress. Then you will have the reassurance you need.'

'But I still can't free associate,' I persisted, 'so there must be a lot about me you don't know. This must hinder you in your treatment.'

'I don't expect you to free associate properly,' he said. 'You are giving me enough to work with at the moment. I'm satisfied with the way you are. You project your personality on to me. You also demand perfection of yourself, and so you think I demand perfection of you. You imagine I expect you to free associate properly, but because you can't free associate properly, it seems to you I am making impossible demands.' He paused. 'You feel I am unreasonable in my demands and I'm putting you in a position where you can't succeed. You believe you are doomed to failure, and your sense of failure entrenches you in your depression. To put it more simply: it appears to you that I am the cause of your failure. This failure is in turn causing your depression, so you hate me for inflicting such pain on you, and you now want to escape from me.'

'What can I do?' I asked anxiously.

'See things as they really are,' he said seriously. 'I am not demanding that you free associate. You are projecting on to me the experiences you had in your childhood.'

I lay quietly. I needed time to absorb all he had said.

I thought of the events of the week. I couldn't bring myself to tell him about my longing for Alan – it would be too distressing. However, I was able to tell him about my resentment towards my brother Brian.

'During the week,' I said. 'My sister-in-law had a baby. I felt bitter about it. My brother had first told me she was pregnant when I was about to have my hysterectomy. I was upset that he had told me about the baby at a time when I had been told I could never have a baby of my own. I don't want to see his baby. Is it normal for me to feel like this?'

'It is normal and natural for you to feel bitter. You cannot escape from these feelings. You must accept that you do feel bitter, and you will feel bitter. Don't add to the pain by feeling guilty as well. There is no reason for you to feel guilty. Bitterness is a natural reaction for a person in your position. You need to learn to accept your emotions, otherwise you will never be able to come to terms with the hysterectomy.'

I thought for a moment, then I brought up another subject. 'This week I've realised how bad I am at making relationships. At the tennis club I'm so awkward. I pretend to be happy when I'm not; at home, too, I'm putting on an act all the time.'

'You won't be good at making relationships until your basic needs are satisfied,' he said. 'You have a basic need for male company, and until you form relationships with men, you will feel frustrated.'

I didn't agree with what he said, at least, I didn't think his theory was relevant. My basic need was to get rid of my depression. Relationships with men could wait.

I didn't want to pursue the topic any further. I let my mind wander back to the other topics we had discussed.

The next day brought more depression. I tried to analyse what was wrong with myself and I concluded I was suffering from remorse over the death of my brother. I also felt bitter about the causes of my brother's illness. I had just arrived at work when Rita came to me. 'I've had enough of seeing you struggle,' she said. 'You must face facts. You are not able to cope with work; you should see your doctor and have a week's sick leave.'

'I can't,' I said. 'I'm frightened to go off sick – I'll get worse if I stay at home.'

'Then go and stay with one of your friends,' she said. 'If you can get away for a while, you'll come back feeling refreshed, then you'll be able to do your job properly.'

I relented and went straight to my doctor. He gave me a week's sick leave immediately. I went home and phoned Pat. She was in. 'Pat, I'm off sick for a week with depression; can I come and stay with you?' I said anxiously.

'Yes, I'd love to have you,' she said cheerfully. 'Come straight away.'

I packed my bags hurriedly and had a quick lunch. Within the hour I was on the way. At first the drive was tedious, but once I had crossed over into Pat's county I felt as though a weight had fallen from me. By the time I arrived at Pat's home, I felt well and happy: it was such a carefree feeling.

Pat had prepared a picnic, so as soon as I arrived, we set off in her car to a nearby forest of fir trees.

'I love fir trees,' I exclaimed. 'They have a philosophy of their own.'

Pat looked puzzled, but I hadn't the patience to explain about my song.

We were both lighthearted, laughing at nothing. When we came to the forest I jumped out of the car and darted off between the trees, rubbing my hands along the branches as I ran. I sang my German song at the top of my voice, and I listened as the echo of my song rang through the trees. Pat lifted the picnic hamper out of the car and carried it to a nearby seat. She sat watching me in amusement.

'You're a real tonic,' she laughed. 'I haven't enjoyed myself so much for weeks.'

After a while I calmed down and ran back to Pat. 'I'm ravenous. Let's eat,' I said.

It was hot weather, but in the shade of the trees it was cool and pleasant. After we had eaten we wandered along the paths between the trees. It was wonderful to be in the lovely dark forest with the smell of the fir trees and the bed of soft needles beneath our feet. I wondered why I had been making such a fuss about my life.

Back at Pat's flat that evening we chatted about my psychotherapy. 'You've been writing quite a lot to me about Dr Goldblatt,' Pat said suddenly. 'Are you in love with him?'

I was so taken aback I couldn't think for a moment. 'Of course I'm not in love with him,' I exclaimed. 'What on earth made you ask a question like that?'

'I thought all patients fell in love with their psychotherapists. It's a side-effect of the treatment,' Pat said mischievously.

'I don't know about other patients,' I retorted, 'but it certainly isn't a side-effect with me. I can't imagine it could happen with Dr Goldblatt – he's too professional and detached. I could only fall in love with someone who needed my love.'

'Nonsense,' contradicted Pat. 'You don't know what you're talking about. Are you trying to tell me you don't feel anything for him?'

'I'm not trying to tell you anything except the truth,' I said seriously.

'But surely you can't feel indifferent towards him,' Pat persisted.

'No,' I admitted, 'he makes me angry and I often hate him because most of the time I'm in a state of despair. He doesn't make me feel better, in fact often he makes me feel worse. He's making me experience emotions I've never let myself indulge in before, and it's quite shattering. When I feel at my worst, I think it's all his fault for not protecting me from such frightening feelings, so I hate him.'

'But why do you keep going to him if you feel like that towards him?' Pat asked. 'You've even turned down a cycling holiday because you can't bear the thought of missing a session with him. I'm sure I would have given up psychotherapy long ago and changed to ECT. What makes you keep going?'

I thought carefully for a moment, then I said, 'There are three reasons. First of all I can't see any other alternative. I was on Librium for a few months but it didn't help, and I don't think ECT would help either. Those treatments only help you to forget your worries for a little while, but in the long run, I don't think they are of any use. I want to understand myself – I don't want to have a part of my memory blotted out for ever. Dr Goldblatt's method is my only hope. Through his treatment I'm hoping it will be possible for me to understand why I think and feel as I do.'

'I can see that,' Pat said slowly, 'but what are your other reasons for not giving up?'

'Rita thinks that psychotherapy is right for me,' I said, 'and I trust her. She knows me as well as anyone, and she understands what psychotherapy is all about. She's seen me at my worst, but she's never given up on me. She believes I'll win through so long as I keep on trying.'

'You are lucky to have Rita,' said Pat. 'She's marvellous, the way she lets you phone her any time when you feel desperate.' Pat paused, then she said. 'What's your third reason for sticking it out?'

'The third reason is the most important one as far as I'm concerned,' I said. 'I'm persevering because Dr Goldblatt's treatment is based on an understanding relationship between doctor and patient. He knows how my mind works, and what's more, he treats me as though I'm a rational human being. If I were on pills I'd only see the doctor for repeat prescriptions.'

Pat laughed. 'I can remember you wrote to me a few weeks ago, complaining that your psychotherapist was cruel and brutal to you.'

I felt caught out. 'Well, he is sometimes. That is a failing in him. No one is perfect. I'm sure he doesn't mean to be cruel, but sometimes he seems to disregard my feelings and he won't show me any sympathy. If he'd occasionally put his hand on my shoulder and say how sorry he was that my life was so frightening, it would make me feel more secure.'

'I think you've got to see it from his point of view as well as your own,' Pat said. 'He'd become more tense than his patients if he allowed himself to enter into their feelings.'

'I suppose you're right,' I said. 'I'm only looking at it from my point of view, but after all, I'm going to him for my own sake, not for his sake.'

'Have you told him you hate him?' asked Pat.

'Yes,' I replied, 'but I know he doesn't take it personally. In free association I can say anything I want. One of these days I'll drink half a bottle of sherry before I see him, so that I can really free associate!'

'I'd like to be a fly on the wall when that happens,' laughed Pat.

We continued joking about my experiences with psychotherapy. My depression seemed a world away: I felt as though I was floating on a cloud and looking down on myself, a tiny figure running up and down Harley Street. It was as though the real me was up there on a cloud, and the disturbed me was down there going through all those terrible emotions. I felt totally detached from my other, suffering self.

We tired ourselves out with talking, and we went to bed. As soon as I lay down I began to feel wretched. I cried myself to sleep.

Throughout my time at Pat's I experienced several sudden swings of mood. Most of the time I felt elated, and Pat shared the elation with me. That helped, because it prevented me from feeling guilty about my childish behaviour. At other times I felt a deep sense of panic suddenly well up inside me, and on several occasions I rushed from the flat and ran along the country lanes until I was exhausted. I was trying to run away from a terrible, unknown force. Then I returned to the flat, feeling drained, mentally and physically, and cried. At those times Pat continued with her work, accepting my behaviour without question or complaint. She would bring me a cup of coffee and say gently, 'It will pass, Margaret, you'll win through in the end.' Her tolerance was very comforting, because she enabled me to accept myself and my emotions that much more easily.

All too soon it was time for me to return home. I left Pat early on the Wednesday afternoon in order to be in time for my psychotherapy session. My feelings of gloom and anxiety increased as I drew nearer to London. With Pat I had escaped from responsibility and the world. Now I had to face my circumstances and the world again.

**28 June 1967**

Later that afternoon on Dr Goldblatt's couch I felt tense and anxious. I hoped that seeing him would make me feel better.

'I've just had a week's sick leave because I was so depressed,' I began. 'I went to stay with a friend who is very understanding, but even with her I still felt disturbed. I had extreme mood changes. A lot of the time I was elated – laughing, singing, shouting – then I became depressed and scared. I kept swinging from one extreme to the other.'

'You became elated,' he said, 'because you feel free as a result of the psychotherapy. You are freeing yourself from your old restrictions and feelings of guilt, and you are now expressing your emotions.'

'But I'm too extreme,' I said. 'I can't stay on an even keel. Why am I in the depths of despair one minute and elated the next? It's really frightening.'

'It's the outward sign of the conflict that is going on inside you. I am putting ideas to you which are making you reconsider the restrictions you have placed on your life. Those ideas are liberating you – causing you to behave in an unrestricted way – but your old ideas keep fighting back and restricting you, and so you feel depressed.'

'What can I do about it?'

'You will not be able to balance your moods until you have come to terms with the conflict and resolved that conflict,' he replied.

'Will it take long?' I asked.

'Yes, there's a lot to be done, but at least you have made a start.'

'I realise I have made some progress,' I agreed. 'I can now make relationships more easily. I'm confident with my friend. I want her to know what my feelings are, and I'm not afraid of losing her friendship by showing my feelings. I've never been so frank about myself with other people before.'

'I think you have made real progress,' he said. We were silent for a while.

'I have felt down today,' I said. 'I'll be going back to work tomorrow, which means I'll have to see mothers with babies. I don't want to see another baby if I can help it. It makes me feel so upset, because I'll never experience having a baby of my own.'

'Do you feel guilty about your feelings?'

'Not any more,' I replied.

'You seem to have lost the bitterness you had last week.'

'Yes,' I replied. I was grateful to him for bringing that to my notice. I was making more progress.

These thoughts should have pleased me, but instead I felt tense, and I began to tremble. I wanted to run away from the fear that was welling up inside me. 'Why am I trembling?' I asked loudly. 'Why do I have this feeling of dread?'

'There's something frightening you in your unconscious mind,' he said.

There was a frustrating silence.

'I feel tense when I can't think what to say, and I get annoyed with you when you sit there and don't do anything to help. It's a waste of time when we say nothing.'

'It isn't a waste of time,' he said. 'You are having a battle in your unconscious mind, and when you speak you have achieved something positive. If I spoke every time you stopped talking, I would not be helping you.'

'I feel very apprehensive,' I said, 'because I don't know what to believe any more.' I trembled uncontrollably.

'The old rules which you lived by as a child are no longer completely appropriate to you, but you can't find suitable rules to replace them,' he said. 'You are afraid to live without rules because that would make you feel insecure, so you are looking for a new set of rules – you want security.'

I didn't comment, but I thought very carefully about what Dr Goldblatt had said. It seemed to me that my religious background was a major problem and, much as I shrank from discussing my beliefs with Dr Goldblatt, I realised that my progress would be hindered if I didn't tackle the subject of my religious beliefs during the next session.

I left Dr Goldblatt with a feeling of dread inside me. As I drove home I managed to keep my composure by telling myself over and over again that Dr Goldblatt's treatment was working. He had explained my unstable moods, and my intense feelings of dread. I hoped I would soon have it in my power to overcome this terrifying illness.

That evening I had a most devastating dream. I felt as if I were hurtling into a black unknown sky with all my old childhood rules falling away behind me in the darkness.

# 11 An Agonising Battle

(5 July 1967 - 23 August 1967)

The thought of discussing my religious beliefs and moral code with Dr Goldblatt caused me some concern. Before my illness I had already begun to question the religious beliefs and attitudes that had been instilled in me since childhood. I had arrived at a position where I felt that one religion had as much to offer the individual as another, and I believed that what really mattered was compassion.

But although I was beginning to see religion in a new perspective, I was still trapped in the web of indoctrination which had been woven into my childhood. A central part of that indoctrination was that non-Christians enter into hell when they die. I was therefore terrified of giving up the beliefs which had been an important part of my life since my early days. I had been brought up within the narrow confines of a strict non-conformist group of Christians. They were almost fanatical about their rules and regulations; many of these rules may seem laughable to the outsider. For example, they believed cinemas were evil places and, no matter what film was being shown, it was wrong for any member of the group to go to the cinema. The rules laid down by the group applied to almost all aspects of life, so that nearly everything I did meant I was in danger of breaking a rule. They had very strict views about Sunday. For example, it was wrong to read non-religious books or literature on a Sunday. Also it was wrong for women to make themselves look attractive by using make-up or by wearing pretty clothes.

I had begun to examine the rules which had been instilled in me, to discover which were really Christian rules and which were not, but I hadn't got far in my quest before I was overtaken by my illness.

Since my operation I had been overwhelmed by depression, and I hadn't been in a fit state to continue with my heart-searching. I had been utterly shaken by the total spiritual isolation in which I found myself when I became ill. Prayer had become meaningless. I found that it was those people who didn't lay claim to a rigid religious belief who had stood by me and understood me most. It was also a Jewish doctor, not a Christian, who was helping me now.

Sad to relate, it was my experiences over the last nine months which continued to undermine the deep Christian faith I had been brought up with, yet I was afraid to abandon that faith. I feared that if I discussed these conflicts with Dr Goldblatt I might lose my faith entirely. I didn't think that he could understand my conflict, and I was afraid he might unwittingly destroy my religious beliefs. I saw my religion as something separate to my psychotherapy, and I had to sort out my beliefs for myself. The attitudes and ideas contained in Freud's work were a philosophy which had a great deal to offer me, but I was afraid of using these Freudian theories against my religion. Religion is a matter of belief, and I thought it inappropriate to subject that belief to the logical argument contained in Freudian theories.

However, I had to conquer my depression somehow, and if in the process I lost my religious faith, then it would have to be lost. I hoped I would find my faith again when my depression was gone.

All week I kept telling myself I had nothing to fear, but I was plagued by nightmares and anxiety. I felt desperate. When at last I set off for Harley Street, I knew I must discuss my problem with Dr Goldblatt.

## 5 July 1967

Lying on the couch and staring at the rosettes on the wall, I struggled to say what I had planned. After fidgeting for a while, I said, 'I've been thinking about my Christian beliefs – I'm in a state of uncertainty. I don't know where I stand. I'm afraid to examine my beliefs analytically with you because I might turn my back on my Christian principles. I'm frightened to go against some of the things that have been ingrained in me since early childhood.' I paused.

'You are afraid to look critically at what your parents have taught you,' he said, 'because you think they might reject you. You are also afraid of questioning your religious beliefs because you think God will reject you. You feel it's wrong to question.'

'Yes,' I said, 'I was always told to accept my parents' teachings, but I wanted to question them.'

'Your desire and your conscience are pulling you in opposite directions,' he said.

I was afraid to pursue the topic any further; I felt I could easily be overwhelmed if we tried to go deeper, so I decided to change the subject without making it obvious.

'I enjoy talking to Rita, and discussing our beliefs,' I said. 'She has unconventional attitudes. She's warm-hearted and she shows her emotions. She's quite different from me. I value her friendship, but what worries me are the times when she doesn't seem to notice me because then I feel unwanted.'

'These strong emotions are there,' he said, 'because you are getting from her what you missed from your mother, and, having experienced the kind of relationship you have needed for years, you naturally feel a sense of loss each time the relationship falters.'

'Is it possible for me to make up what I missed in my childhood?' I asked.

'It will be difficult, but it is possible,' he said. 'The first step is to recognise what you have missed.'

'But even if I am aware of what I've missed emotionally, I can't demand constant attention from my friends.'

'You can have a relationship of interdependence with your friends,' he said. 'You can give, and you can receive. Your needs can be shared with your friends. It will take time, but once you understand yourself, it will be possible.'

For the rest of the session I kept the discussion revolving around relationships because it was comforting to me. In that way I avoided touching on anything that caused conflicts. I felt too weak, too tired, too anxious to bring anything new to the surface. I wanted to gather all my strength before entering into an agonising battle.

But my strength never came. That next week I wasn't ready for any battle. It was all I could do to keep going. I was stuck with my depression. I wanted to see Dr Goldblatt and tell him just how bad I felt. If only I could go more often to see him. How I longed for someone who could take all my anxieties and conflicts away from me.

By Sunday night my nightmares had become so frequent that I was afraid to go to sleep. I felt exhausted, so I took a sleeping tablet to give me one night's peace.

I was reluctant to take tablets of any kind as Dr Goldblatt had advised me against medication unless it was really necessary. There were conflicts and difficulties in my mind I had to work through, whether I took tablets or not. Tablets might reduce my symptoms, but in the long run they could slow down my recovery. Deep down I wanted to end my depression, not just reduce the symptoms.

On Wednesday I worked up enthusiasm for the mothercraft class but then I sank back into my depression. At last it was time to go to Harley Street.

## 12 July 1967

Even the drive was a nightmare. Torrential rain beat down on the roof of my car, and I could scarcely see the way. To add to my difficulties I couldn't control my tears. By the time I reached Harley Street I was almost knee deep in wet paper tissues. I ran through the pouring rain to Dr Goldblatt's rooms. I got soaked. There was a towel in the cloakroom, so I dried myself off as best I could, and then I went into the waiting room. I hung my wet raincoat on a coat stand and sat down. I felt totally dejected. I was shivering with cold.

I asked myself why I continued coming to this place even though I felt no better. I didn't know the answer, but I did know that nothing would induce me to stop coming. Deep down, despite my despair, I somehow believed in psychotherapy, and my belief was reinforced by my two most trusted friends. They believed I was doing the right thing.

Discouraged and weary though I was, I knew I would keep coming, whatever the cost. I needed Dr Goldblatt, I trusted him, and I believed in him.

No sooner had these thoughts crossed my mind than I had a sinking feeling. I should place my trust in God, not in man. Yet how could I believe in God, when none of my prayers had been answered? I had not deliberately turned my back on God – he had turned his back on me. Now I believed in Dr Goldblatt. It had just happened that way, and I couldn't alter it.

'I don't want to alter it,' I whispered to myself, even though I felt a cold chill of guilt.

The receptionist suddenly called my name. Wearily I made my way to the staircase and looked up. There was Dr Goldblatt on the landing smiling kindly. I watched his face as I climbed the stairs. His expression was gentle. As long as I could see his face I felt I could relate to him more easily. We walked into the consulting room, and I backed away from the couch. 'I'd rather have a chair this week please,' I stammered.

'Of course,' he replied softly, and arranged two armchairs at right angles to each other.

For a while I sat and stared at the carpet. I fiddled nervously with my hands, struggling to find words that would express the true state of terror in my mind. I turned my head and looked straight at him. Our eyes met. The contact was made. The gulf had been bridged.

'I've had a horrifying week,' I said. 'Such terrible nights. I keep dreaming I'm lost and wandering on a dark and empty moor. I roam for hours in solitude. I dread each night.' I hesitated, and looked down at the carpet. I felt ashamed. 'I often find myself imagining I'm committing suicide.' I looked at him again, hoping for sympathy. His expression hadn't changed. 'Whenever I have a bath I imagine myself slipping beneath the water and breathing.' I looked down at the carpet again, and waited for him to speak.

'I encourage you to question your beliefs,' he said, 'and you hate me for it. This questioning has made your life so difficult that you want to destroy me. But at the same time you want me to encourage you, and as result you are in conflict with yourself. You want to get rid of me, but at the same time you want me. You feel so guilty about wanting to destroy me, that your destructive feeling has turned against yourself. You are being consumed by your own hate.'

His words shocked me. 'I don't want to destroy you,' I protested loudly.

But he persisted. 'You are like a girl who has enjoyed sexual intercourse, but who feels guilty afterwards. You believe I've seduced you into disloyalty to your religion. It's true. I'm encouraging you to see things differently at a time when you are at your weakest. You are totally overwhelmed with guilt because you are being made to question matters which you have never questioned before. You think I'm to blame, so you want to destroy me.'

I was not prepared to accept his theory. I did not want to destroy him. I was not that wicked. Just thinking about it filled me with horror. I had to get away from his accusations by changing the subject. I recalled his sentence about intercourse.

'I don't like the way you refer to sexual relationships to illustrate your arguments,' I said.

'Why not?' he queried.

'It's as if you are mocking me.'

'Why should I mock you? were you mocked as a child?'

'No,' I replied. 'I always avoided situations where I might be mocked. I was brought up outside the mainstream of the life of children around me. I was led to believe I was different, but I learned how to conceal the differences in order to prevent them laughing at me.'

For a few seconds neither of us spoke.

'Where is all this self-analysis getting me?' I said at last. 'Will I ever make progress?'

'You are making progress all the time,' he said. 'You are more able to express yourself now than when you first came here. You were not always able to speak to me as you have spoken today. You are impatient because it's taking so long for your unpleasant symptoms to go. It's a natural impatience, because you want to get well.'

'But surely if I am getting better, there should be a corresponding improvement in my symptoms. Instead, I seem more depressed now than I used to be.'

'That's because each time you make progress, you feel a corresponding sense of guilt. Progress in your case involves fighting against what you have been taught to believe since childhood, so your conscience tells you that progress is wrong, and your guilt causes you to feel depressed.'

'I wish I could see you more often. I'd get over my depression sooner. A week is a long time to wait.'

'A week is a long time,' he said. 'In some ways more frequent visits would be advisable, but at present it's impossible. My time is fully booked.'

'Am I likely to go through many more bad patches, or do you think I am nearly over my depression?' I asked.

"Your depression will probably continue for some time.'

'I feel so terribly alone. Will this feeling of loneliness persist?'

'Yes,' he said, 'because you are alone. You are alone with your conscience and your beliefs. You are alone in deciding what sort of person you are going to be.'

'But I'm frightened of being alone,' I whispered. 'That's why I'm coming to you for help.'

'I am giving you the tools you need for your recovery, and I'm showing you how to use them,' he said firmly. 'I can't go further than that. It's up to you to use the tools for what you decide should be done.'

I left the consulting room, bewildered. Dr Goldblatt had retained his kind, gentle expression, yet the things he had said to me were hard and brutal. He had reassured me by saying I was making progress, but he had spoilt everything by telling me I would continue to be depressed for some time, and that I was alone in my struggle. My feelings of desolation remained as intense as ever.

That week my depression continued to be as bad as before, but it was interspersed with feelings of anger towards Dr Goldblatt for being so blunt towards me and for not comforting me. After a few days, however, I resolved not to allow myself to wallow in misery. Dr Goldblatt's words, 'Your conscience tells you that progress is wrong' kept ringing in my ears. I realised it was my conscience that was hampering my recovery and intensifying my depression, so I made up my mind to wage an all out battle with my conscience. I decided

I would deliberately do the opposite to what my conscience dictated, where I could see no reason to think I was doing wrong.

I decided to begin drinking. Already I was drinking sherry at nights, but that was from sheer desperation. I would drink for the pleasure of drinking, which my conscience told me was wrong.

During a lunch break I bought some cider and martini. In the evenings I began pouring myself glasses of cider and martini. I felt conscience striken, but I was determined to defy my conscience, believing that eventually I must wear it down. The sherry was reserved for night times to 'drown my sorrows'.

## 19 July 1967

On the Wednesday I looked forward to seeing Dr Goldblatt. I imagined he would be sympathetic and have a chair arranged for me to sit on. However, when I entered the consulting room I was disappointed. He walked in behind me, closed the door, walked across to the armchair beyond the couch and sat down. He lit a cigarette without even looking at me. His manner seemed to indicate that he was not prepared to tolerate any nonsense.

I felt like protesting, as I waited to sit on a chair, but I didn't dare. I longed for sympathy, not a battle. Discouraged, I climbed onto the couch. How could I show my feelings to someone so unsympathetic?

I fidgeted. I wanted to tell him I felt angry with him, but I couldn't. For such outspokenness I needed to watch his face. I decided to express my feelings in the past tense. 'I was angry with you last week,' I said.

'Why were you angry with me?'

'You were unkind to me. You told me I would be depressed for a long time. You said I'm alone. You didn't comfort me when I needed it.'

'I was answering your questions,' he replied. 'You wouldn't have wanted me to evade your questions, or to be dishonest with you.'

'No, that's true.' I paused. 'I shouldn't have been angry with you,' I continued. 'It was wrong of me. You are the last person I should be angry with. You are doing all you can to help me.'

'It wasn't wrong of you to be angry with me,' he said. 'You need to express your anger and to understand it.'

'Twice I burst into tears at work,' I said. 'I sat at my desk and sobbed. One of the clinic nurses put her arm around me, and it helped a lot.'

'Last week you wanted me to put my arm around you, to love and to comfort you,' he said. 'But if I had done that, you wouldn't have liked it. You would have felt cheated, because I'm your analyst, and it's my task to help you to look at yourself, to understand yourself, to accept yourself.'

'Yes,' I said thoughtfully. 'You are right.'

We were quiet for a few minutes. It was not an uncomfortable silence. It was restful, soothing. I grew more confident.

'I've been working on my conscience this week,' I said. 'Every time when I thought I shouldn't do something, I asked myself why, and if there was no good reason, I made myself do what my conscience said I shouldn't. That made me feel very uneasy.'

'Your conscience is very narrow and forbidding,' he said.

'Yes, but I'm going to keep fighting it until I wear it down. Then I'll be free to choose properly what's right and wrong.'

'Don't underestimate the power of your conscience,' he warned. 'You have set yourself a very difficult task.'

'I can't turn back now. I can only go on, as quickly as I can.'

'Remember your conscience is just a part of you, not the whole of you,' he said. 'Keep looking towards that other part of yourself.'

'My conscience tells me it's wrong to think of myself: I feel I should be self-sacrificing.'

'That's why you find it so difficult to consider the whole of yourself,' he said.

'It's strange,' I said, 'At the beginning of this afternoon's session you seemed to be cold and impersonal, but now you seem to be warmhearted and caring in your dealings with me. I expect when I've left here I'll think you are indifferent again. Most weeks I feel like that.'

'Your conscience is too severe,' he said, 'and you project that severity on to me, and on to every other relationship you have.' We both fell silent. I felt resentful at having to lie on the couch. I wanted to let him know my feelings but I could do so only in an indirect way.

'Why do you prefer your patients to be on the couch?' I asked.

'Because it gives freedom to me and my patient,' he replied.

'I don't feel free lying on a couch,' I said. 'I'm more able to say what I think when I sit in the chair.'

'The reason why you want to sit in the chair is so that you can watch me, and see if I am listening sympathetically.'

'Why won't you alter your methods to take account of my need to watch you?' I asked.

'My task is to help you,' he said. 'I want you to study your own reactions, not mine.'

There was a pause. It was apparent to me he had no intention of letting me sit in a chair.

'I've been more outspoken today than ever before,' I commented.

'You are certainly more outspoken than you used to be,' he agreed.

When I left him that week I felt encouraged at my outspoken manner, but I was annoyed at his reluctance to let me sit on a chair.

During the coming week I still longed to hide myself away and wallow in my misery. I felt exhausted: everything I did was a tremendous effort. On the Monday evening the phone rang. A strange woman's voice was speaking.

'I have a message from Dr Goldblatt,' she said. 'He is indisposed and has to cancel your appointment for Wednesday next. Unless you hear otherwise, please come the following week.'

I put the phone down, feeling stunned. It had not occurred to me that Dr Goldblatt could ever be ill.

Somehow I drifted through the week. I couldn't think constructively. I just existed, just keeping my head above water until Dr Goldblatt could take my hand again.

On the Sunday evening I went to Church; not because I expected to enter into the spirit of the service, but because I knew I needed to relate to people. Desolation remained in me, and after the service I wandered slowly out of the building, fighting back my tears. Everyone seemed to be so happy, but I was alone, and left out in the cold.

Suddenly I realised I was being spoken to. 'Hello,' someone said.

I turned round. A young man whom I had seen occasionally at the Church walked towards me. 'Hello Peter,' I said listlessly.

'Would you like to join me for a coffee back at my flat?' he said boldly.

'I feel terribly depressed,' I said, 'but I'll join you for a while; it might cheer me up.'

We drove to his flat. He lived alone; his parents were dead and he had no brothers or sisters. The flat was cosy, with one or two interesting pictures on the walls. Peter made some coffee, and we sat down and listened to some classical music. It was very comforting.

Peter said, 'I like being friendly with girls, but I only want platonic friendships. I never want to get involved. I like to be free to come and go, and to have lots of friends.'

'That suits me,' I said. 'I don't want to get involved either.' I meant it. I was not ready for involvement with the opposite sex. I had to sort myself out first; to find out what I stood for, and what I wanted in life.

It seemed strange to be sitting in Peter's flat. He was a comparative stranger to me and yet I felt relaxed. Later that evening he drove me home. He was sympathetic towards me and I felt less lonely.

That evening with Peter seemed to restore my will power, and I resolved to make a new effort to carry on the battle against my conscience.

On the Monday evening Peter phoned me. 'I'm going out for a drink,' he said. 'Do you want to join me?'

I had been brought up to believe that drinking in pubs was an evil pastime. Once more I could do something against my conscience. 'Yes, please,' I replied. 'Give me half an hour to get ready.'

Peter came for me in his car, and we drove to a marvellous little pub in the country. We drank lager and lime. I had never drunk beer before, but I enjoyed the taste. The atmosphere in the pub was charming. I looked around in amazement. How could anyone think it wrong to go into a pub if the pubs were all like this? We had a really happy evening and later we drove back to Peter's flat for coffee and music. I arrived home at about 1 a.m. in a rare mood of contentment, but that night I paid dearly for my adventure. I had a most horrifying dream.

I dreamt I had turned into twins. One twin was plump and happy the other was thin and miserable. I felt sorry for the thin one because it was starved and desperate, but I was also afraid of it. I was attracted to the plump twin, but in my dream I was inside each twin and outside them at the same time. I wished I could only be the plump twin, and for a while that did actually happen and life seemed suddenly wonderful, but this feeling soon changed as the thin twin took over and I began to feel a deep sense of dread and confusion. I realised I had become a pair of Siamese twins. Each twin was tearing at the other, refusing to let the other have its own life. Suddenly I realised I was hovering over both twins as they clawed at each other, but in seconds I had become the twins again, and I was fighting desperately with myself. I felt myself telling the plump twin to kill the thin twin, so that I could become the plump twin for ever. The thin twin suddenly began to writhe in agony and to shrivel up before my eyes, its body curling and twisting in a grotesque dance of desperation. I actually felt the agony of the thin twin as it writhed before me.

'Destroy it,' I shouted to the plump twin, but the plump twin hesitated at the sight of such agony. Suddenly the thin twin curled its horrid body forwards and sank its teeth into the pump twin's neck. Within moments the tables were turned and the plump twin began to cry for help as the thin twin slowly devoured it. I struggled against myself, desperately wanting the plump twin to survive and the thin twin to be destroyed, but I had no control over this ugly scene. After a long, excruciating struggle the plump twin was totally devoured and I was now the thin twin, destroying all that was free and happy. I awoke, shaking in terror, my body was soaked in perspiration, and I imagined I could still see the twins writhing in the shadows before me.

The dream left me shaken and I felt haunted. I wondered how much more madness I would have to go through.

**2 August 1967**

Once more I entered Dr Goldblatt's consulting room, feeling all was lost. I climbed dismally onto the couch, and for some time I couldn't bring myself to say anything. Eventually I told him about my dream. He listened with interest, then he said. 'The thin twin represents your conscience, and the plump twin is the person you would like to be.'

'Does this mean my conscience will always win, like it did in the dream?' I asked.

'No,' he replied, emphatically. 'You are afraid your conscience will win because it's so strong. But your conscience is just a part of you. It is my task to help you to master your conscience.'

'Will I ever achieve that?'

'I believe you will,' he said, 'but your conscience is a very powerful element in your make-up.'

He paused. Then I talked about my job. 'I'm preoccupied at work,' I said. 'Sometimes I can't concentrate on what the mothers say to me. That makes me feel guilty.'

'You are bound to be preoccupied because you have to think a lot about yourself in order to solve your problems. Your life is more important than your job. Even one constructive thought in a day makes that day worthwhile for you.'

**9 August 1967**

At my next session I talked again about my dream. 'I can't get the dream out of my mind,' I said. 'I keep reliving the horrid experience of being devoured by that part of myself which I despise.'

'Your dream means that your superego, that is, your conscience, will dominate unless you destroy it. But that isn't necessary. What you have got to do is to get your conscience and your desires into harmony. Until you do that, you will not be able to form good relationships with other people.'

'I believe I have begun to harmonise the two,' I said. 'At work the medical officer chose me to do a job because she believed I was the most suitable for it. I felt very encouraged, even though I felt guilty for being pleased. I used to think it was wrong to admit I was good at something. I thought I should be humble and think myself inferior to others. Now I know it's healthy to recognise what I'm good at.'

'That's the way to recovery,' he said. 'In the past your conscience has played tricks on you.'

'People at work tell me I should get a boyfriend. That makes me feel angry.'

'Why is that?' he asked.

'Because I would like to have a boyfriend, but I don't seem to meet the right people,' I replied. (I didn't think of Peter as a boyfriend.) 'It doesn't help when people keep on about it.'

'You must not let your anger over this boyfriend issue cloud your judgement. It's right for you to feel angry, but at the same time you should also think in a positive way whenever you do get angry. Don't let your anger drive you back into a shell; that way leads nowhere. Respond to your anger by facing up to your loneliness, and do something positive about it.'

That week my nightmares continued, and I needed all my willpower and determination to continue with my job. The only respite from my torment was an evening out with Peter at a country pub.

## 16 August 1967

As I drove to Harley Street again, I realised it was my twenty-fifth meeting with Dr Goldblatt and I seemed as depressed as ever. Wearily I climbed onto the couch. After a while, I said. 'Last week you told me I should use my anger constructively, but anger doesn't help me. It leaves me depressed and paralysed.'

'That's because you are frightened of your anger,' he said. 'Your conscience tells you anger is wrong, so you feel anger is a destructive force, but, in reality, anger is not always wrong.

You need to learn to use your anger to help you.'

I couldn't imagine I would ever be able to learn that lesson. Discouraged, my thoughts wandered to another area of failure.

'I go to a tennis club on Saturday afternoons,' I said 'but it's difficult. If I play a bad shot I criticise myself so much I lose my confidence, and then I'm hopeless. I feel everyone is criticising my tennis in an unkind way.'

'You are projecting onto other people the attitudes you have towards yourself,' he said.

'But I'm struggling with myself all the time,' I said. 'I want to stop going to the tennis club because the people aren't friendly, but I make myself go. Am I wise? How much will-power should I use? Am I driving myself too hard?'

'You must decide that for yourself,' he said carefully. 'If you believe that what you are doing is helpful, then do it, but if the tennis club is distressing you, there is no reason why you should continue to go.'

After a pause, I said, 'I've been having bad nightmares again this week.'

'Tell me about them,' he said.

'I can't remember what they were about, but I was very frightened.'

'It doesn't matter if you can't remember,' he said. 'If you have any more bad dreams we can discuss them next week.'

I could find nothing more to say, and Dr Goldblatt didn't break the silence. I wriggled uncomfortably, feeling desperately miserable. How could I keep up my single handed battle against my conscience? I asked myself in despair.

Dismally I drove back through the London streets, unable to think. When I arrived home, I felt angry with Dr Goldblatt and I wished I could tell him what was in my mind. All evening and the next day I couldn't rest. On Thursday evening I felt so frustrated I decided to write a letter to him.

This is the actual letter I wrote.

Dear Dr Goldblatt,

I am writing to tell you how I feel after seeing you last Wednesday. I react similarly most weeks, but after a few days I usually overcome or suppress my feelings and therefore when I next come to you I find that I do not say all I meant to.

Probably most of my grievances are merely a projection of my own personality, and certainly I do not believe completely all that I shall write. Indeed, part of me believes the contrary, but if I do not express these feelings now, I shall try to perpetuate them until Wednesday, which will make me depressed unnecessarily.

My main complaint is that in some respects you either do not care about, or do not understand, my feelings. During my first consultation with you, and on subsequent occasions, I said that I prefer sitting on a chair to talk to you. Periodically I have the courage, or I am sufficiently desperate, to ask to sit down, but at other times I have to cope with staring at the walls or ceiling, wondering how you are reacting to what I am saying, and whether in fact you are listening to me at all. Certain things I cannot say to someone who might be disinterested. Only by seeing your face can I know your attitude to me.

Secondly, I do not understand why you must keep so rigidly to generally accepted methods of psychotherapy. When I have nothing to say, why can you not ask me questions in order to obtain a more accurate knowledge of certain points? I am anxious in case my inability to tell you what you need to know might affect your ability to understand and help me.

Thirdly, you seem to be indifferent about a matter which worries and frightens me. When I told you of my fear of suicide you showed no concern. At the same time you gave me the impression that patients were easy to acquire, and one lost could soon be replaced. You have not since asked if I am still afraid. I expect you to care sufficiently to want to know. Obviously you expect me to tell you without your questioning, but this is difficult for me to do, as twice I have mentioned this problem, and on both occasions you have shown little interest. This is not a subject I can raise just for something to say. A response of cold indifference from you is harder to take than doing without talking to someone who will care.

Please understand that I have misgivings about what I have written, as I recognise that you show exceptional understanding and patience. In addition, you bear in mind my background. This impresses me most, as my chief criticism of psychiatrists has been that they do not bother to find out enough about the patients' environments to enable them to have adequate understanding.

You have at least got through to me to the extent that I may say to you what I wish, and I feel better now for doing that. Possibly writing this letter shows that I am beginning to use my anger constructively.

Yours very sincerely,
Margaret

**23 August 1967**

The following Wednesday I felt uneasy as I walked into Dr Goldblatt's consulting room in case he was annoyed by my letter. To my relief I saw two chairs set at right angles to each other. That suggested to me that he was willing to adapt his methods to suit my needs. I felt as though a weight had been lifted from my shoulders. I would be able to express my thoughts and feelings more easily.

I was about to sit down when he said, 'It's important you lie on the couch to start with.'

I was taken aback. 'Why?' I asked, bewildered.

'You wrote to me about your feelings in that respect,' he said. 'We need to discuss those feelings.'

'I can discuss my feelings much better if I'm looking at you,' I said boldly. 'I don't want to lie on the couch. It inhibits me.'

I expected him to give way, but I was disappointed. 'I want you to do as I ask,' he insisted. His face was solemn.

I hesitated. I wanted to refuse, but I didn't have the courage to go against his wishes.

'It's important to discuss your feelings,' he continued, 'and since it's through lying on the couch that you have those feelings, it's more appropriate you lie on the couch while we discuss the matter.'

I felt he was being unreasonable, but his firm manner stopped me from saying so.

Reluctantly I walked to the couch. I slipped off my shoes and hesitated. The barrier between us felt insurmountable. Somehow I had to try to break it down, or I might as well go home.

I looked at him. He was standing just a few feet away, waiting. He didn't look impatient or annoyed. He seemed relaxed; there was even the hint of a smile on his face. I had to know what his attitude was towards me, and I could only know by watching his response. I thought quickly. 'I want to ask your advice on something first,' I said.

'All right,' he said quietly.

'How should a person set about getting private treatment if their GP doesn't give them any help?'

He was evasive. 'Why do you think a GP wouldn't help?' he asked.

'I don't think, I know,' I said. 'My doctor wouldn't help me.'

'You are projecting your feelings onto others,' he said. 'You feel that doctors have failed to help you, so you believe other people will have the same experience.'

His reply gave me what I was looking for. He was the analyst, I was the patient. He decided on the rules of the game, I was expected to obey those rules. Only he could decide when a rule could be broken, and now was not a time for breaking rules. In this case, he wouldn't answer my questions, neither would he let me sit and watch him. I had no choice.

Miserably I climbed onto the couch. I felt desperately alone. I heard him walk to his chair and sit down. No, I wasn't alone, but much worse: I was with a horrid psychiatrist who refused to see me as an individual, who treated me merely as an interesting case. He refused to accept that I had feelings and a mind of my own.

He was waiting for me to talk, but there seemed to be no point. I had told him about these feelings on many previous occasions. There was nothing new I could tell him. I stared at a broken rosette on the plaster ceiling. Perhaps Dr Goldblatt believed there was a strange psychological reason behind my dislike of his couch. If so, it was important for me to co-operate with him. Somehow I had to let my thoughts drift freely. I felt tense and anxious. Then Mozart's Jupiter Symphony came to my mind, so I hummed it to myself. Music always helped me . . . .

I recalled the gynaecological examinations I had had several months ago, lying in this position. Then I was a body with symptoms of an interesting disease which had to be diagnosed. I felt the clumsy handling I had been subjected to, and the pain caused by the carelessness and inexperience of the doctors. I flinched. I had wanted to cry out to be recognised as a sensitive human being, but as long as I had been on the couch, I had been just another body to the doctors. The only time I had been treated kindly was when the consultant had explained what was wrong with me, and had asked me what I thought. On that occasion there had been no couch. We had sat opposite each other and I had watched his face. I had seen then that he genuinely cared about me. He had seen me as a real person, with a life ahead of me, not merely as an unusual, challenging case . . . . I continued humming Mozart's music to myself, and I began to relax.

Dr Goldblatt was sitting quietly. I realised it was time to talk.

'Lying on the couch reminds me of the gynaecological examinations I had when I was ill,' I said. 'It was a shattering experience. It was physically painful, and the doctors treated me merely as a body with no feelings.'

'You feel I am treating you in the same way,' he said.

'Yes,' I replied. 'I've no reason to think you are like that, but I still feel that way. Every week I have to struggle against these feelings before I can say what's in my mind.'

'That shows how strongly you feel that no one really cares about you,' he said. 'You must learn to recognise those feelings, and decide whether or not you are justified in believing that people are indifferent to you.' He paused for a while, then continued speaking. 'If you still want to sit on the armchair, please do. I don't want to make an issue out of something that isn't an issue for me.'

'No, it's all right, now,' I said. 'The ice has been broken. Those feelings about you have gone. I don't need to watch you any more this week, because I now realise you're sympathetic towards me.'

'No wonder you have difficulty in forming relationships with people when you feel they don't care about you. That feeling in itself makes it impossible to be happy and relaxed in any relationship.'

'A lot of the time I believe my friends care about me,' I said.

'That shows you are making progress,' he replied, 'but you must learn not to assume that people don't care, when you have no real evidence for thinking that.'

We were quiet for a while. Then I remembered my dreams.

'I've had several nightmares this past week but each morning I've forgotten what the dreams were about. I really wanted to remember so that I could tell you: I even kept a pen and paper by my bedside, intending to write down what I had dreamt as soon as I woke up. That didn't help. Since then I've woken up terrified each night – sometimes several times in one night – but I've not been able to remember a single dream, even one second after waking.'

'That shows the extent of the resistance in your unconscious,' he explained. 'It means you have a very hard battle ahead.'

I let my mind wander to something that had bothered me for years; something I had tried to forget. I didn't want to talk about it, but I couldn't get it from my mind.

'Will I lose anything by not telling you all that's in my mind?' I asked.

'If the patient–analyst relationship is a good one, anything important will eventually be brought into the open,' he replied.

'How obvious was my confused thinking and my anxiety when I first came to see you?' I asked.

'Everything about you was contained in that first interview,' he replied.

'So you knew there was a lot in my mind that I didn't dare talk about, yet you agreed to help me.'

'Yes,' he replied.

I felt reassured. He knew the worst side of me, yet he persevered with me. I was no longer afraid of being rejected by him if I told him all that was on my mind.

'I think I can tell you what's bothering me. It's a relationship I once had,' I said. 'I was a student nurse and I liked to be friendly with everyone but I didn't want to become too involved. The uninvolved relationships were easier to cope with. Some of the students were from overseas. One in particular was very homesick when she returned from her holidays. I felt sorry for her, so I lent her my radio. She began coming to my room in the evenings, and if anyone else was with me she became jealous. Soon I noticed she was going out of her way to sit beside me at mealtimes, and to be near me whenever she could. I couldn't understand it, because she was popular with everyone. When I suggested she spent time with other people she said she preferred my company, and when I went with other students she became upset. I realised she was homosexual. Later when I tried to break away from her she threatened to kill herself. These threats made me comply with her wishes. At that time I felt partly responsible for my brother's death. I couldn't bear the thought of another death on my conscience. For nearly three years I was stuck with her. There were some positive aspects to the relationship of course. She was demonstrative, and that helped me to show my feelings. On three occasions I went on holiday with her to the continent. I learnt a great deal about Europe. Also we saw a lot of London. She was kind and generous, but it was her possessive nature that I came to hate. Eventually we met another nurse who was attracted to her, and I managed at last to break away. I still worry when I think about that friendship.'

'Why do you worry, when you apparently resolved the problem satisfactorily from your point of view?' he asked.

'As a result of that friendship I don't like being touched.'

'Your fear of being touched goes back further than that,' he replied. 'In your childhood both homosexual and heterosexual relationships were taboo, so you feel guilty anyway.'

'What can I do about it?'

'You are able to work that out for yourself.'

'I suppose I should disregard my fear, and do what I want

to do.'

Lying there quietly I felt relieved from having told him about that relationship which had caused me such anxiety. The anxiety was now gone, and I was able to look on those years as an experience in which I had learnt about life. The happy times we had had together could now be seen in a positive wholesome light. I saw my friend as someone who had been troubled in her mind. Her friendship with me had enabled her to complete her training and to make something of herself in life. Now, all the worry and the resentment were gone.

Dr Goldblatt was to have four weeks' holiday. At the end of the session I thanked him for the ways he had helped me over the past six months.

'I believe you will cope with this break in your treatment without too much trauma,' he said. 'Remember not to drive yourself too hard. Do things because you want to, not just because you think you should.'

As I drove home I suddenly realised I no longer felt resentful and angry towards Dr Goldblatt. Instead I felt grateful. He had helped me understand why I had such a dread of the couch. His firm but kind attitude towards me had given me sufficient confidence in his treatment to tell him about a relationship that had been playing on my mind for years. I had unburdened myself, and I felt better for it.

# 12 The Summer Holidays

(23 August 1967 - 27 September 1967)

After my meal that evening I went to my bedroom to draw up a plan of action for the coming five weeks until I could see Dr Goldblatt again. I was determined not to regress while he was away.

I was due for two weeks' holiday, and as I imagined that life would be more difficult the longer I had to cope without treatment, I decided to leave my holiday until just before Dr Goldblatt returned. I would stay with Pat, as I always felt free in her company. She would help me through.

During the three weeks before going to Pat's I planned to go out with Peter. I was like a trapeze artist swinging from one safe hold to the next. One slip and I would go crashing down into depression.

The sixteen guineas I would save by not seeing Dr Goldblatt would go on a spending spree to boost my morale.

This positive approach paid off. On the Thursday and Friday I did a record number of successful visits to mothers.

On the Saturday I set out to spend my sixteen guineas with no idea what I would buy. I started off in my local book shop but none of the books appealed to me. At one time I had been an avid reader but now I couldn't concentrate. Then I tried a dress shop but the dresses didn't look right. I wandered on from one shop window to the next: suddenly I saw a portable record player for sixteen guineas. Just what I needed. I could play my own records in my own room whenever I wanted to. I went quickly into the shop and bought it.

When I got home I went straight to my room and tried it out. I was delighted. The first record I played was Mozart's

Jupiter Symphony. Over the months of my depression I had played it many times. Whatever my mood I always found that Mozart's music appealed to me even if it didn't make me feel better. At least I felt less lonely. The first movement of Jupiter suited me when I felt angry. I played it loudly and beat my hands on the chair in time to the music. The second movement of Jupiter suited me when I became depressed. My moods seemed to be portrayed in its melody. Whenever I listened I felt there was a kindred spirit within the music which comforted me. The third movement of Jupiter is balanced and happy. I looked forward to the time when I could also be a balanced, happy person.

During the next week there were periods of depression and elation but I was able to understand why they occurred and I accepted my feelings. Then suddenly I seemed to lose my grip. I was caught in a whirlpool of indecision. One evening Peter asked me out. I felt tired and I had planned an early night. I remembered that Dr Goldblatt had advised me to do things because I wanted to, and I tried to do what he had told me, but to my dismay I became so confused that I lost my confidence. I went out with Peter but I felt totally depressed.

It was my birthday during the second week of September, and Peter wanted to take me out for a meal. He invited two friends to join us. I didn't really want to go, but as Peter had booked a table, I couldn't refuse.

I was tense and miserable when Peter called for me, but I tried not to show it, as I didn't want to spoil his evening. In an attempt to get out of my depression, I mixed a sherry and martini and drank it before I left.

The four of us had a drink in the restaurant bar and then went to a table for our meal. I began to feel light-headed, and in order to retain the feeling I drank glass after glass of wine. Soon I felt distinctly carefree: my sadness had evaporated.

After the meal we all went back to our friends' house. We played some music and soon we had a good party going. Peter had brought along a lot of drink, and I began sampling a different drink every time. I wanted to have a good time. Before long I became merry, and to increase my merriment I went round drinking everything I could lay my hands on.

Suddenly I found myself sitting on the floor in the middle of the room – there were two of everybody. I started crying. Between my sobs I began saying everything that came into my mind. I even started to insult everyone.

The next thing I remember was being dragged into the bathroom where I was sick. My head was throbbing and the room seemed to be going round and round. I let myself go; laughing, yelling, crying, shouting and kicking out in a marvellous moment of drunken madness. The rest of the party were amused at first; then they became alarmed at my hysterical shrieks. They grabbed me and, like a grotesque wobbling dummy, I was dragged out of the toilet and dumped onto the settee, while a jug of black coffee was being made in the kitchen. Through a wine-soaked haze I was dimly aware of what was happening, but I had no control over myself. I only knew that for the first time in my life I felt totally indifferent to what anyone thought of me. I was having the time of my life.

After forcing me to drink large quantities of black coffee, my friends decided to take me home.

They had to carry me out to the car. All the way home I was singing loudly, and laughing and sobbing at the same time. It was marvellous. I hadn't a care in the world. Let the others do the worrying, I thought.

When we got to my house, they dragged me out of the car, but I still couldn't stand. I collapsed in a heap on the pavement, still singing.

'We can't leave her like this,' a voice said. 'She'll wake the neighbourhood. It's long past midnight.' I felt someone grab hold of me. 'Where's your key?' I just giggled. They rummaged through my handbag, and the key fell onto the pavement.

'We'll have to carry her into the house,' said Peter. 'Let's hope we don't wake her parents. They'd be horrified to see her in this mess.'

As they dragged me up the stairs, I continued singing loudly. They carried me into my bedroom and dumped me onto the bed. 'She's too far gone to undress herself,' one of them said. 'We'd better undress her.'

After a long struggle and a lot of noise, I was tucked up in bed and kissed good night. The party tiptoed downstairs and

I heard the door close behind them.

Next morning my head felt like thunder. I staggered downstairs for breakfast. My parents didn't seem to notice anything and they didn't comment on the noise in the night.

Carefully I drove to work. When I arrived, I was greeted by a chorus of shocked voices: 'Good God, what on earth have you been doing? I've never seen anyone look so awful.'

'I got drunk last night. It was marvellous.' I laughed. 'It's worth the headache.'

Reflecting on the party later that day I didn't feel guilty. It was an enjoyable experience which harmed no one; but I was concerned about the pleasure I was deriving from drink, and I worried in case I was on the way to becoming an alcoholic. That was not what I wanted. I wanted to overcome my sorrows, not to drown them in drink. After my wild party I resolved never to drink in order to cope with depression, and I never used drink again to see me through the night.

At last it was time for my holiday at Pat's. I was relieved at the prospect of two weeks without responsibility. I would be free to do as I liked. As I drove across the county where Pat lived, I felt elated. Pat was in when I arrived. We had lunch together and afterwards, while she went on her afternoon visits, I strolled around the village. How I loved that place. There was nothing particularly beautiful about it: an ordinary looking village school, a pub, a police station, a general store and a butcher's shop awkwardly placed on the crossroads in the centre of the village. Yet I felt welcomed there. The shopkeepers were friendly, and the village people nodded as I passed them in the street. It was playtime at the school as I walked by, and the children waved. On returning to the flat I felt really happy. Pat was not yet home, so I relaxed in an armchair and listened to music on the radio.

Just before 4 o'clock there was a clattering up the stairs: four children from the school came running in to welcome me. The children were friends of mine, and they sat down and began chatting away. One of the children was a boy called Johnnie. He was eight years old, and fostered by a family in the village. He always looked sulky and hardly ever spoke, but he gained attention by opening cupboards or moving ornaments around. That day he looked particularly sad, so I held my arms out to him and said, 'Come here, Johnnie.'

He came towards me and I reached out and sat him on my lap and cuddled him while the other children continued telling me what they had been doing at school. I loved Johnnie. He needed affection, and I needed to give affection. I gave him lots of cuddles.

Johnnie had tears in his eyes so I asked him what was wrong. He didn't answer. He just pressed himself closer to me. 'He doesn't like being laughed at,' one of the children explained.

'Why is he being laughed at?' I asked.

'Because he's stupid. He can't even tell the time.'

'Laughing at him won't help,' I said.

Just then Pat came in, so the children turned their attention to her.

'Do you want to learn to tell the time, Johnnie?' I asked.

He nodded.

'Then I'll teach you,' I said.

For the rest of my holiday Johnnie would come in straight from school for his cuddle and a lesson on telling the time; then he would have a drink of orange and a biscuit. When I left him two weeks later he could tell the time, like the rest of the children. He had tears in his eyes when we said goodbye; I wanted to take him with me. It was a wonderful example of interdependence from which both Johnnie and I benefited.

On Pat's day off we arranged to meet her sister in a nearby town. On the outskirts of the town was an old castle in its own grounds. The castle was unsafe and railings surrounded the ruins.

'Let's go in for fun,' I said. 'We can easily climb over these railings.' Pat's sister was horrified but Pat, who always entered into my moods, was climbing over the railings before I knew what was happening. We chased each other around the grounds, and then we ran to the castle walls for a rest. Soon we began running again, calling out and laughing to each other, thoroughly enjoying our adventure. Suddenly we heard a man's voice, shouting furiously at us. We looked in the direction of the voice and saw a blue-uniformed man coming towards us.

'Quick, let's get out,' called Pat, so we rushed back to the railings and climbed over and joined Pat's sister. By now the man was running. 'Dash for it,' gasped Pat, so we ran away. Unfortunately, Pat's sister was so dumbstruck by our behaviour that she stayed rooted to the spot. The man reached her and seized her by the shoulders. He spoke to her roughly, ticking her off for disregarding a public notice. He cautioned her.

Pat and I thought the incident was a huge joke, but her sister was not amused. She vowed not to keep company with us again. Nothing could dampen our spirits, and we laughed all the way home.

Pat and I had several other escapades, triggered off by my elation. We both enjoyed ourselves, and I was delighted when I realised my conscience didn't worry me so much.

One evening Pat said, 'I can see a real change in you. You aren't as anxious as you used to be and you don't keep trying to hide your feelings any more. Dr Goldblatt deserves a gold medal for what he's doing for you.'

'I think I am getting better,' I said seriously to Pat, 'but I'm still not as I would like to be. I'm very unstable and temperamental, and I'm afraid sometimes I'll never be normal.'

'Of course you will,' Pat reassured me. 'You're over the worst of it now, and it's just a matter of time.'

# Part 2
# REBUILDING MY PERSONALITY

# 13 Taking Stock

(27 September 1967)

On Wednesday 27th September 1967 I woke up feeling tense. My holiday at Pat's was over. Two weeks' of freedom and happiness were at an end. Soon I would be leaving the haven where I felt wanted and accepted. Pat was like a sister to me, the village had become my village, and the village children were my friends. That morning I felt like a teenager, about to leave home for the first time. Before me was a hostile world and a terrifying, unknown future. I felt totally unprepared for what might lie ahead.

I was so frightened that I forced msyelf to think of the present. I got up quickly, washed and dressed, and went into the kitchen. Pat was still sleeping but I decided to wake her with a cup of tea.

While waiting for the kettle to boil I gazed out of the window, hoping for some kind of inspiration from the countryside. It was very windy and the sky was overcast. Grey, ragged clouds chased each other and in the distance I could see a line of fir trees bending in the wind. 'Hope and endurance give fortitude and strength at all times,' I whispered to myself. 'Dr Goldblatt is my only hope, and I'll be seeing him again this afternoon. He'll help me cope with the future.'

Thinking of Dr Goldblatt calmed me. He understood me more than anyone, and he had the knowledge and the skill to help me through the coming months. In one sense he was an island of trust and confidence in my uncertain life. To be in my condition with no one to turn to would be a hell on earth: but as I gazed out of the window at the stormy sky a sudden feeling of excitement came to me because I realised I had one true and reliable human being who was going to help me out of the torment and terror that my life had become.

The steam from the kettle began swirling around me. I made the tea and went in to wake Pat. She sat up in bed yawning. I perched on an armchair and sipped my tea quietly. Neither of us spoke. The silence was our sadness and the bond between us grew stronger in that moment.

I left Pat to rouse herself and went into the kitchen to cook breakfast. Soon we were eating our eggs and bacon in silence. After breakfast I said to Pat, 'I'd like to walk around the village before I go. Have you got time to come with me?'

'Yes, of course,' she replied.

We walked along the country lanes for a little while, battling against the wind, then we turned back to the centre of the village. As we walked past I whispered goodbye to all the familiar places; then we came to the signpost which pointed to the forest of fir trees. I reached up and traced the letters with my fingers, and imagined I was running my fingers along the branches of my favourite tree. I looked at Pat. All I could whisper to her were the words, 'Hope and perseverance.' We were both fighting back our tears.

It began to rain so we hurried home. I collected my luggage together and carried it to my car. Pat made me a packed lunch and filled a flask with coffee for my journey. I planned to drive direct to Harley Street, with a number of stops on the way.

It was 9 o'clock and my appointment with Dr Goldblatt wasn't until 5 o'clock that afternoon. I had all day for a journey that would normally take about three hours. Yet I had to leave now. I had said my goodbyes to the village, and I wanted to say goodbye to Pat before she left for work. I had to be the one to leave. I felt I would break down completely if Pat left for work while I stayed at the flat. I sat in the car and waited for Pat to bring my sandwiches. Soon she appeared and handed a neat package through the car window. 'Come and see me whenever you want,' she said. 'I'll miss you. It's been fun having you here.'

'Thanks', I said. 'You've stood by me through the most terrible experience of my life. I can never repay you.'

I started the car and drove slowly down the driveway. At

the end of the drive I paused and looked back at Pat. I felt nervous and apprehensive.

'You'll make it,' she said. 'With Dr Goldblatt's skill and your determination nothing can stop you.'

I waved goodbye and turned the car into the lane. I was on my own for the first time in two weeks.

The early autumn countryside matched my mood. The warmth of summer had gone and the cold, bare reality of winter lay ahead. It was a windy day and the trees seemed to be clinging to the ground by their roots. I, too, would clutch desperately to Dr Goldblatt's ideas, or I would be blown off course and lost for ever.

Soon I was driving on the road that ran through the forest of fir trees. Before the forest ended I stopped at a grass verge and gazed at my trees. The deep silence of the forest held me. 'You aren't running away from the winter,' I whispered to the trees. 'You'll keep hold of your leaves, even though other trees give up and shed theirs. I'll be like you. I'll hold on, however bad the winter. I'll keep hoping and trying until spring comes.' Despite the rain, I got out of the car and walked towards the trees. I broke off a twig of fir needles to keep with me. It would remind me of my resolve never to give up. I drove off leaving the forest far behind.

After about an hour's driving I pulled into a lay-by for some coffee and a snack. I suddenly realised that, although I was tense and anxious, I didn't have the usual feeling of dread that overcame me as I approached London. I was afraid of the future but I didn't dread it because I hoped and believed that the future held the key to my recovery.

As I ate my sandwiches I began to recall my life. Just one year ago I had been in hospital, fearing I might be suffering from a fatal disease. Yet it was the resulting mental illness that nearly destroyed me. If at that time I had known of the terror that lay ahead, I would have wanted to die under the anaesthetic. Now as I sat in my car at a lonely lay-by I wondered if I really was recovering, or whether I would have to face another year of terror. I thought I could judge whether I was making progress by comparing my state of mind when I first consulted Dr Goldblatt seven months ago with my state of mind now.

I tried to imagine how Dr Goldblatt would do that. I thought he would study the three areas of my personality he said were out of balance: my ego or self-image, my emotions and my conscience.

When I first went to Dr Goldblatt my ego had been underdeveloped. I had tried to conform too much to what I thought others expected of me, and if I couldn't detect what I thought was expected of me I became confused. I had brought those feelings into my relationship with Dr Goldblatt. In the early months of my psychotherapy, free association was difficult for me because I couldn't even believe that Dr Goldblatt was interested. I tried to select what I thought he would want to hear, but he deliberately avoided giving me leads. I became confused and irritated. I realised I thought differently now. I knew he was interested in everything I had to say.

Another manifestation of my underdeveloped ego was that I had believed I had no rights. I shuddered as I recalled a consultation with Dr Goldblatt last May when he relentlessly drove me to face up to my illness. The terror of that time was still with me – I didn't need my diary to remember. Now I realised that if Dr Goldblatt ever tried to make me think about things against my will again, I would protest or walkout on him. I knew I had changed, and was changing. I now believed I had rights, and if necessary I would exert those rights. I had the right to end my own life if I wanted to; I had the right to question all I had been taught as a child; I had the right to make up my own mind about the kind of person I would become.

I poured some more coffee. Already I had evidence that I had made progress. I was encouraged to continue with my analysis. I drank my coffee slowly and reflected on the second area of my personality: my emotions.

I used to hide my feelings all the time. I would try to convince myself that I was never jealous or resentful or bitter. I even tried to stifle feelings of happiness or disappointment. I used to have long discussions with myself over the rights and wrongs of everything. For example, if I was looking forward to going out for the day and the trip was cancelled, I would tell myself it was wrong to feel disappointed. I might be turning this over in my mind for hours, trying to convince myself I wasn't disappointed. Sometimes I would put on an act for days on end without saying anything to let people know what my true feelings were.

Now all that was behind me. Under Dr Goldblatt's encouragement I let myself experience any and every emotion that came my way. I still didn't show my emotions easily, but at least I allowed these feelings to run their course. In a sense Dr Goldblatt had begun to change my life by helping me to liberate my emotions.

The third area of my personality that Dr Goldblatt had drawn attention to was my conscience. I had been dictated to by an overdeveloped conscience, but at last I was beginning to break free. I still had a very active conscience over important matters, but my conscience no longer condemned everything I thought and did. Most of the time now my reason and my conscience were in harmony.

It was no longer raining so I got out of the car and walked across the grass verge to the fence which encircled the field beyond. I looked at the trees at the edge of the field. A feeling of relief came over me. My self-analysis showed me that a fundamental change had taken place in my personality. My ego, my emotions and my conscience were being brought into harmony. With Dr Goldblatt's help the process of rebuilding my personality was beginning to take place.

The noise of lorries thundering past jolted me out of my reverie. I looked at my watch – nearly one o'clock. I still had plenty of time. I got back into my car and began to eat a banana.

Gradually my sense of wellbeing turned to anxiety. There was ample evidence that I was changing, both in my thinking and in my behaviour, but how could I be sure the change was for the better? I suddenly felt alarmed. The change in my personality might not mean that I was recovering. My father wouldn't think so. He would say I was turning my back on my Christian Faith. I began shaking and suddenly I felt sick. It came home to me with great force that over the past few months I had discarded my Christian teaching and the attitudes I had acquired from childhood, and taken up a set of new ideas based on Freudian psychology. Yet how could I be sure that these new ideas would really cure my depression?

I suddenly felt like a person on a sinking ship. The steep sides of the vessel were sliding into the water. Dr Goldblatt was calling me to jump his way; my father and my Church were calling me to jump their way.

I was alone. I had to decide for myself which of the two sets of ideas would lead me out of my depression. My Christian Faith had suffered a nasty jolt. I had been seriously ill and I was now in a strange mental state which frightened me, and it seemed that none of my prayers were being answered. My salvation seemed to lie in the hands of a psychoanalyst, but even his treatment might not cure me.

I had evidence that I was changing, but my purpose in persevering with the treatment was not to be changed, but to be cured. It seemed reasonable to expect that after seven months there should be some indication that my symptoms were becoming less acute. I began to consider my symptoms to see if there was any improvement.

Throughout my illness the nights were the worst because once I was asleep I had no control over the nightmares which possessed me. I was at the mercy of my disturbed and troubled mind. My bedroom was a torture chamber. Most nights and sometimes several times each night I awoke with a start, cold yet bathed in perspiration, my mind filled with fear and dread. When I first consulted Dr Goldblatt my dreams were about my brother Alan, who was usually begging me to help him, but I was unable to do anything for him. Some of the dreams became more violent, with Alan shaking me and gripping me around the throat. In many of my dreams I was wandering in a maze, feeling confused and unable to find my way back to familiar surroundings. Night after night I was sucked into whirlpools, dropped over cliff edges, plunged into tumultuous seas and suspended over raging furnaces. Then I even dreamed of battles with myself as twins: the thin twin devouring the plump twin . . . I shuddered and looked out across the fields. I couldn't bear to think any more about those nightmares. Over the last few weeks I had almost forgotten the intensity of my night-time terrors because my dreams were now less frequent and not so frightening.

It suddenly dawned on me that these nightmares which were my most horrible symptom had lessened since I last saw

Dr Goldblatt at the end of August. This was encouraging.

My other night-time terror was also subsiding. These were the 'fits' which I experienced at frequent intervals. My body would go into spasm, or my legs and arms became like lead and I was unable to move. During May to August these 'fits' were at their peak, occurring nearly every night. Recently, however, they had become less frequent. I could remember only one night when it had occurred at Pat's.

Next I considered my longing to withdraw myself from people, to sit and cry and to relinquish all my reponsibilities. I was still tempted to withdraw whenever conflict or sadness came my way, but I believed if I gave in to that longing I would deteriorate into a state of schizophrenia. I feared schizophrenia more than anything – more than my nightmares, more than my uncertain future, more than cancer. I couldn't judge whether my isolationist symptom was decreasing, because it always disappeared when I was with Pat.

I didn't want to dwell on that topic so I thought about my only pleasant symptom, which was extreme elation. It came over me mostly when I was at Pat's. It was like being merrily drunk. I recalled some of the instances of the last few days, and chuckled. That symptom was certainly not declining. For a while I mused over my crazy antics. Then I thought seriously about my emotional instability.

Before I became ill I was a very stable and unemotional person. I was in control of my reactions and behaviour. This new experience of behaving and reacting in ways which I didn't expect alarmed me, and my inability to control my moods frightened me. However, I now realised that it was necessary for me to experience a variety of emotions, and I was learning to accept that my feelings and behaviour would be changeable like the weather. My emotional instability was persisting, although my attitude to it was different.

Next I thought about the constant sense of dread and foreboding which I had experienced over the past year. Now suddenly I was free of it. I tried to work out when that feeling was last with me. I believed it was at the time of my last session with Dr Goldblatt. When I left his consulting room on that occasion I felt relieved. Now, even though I would soon be back in London, I felt no dread. I was delighted that at last I could see an improvement.

I remembered next the sudden panic 'attacks' which I experienced, when I ran through the streets or phoned Rita. The last 'attack' was a month ago.

My shopping phobia came to mind. My dislike of going into shops varied according to how confused or inadequate I felt. At Pat's I enjoyed going into the village shop because everyone was so friendly. I would have to wait until I shopped in my own home town before I could tell if shopping was still a problem.

The thought of going home reminded me of my job, and of how difficult I found the visiting. That difficulty remained up to my holiday. I wondered how I would be when I returned to work the next day.

I suddenly became aware I was gripping the steering wheel so tightly that my hands hurt. Thinking about work was making me very tense. My car seemed like a cage, and I had to escape. I opened the door and ran across the grass verge to the fence. Tears began streaming down my face. 'Relax,' I told myself. 'Practice what you teach the mothers in the relaxation classes.' I breathed in and out deeply for a few minutes, and then I relaxed my muscles one by one. I concentrated my mind on what I was doing, and gradually I calmed down. For a while I stood gazing across the fields, letting my mind drift freely. Slowly it dawned on me that I had actually managed to control and overcome a panic attack.

I began to shiver in the cold autumn wind so I got back into my car. There were still other symptoms to examine, but I wasn't sure if I could take the strain of thinking about them. Life seemed to be one continuous strain. I wondered if I would ever be free from this struggle with my mind. How weary I felt.

Lorries continued to thunder past. Often, driving home from Harley Street, I had imagined swerving into the path of a lorry. I let my mind drift back and I remembered really believing I was in danger of acting out my fantasies. Now I felt safer because I believed I would be able to overcome the urges to end my life.

With fresh confidence I decided to consider my remaining symptom – my muddled and confused thinking. When I first consulted Dr Goldblatt I was unable to think constructively. Over the months I learnt to trust him and to understand his methods, so that sometimes I could work out what Dr Goldblatt would advise me to do. However, there were still many occasions when I felt bewildered and uncertain about what I wanted and what I believed in and what sort of person I wanted to be. I feared that without psychotherapy from Dr Goldblatt I would be utterly lost.

I gazed out of the window and let the impact of my evaluation penetrate. It seemed that all my symptoms had persisted in their intensity right through until the end of August, but now, almost imperceptibly, a gradual improvement in a few of them was taking place. Yet I couldn't be sure the improvement would be maintained. I had just spent two weeks in a happy environment, so it was natural I should feel better at the moment. I wondered what would happen once I returned to the emotional isolation of home and the responsibility of work.

I began to feel really confused as to whether or not I was making progress, and I grew anxious. Logic, self-analysis and past evidence could be interpreted either way. All I had left was instinct. Instinct told me to trust people who understood me and who cared about me. Instinct told me to persevere.

Resolutely I packed away my flask and lunch box, fastened my seat belt and eased the car off the lay-by to continue my journey to Harley Street.

# 14 A Change in My Relationship with Dr Goldblatt

(27 September 1967 - 11 October 1967)

**27 September 1967**

I arrived early for my appointment at Harley Street. I went into the waiting room and sat down on the comfortable settee, relieved that soon I would be sharing my thoughts with Dr Goldblatt. My attitude towards him seemed changed. Before he went on holiday I was afraid to tell him everything in case he confronted me with ideas which threatened my own way of thinking. He might have made me face facts which would disturb me. I had been aware of conflicting emotions towards him. I had been afraid of him, and I had even felt anger towards him, and I hated him for 'allowing' me to suffer for so long. Yet even after he withheld comfort and sympathy from me, I had counted the days and hours to when I would see him again.

But these contradictory emotions were gone. Instead I felt grateful to him for persevering with the treatment despite my resistance. Now I felt I was ready to work with him as an equal. I saw him as a friend who had proved himself worthy of my trust and respect.

The receptionist called my name, and I walked up the stairs and entered Dr Goldblatt's room. He looked relaxed and his manner was informal and friendly towards me. After asking him if he had enjoyed his holiday I looked around the room. There in the centre were two armchairs. I looked questioningly at Dr Goldblatt. He smiled and murmured, 'I thought it might be easier for you to talk straight at me.'

I was happy. Our one remaining obstacle was gone. I no longer had to fight against memories and feelings of insignificance that the couch created.

I chatted easily to Dr Goldblatt about my activities during the holiday, and he seemed genuinely interested. As time went on I realised I had changed quite dramatically. My thoughts came quickly and I spoke with ease.

I told Dr Goldblatt I believed I had changed, but I still felt far from well. He said he could see a big difference in me, which showed I had made progress. However, he said I still had more progress to make before I could feel I was on the road to recovery.

A sense of desperation came over me, and I looked appealingly at Dr Goldblatt for help. I felt mentally exhausted and I needed encouragement in my struggle.

Dr Goldblatt responded. 'You must appreciate that you really have improved,' he emphasised. 'You continued to make progress during my absence, which shows you have understood what I've been doing, and you can apply what you've learnt to different situations. My work with you has been very worthwhile, and you are giving me a great deal of job satisfaction.'

I left Dr Goldblatt feeling very encouraged. From then on his consulting room became a haven to me, a place where I could find the strength and encouragement to continue on the arduous road to recovery. The chairs were always there for me, and the couch was gone for ever.

When I arrived home that evening I longed to tell my parents about the thoughts that had gone through my mind that day, but all I could say was that I'd enjoyed my holiday and I felt better for it. I knew they would be distressed to know I had renewed my vow to persevere with psychotherapy, even though it conflicted with their Christian faith. I realised I had changed but they hadn't. My attitude to life was different and I assessed myself by a new set of standards. What was progress to me was backsliding to them. To them, my perseverance with psychotherapy and my receptiveness to

Dr Goldblatt's ideas were not strength of character, but defiance against God. If I told them I didn't know what I believed they would be deeply shocked.

It seemed to me that nothing positive could be achieved by letting my parents know the true state of my mind. It would cause distress to all of us. I had to let them think I still saw things their way – but it was difficult. I was living a double life at a time when I needed to share my hopes and fears with others, and to try out my new ideas.

I went to bed that night feeling I had become an outcast. I dreamt I had wandered onto a fog-shrouded moor. I heard a voice calling me, so I turned towards the sound. Then a voice called from the opposite direction, so I turned back again. Then the first voice repeated its call. I didn't know what to do. I didn't know which voice to trust. In despair I buried my head in my hands and sobbed. Then I became Lot's wife who, according to the Bible story, was turned into a pillar of salt for looking back at the city she was leaving.

The next day was a Thursday and I returned to work. My colleagues welcomed me back and I felt happy. Over coffee I told them about my escapades with Pat. They were highly amused.

Soon it was time for visiting, and I set off determined to keep my anxieties at bay. Everyone I visited had problems, and they poured out their worries in great detail. I found it difficult to concentrate, and at times my mind wandered to my own problems, which seemed much greater. I struggled on till lunchtime, when I returned to the clinic and had my snack with the dental nurse. We chatted through the lunch break, and I enjoyed listening to her opinions.

That afternoon my mind was full of questions about the purpose of life, and my place in the vastness of the universe. I wanted to talk to other people, yet I was employed to advise mothers on practical matters, such as how to wean their babies, or how to handle their difficult toddlers. The demands of my job were incompatible with my own psychological and intellectual needs at that time. My own needs won the battle, and I spent the rest of the afternoon at my desk, looking out of the window and pondering over the meaning of life.

After two weeks at work I began to feel desperate. Every day was a battle between the demands of my job, and my own need to philosophise. I wanted to give up but the fear of going downhill made me persevere. Because I had relinquished my old ideas and attitudes I felt empty and destitute, with no established personality. I didn't know what to believe, I didn't even know what I was really like, or what I wanted to be like. All I could feel was the need to sort myself out as quickly as possible, before my lack of personality drove me to despair. I could never again go through another mental illness. Death stared me in the face and I shuddered.

The feeling of emptiness sapped my confidence so much that in spite of the greatest possible effort, I could only cope with my Tuesday afternoon and Wednesday morning clinics. I wanted to spend all my time asking my colleagues their opinions on a wide variety of topics, and discussing my own tentative views. There was usually someone around at lunchtimes, and often Rita sat and talked with me at the end of the working day. She realised I was trying very hard at my job, but with little success. On one occasion she suggested I went off sick so that I could have a few days to concentrate on getting well. I was torn between a desire to relinquish my responsibilities to give myself time to think about my life, and the fear that if I did give up I would never recover.

In desperation that evening I wrote the following letter to Dr Goldblatt asking for his advice.

Thursday, 5th October 1967

Dear Dr Goldblatt,

I am writing to ask your opinion, as I would like your comment next Wednesday. In a letter I can more easily give you a clear picture.

This week I have had real difficulty at work – in fact, apart from my Tuesday afternoon and Wednesday morning clinics I have done very little. I resent having to listen to other people's problems when I feel swamped by my own. I long to talk to people and to get help from them. If I felt that I would soon get beyond this phase, I would struggle on, but with so much to work through, I cannot see how I can cope any longer.

At my request my colleague spent half an hour with me after work this evening. I told her that I felt she was avoiding me, and that I was a burden to everyone. She said she understood, but that it wasn't so; but I must realise that she couldn't act as a mother towards me, just when I wanted her to. I told her that I would like to see you twice a week if ever you had a spare appointment, but with so much to think about I would never cope with work. She said that perhaps I should be off sick with depression, and this would give me as much time as I need to think about my problems.

The thought of not working fills me with horror; I might give up everything and get worse. I remember how quickly my brother gave up when he stopped work. He spent most of the day in bed. It is silly to associate myself with him, but I do this automatically. Sometimes I wish I could get away from work and let myself do what I want to do, but do you think that it would be good for me?

Please don't tell me that I must work this matter out for myself. I have been concerned about work for a long time, and still I don't know what to do.

I am glad that you have not expected me to lie on the couch for the past two weeks. Thank you for understanding my feelings.

I hope that this letter makes sense, since even forming sentences is difficult at present.

Yours sincerely,
Margaret

**11 October 1967**

When I saw Dr Goldblatt he was very positive in his advice. He said that no matter how difficult I was finding my job, it was important not to give up. I should go to work and do my best, and be content with that. He emphasised that I was an adult, I needed to behave as an adult, and to be treated as an adult. My needs could be met without giving up work.

Dr Goldblatt considered that the more I came to him for

psychotherapy the better. He agreed I needed to discuss my thoughts and feelings with him as much as possible so that I could make a more speedy recovery. He emphasised that he could not act as a father towards me. It was not his job. He could not form a close relationship with me either. He could not even guide my thoughts. His sole function was to analyse my thoughts and explain them to me, so as to aid my recovery.

His positive, firm advice strengthened my resolve. I was no longer indecisive about work. I would do the best I could, even when it seemed my best wasn't good enough. I knew Dr Goldblatt wouldn't tell me to do something that was impossible. He was the expert, and if he believed I could cope with work, I should believe it. His confidence in me increased my confidence.

The next week I worked better than I had ever worked since the onset of my illness. At times I needed all my willpower to concentrate on what the mothers were telling me, but I kept going, and I managed to visit the families on my list. The advice I gave seemed to satisfy everyone, and I contented myself with that.

From Monday 23 October I began seeing Dr Goldblatt twice a week, and I continued twice weekly until my treatment was completed. Knowing that there were only a few days between each visit I was less anxious. I knew that however low I felt, I would not have long to wait before I could get help from Dr Goldblatt again.

# 15 I Learn to Overcome the Symptoms of My Illness

(October - December 1967)

Following my session with Dr Goldblatt on 11 October my symptoms rapidly declined. I was able to work satisfactorily and I no longer felt constantly sad and anxious. Those last two weeks of October stand out in my mind as a time of freedom and happiness. For the very first time since the onset of my illness I didn't feel fatigued or mentally disturbed. I enjoyed my work, and I worked properly throughout the two weeks. Peter and I went out together most evenings and life was suddenly pleasant.

The relief I felt is indescribable. At last I had real evidence I was recovering. The intermittent feelings of sadness I experienced each day were so short lived I ignored them. In that bright fortnight it didn't matter that I was confused about my beliefs. My only plan for the future was to recover from my mental illness. The void in my life was filled with happiness over my marked improvement. My confidence increased, and I felt I would never be depressed again. At that point I believed that within a few weeks I would be completely well.

Dr Goldblatt didn't share my optimism; he was pleased I was enjoying life, but he told me I still had a long way to go. He judged my mental state by the depth of insight I had into my thinking, and by the spontaneity of my reactions.

Suddenly I had a relapse. On Monday evening, 30 October,

Peter and I spent a very happy evening with some friends in their home. After I said goodbye to them I felt unaccountably upset and dejected. That feeling remained with me the next day at work. When I attempted to visit families, tears poured down my cheeks and I couldn't control myself. I didn't know what was wrong. All I could do was wait for Dr Goldblatt's help.

## 1 November 1967

On the Wednesday I told Dr Goldblatt about my setback, and that I couldn't account for it. He said there was always a reason behind the way I felt. If I was unhappy, something must have caused that unhappiness. The first step towards overcoming my debilitating symptoms was to understand why I felt as I did. Once I understood that, I could work out what I should do to feel better.

Dr Goldblatt explained that there were three major causes for my persistent feelings of sadness: firstly, my forbidding conscience, which to a large extent I was able to deal with; secondly, I continued to have a low opinion of myself, which undermined my confidence; and thirdly, I still didn't accept that I had the right to satisfy my needs.

Dr Goldblatt said that whenever I felt depressed I should systematically think about the preceding events so as to isolate the root cause. Something must be causing me to feel guilty, or worthless, or deprived. Dr Goldblatt used my present feeling of unhappiness as an example of how to use his formula.

'Think hard about the events on Monday. Did anything happen to upset you?' he asked.

'No,' I replied. 'I visited families all day, and at the end of the day I was happy because all the visits had gone well, and my work had been worthwhile. After my meal I went out with Peter, and I was pleased when we spent the evening with friends. We left their house at midnight. Peter asked me back to his flat for a drink, but I felt tired and said, "No." There was no bad feeling, but as soon as I arrived home I felt terrible.'

'Perhaps you feel that if you do what you want to do you will be rejected,' Dr Goldblatt suggested.

'Maybe,' I said, not really convinced. Still I felt wretched. Dr Goldblatt said no more, so I rested in the armchair and let my mind wander. Soon I would have to leave the presence of someone who understood me and who cared about me. Soon I would be back home; back to the place that reminded me of my brother's tragic illness, back to the place where my true thoughts and feelings had to be concealed. I wanted to tell Dr Goldblatt how I felt, I wanted him to understand, but I couldn't think of words that would convey my thoughts. At last I managed to say, 'I'd like to have a flat of my own.'

'I've been very stupid,' he exclaimed. 'I'm almost inclined to take back what I said about your feeling rejected. You enjoyed the family atmosphere at your friend's home, but when you got back you wished you could entertain in the same way. Your need for a home of your own is not being satisfied.'

'You're right,' I said. A sense of relief came over me. Then I remembered a dream I had the night before. 'I dreamt I was exploring a room,' I said. 'I was alone, so I looked in all the cupboards. Then someone appeared in the doorway watching me. I knew I shouldn't be in the room, but it was so interesting. I took no notice of the person in the doorway. Then I did something wrong. I don't remember what it was, but I began to feel terribly ashamed. I begged for mercy.'

'Obviously you feel very guilty about your wish to leave home,' said Dr Goldblatt. 'You can't relate to your family in the way you would like, so you feel dissatisfied. Instead of accepting that it's natural for you to feel dissatisfied, you blame yourself for what is lacking in your relationship with your parents, and this increases your unhappiness. You think you shouldn't feel the way you do about your own home, so you conclude that you have no right to enjoy the atmosphere of other people's homes, and that it's wrong to think about having a home of your own.'

'I don't want to hurt my parents,' I said.

'You should think about what's right for yourself,' said Dr Goldblatt.

By the time I left the consulting room I was once more

able to cope with life. Dr Goldblatt had increased my understanding of how my mind was working and why I was still plagued with feelings of intense sadness and inadequacy. He had shown me how to work out the cause of my depressions as they occurred.

From then on if I felt unhappy I concentrated my mind on that unhappiness and thought about the circumstances surrounding it until I discovered the cause. It became apparent to me that my 'depression' usually occurred when I felt unwanted. I found it took very little to trigger off this feeling.

One night I lay awake thinking about my low opinion of myself. I felt no one would want my friendship or my company if they knew what I was really like. I believed that Dr Goldblatt continued to treat me because he was a responsible doctor who wouldn't abandon a patient. Rita spent time talking to me because she found my strange way of thinking a challenge. It was her influence that made my other colleagues tolerate me. Pat welcomed me to her home because she was lonely and any company was better than none.

I assumed that Peter went out with me because he didn't have anyone else. He reinforced my assumptions by telling me that I was just another friend; he didn't want to get 'involved' or have a special relationship with me. Instead of accepting his explanation I took it personally. I believed it was my personality that caused him to be so casual with me.

At my next session with Dr Goldblatt we discussed my interpretation of other people's attitudes. He showed me I was still thinking I was worthless. As long as that continued I would not see people as they really were, and I would misinterpret their behaviour towards me.

Dr Goldblatt said that I must analyse the feeling of not being wanted every time the feeling occurred. If I felt no one really wanted me, then I should disregard this feeling and tell myself I was wanted. I should only let my feelings affect my behaviour if I had a very good reason. He emphasised that people did like me, and I should relate to people with that fact in mind.

The following Saturday I had a chance to put Dr Goldblatt's advice to the test. I woke up, feeling sad and disinterested in life. As I lay in bed I thought about my sadness and I realised I was upset because Peter hadn't contacted me. I thought our friendship must be over. He had become bored with me, I thought, because I was a boring person. I looked for evidence to support my assumption, but there was none. When I was with Peter he seemed happy and interested in anything I said. I changed my premises from, 'I am a boring person' to 'I am an interesting person.' I thought again why Peter hadn't been in touch. Perhaps he had phoned me, but the line might have been engaged. Perhaps he had been busy, or just hadn't felt like going out. I couldn't be sure. I decided to phone him.

I got up and phoned Peter straight away. He said he was glad I'd phoned and he suggested we went out that afternoon. He seemed happy on the phone and before he said goodbye he said he was looking forward to seeing me again.

I was amazed how much my opinion about myself affected my behaviour and other people's response to me. This incident gave new encouragement in following Dr Goldblatt's advice.

From then on I followed Dr Goldblatt's advice regularly. Sometimes I could analyse my way out of my sadness in just a few minutes; sometimes it took hours. Playing my piano helped. I discovered that by playing music which matched my feelings, I could relax. I didn't have to think in words. Through the music I became aware of what was upsetting me. I would continue to play whatever I felt in the mood to play, and the music helped me to see things in perspective. I was actually learning to control my symptoms at least.

On Saturday 25 November I had a sudden setback. I felt so miserable that I shut myself in my bedroom. I wanted to go into a trance and give up the struggle between my feelings and my reason. I wanted to get away from everyone. I wanted to drift off into oblivion. Life had become too difficult, too sad and too confused for me to want to go on.

I got into bed and my tears began to saturate my pillow. I slept fitfully. In the morning I heard my mother moving about the house. I called out to her that I felt tired and didn't want to be disturbed. My tears continued and it seemed to me that if I could ignore everything my problem would be over.

For several hours I lay quite still. I told myself I didn't feel anything. I told myself I didn't exist. The world was an illusion. Nothing existed any more.

Suddenly I heard my mother calling; it was nearly time to visit my father in hospital (he had been admitted to intensive care ten days previously following a heart attack). I sat up in bed, realising I had begun to give up my struggle against mental illness. Fear gripped me. To my way of thinking, giving up was the first step towards schizophrenia. I knew I could never solve my problems if I let myself give up.

Listlessly I got out of bed. I didn't want to meet people; I didn't want to accept responsibilities. I forced myself to do what was expected of me, and I pretended to feel happy.

I drifted through the weekend, pinning all my hopes on my next session with Dr Goldblatt. I kept telling myself that he understood me and would help me.

## 27 November 1967

When I arrived in Dr Goldblatt's consulting room I told him I felt ashamed because I had given up. He asked me what caused me to feel so miserable. I explained that on Saturday mornings Peter usually called round, but recently I hadn't heard from him. On the Saturday afternoon I went to visit my father. Now he was out of intensive care, and he no longer needed me to sit beside his bed. He was ready for livelier visitors, and the close relationship that had grown up between us while he was in danger was no longer necessary. I felt unwanted by my father. I felt unwanted by Peter. I could see no way out.

'Did you show anyone how you felt?' Dr Goldblatt asked.

'No,' I replied. 'I deliberately didn't show my feelings, because I felt guilty. I shouldn't expect Peter every Saturday, and I should be pleased that my father is improving.'

'When you feel upset you need to show it to the person concerned, and talk about it to them. Why not tell Peter you were looking forward to being with him and you were upset that he didn't contact you? Ask him why he hasn't been in touch with you. He might feel just as unwanted as you do. If you discuss your feelings together, your understanding of each other will grow.'

I left Dr Goldblatt and felt lost. I couldn't imagine being able to tell anyone I was upset over them. I drove to the hospital to visit my father, expecting that he would be indifferent to me. When I arrived he welcomed me and said he was very pleased to see me. Straight away my sadness was gone.

When I got home I phoned Peter. I needed to know if he still wanted my friendship. To my surprise he said he was pleased to hear from me. I forgot about Saturday, and we spoke for a long time. My longing to give up and hide away from people was over.

The next day I worked well, but I was concerned that when I felt sad my job was adversely affected. That evening I sat alone in my bedroom and analysed my work very carefully. I began by thinking about the areas which I always did well – the child health clinics and the mothercraft classes. The reason why I felt confident in these two areas was that the mothers wanted my advice. They came to my clinic sessions because they wanted to, and they took the initiative by asking me questions. Mothers often returned the following week to tell me that my advice had worked. I was having constant feedback that I was doing that part of the job properly.

I analysed which visits I found easy and which were impossible. I realised that the easiest visits were those where mothers asked me to call. On those occasions I knew the mothers wanted my advice, and I knew I had worthwhile advice to offer. Another type of visit I could always cope with was to the elderly and to mothers with postnatal depression. They needed to talk and I encouraged them and listened to what they said.

The most difficult visits were the routine visits to families I didn't know. I had to work out a way of overcoming that difficulty.

It occurred to me that with careful planning, these visits could be made easier. I decided to reserve these visits to times when I felt really confident, and to reserve my easy visits to times when I felt low.

In this way I managed to steer a reasonably straight course and my planning paid dividends. From the end of November I worked well, with just occasional lapses. By constantly analysing my moods and the visits, I was able to overcome most of my difficulties.

Step by step Dr Goldblatt had shown me how to cope with my problems. With practice it became easier to analyse my thoughts and feelings, and I was able to work through my problems each day with very little help.

# 16 Dealing with the Causes of My Depression

(October 1967 - February 1968)

From October 1967 there were definite indications that I was recovering. I became obsessed with the idea that I must never have a relapse. On one occasion I told Dr Goldblatt of my fear of recurrent mental illness. He assured me he would continue the psychotherapy until he was confident I was better. He hoped I would become stronger in my mind than I had ever been, so that I would be less likely to suffer from a mental illness again.

Dr Goldblatt explained that my problem lay within my personality. My mother had been shocked when she knew she had conceived me, and throughout my childhood I had sensed something of her anxiety. She wanted me to be a good girl. She wanted me to play with dolls, and to like pretty things, but I hated dolls; I wanted to climb trees and to go swimming, and generally pursue 'boys'' activities. I grew up in a situation of inner conflict. To get my mother's approval I had to do things I didn't like, but when I followed my own inclinations I caused my mother a lot of anxiety. I came to believe that my natural inclinations were wrong, and this belief was intensified by my religious education. From childhood I had been made to believe that I was born in sin, and all my desires were evil. I had coped with the conflict by keeping my normal desires at bay. I even pretended that those desires weren't there. But that method of dealing with my inner conflicts had prevented me from coping with my hysterectomy, and I had become mentally ill.

Now Dr Goldblatt was helping me on the premise that I had basic psychological needs which should be met in order for me to lead a mentally healthy life.

Initially I had to 'discover' myself. Before I consulted Dr Goldblatt I had governed my life according to what I thought other people expected and wanted of me. Now I was beginning to recognise my own wishes and expectations. At work or with Dr Goldblatt or Pat I usually expressed myself as I wished, but at home and at church I hadn't been able to break away from the feeling that I had to conform to other people's wishes.

I needed a purpose in life. I wanted to achieve something worthwhile, but I wasn't sure which direction to take. Dr Goldblatt advised me not to be in a hurry.

From October 1967 I was aware that Dr Goldblatt was using our sessions to help meet those psychological needs. He maintained his professionalism, yet at the same time he showed me that he cared about my progress. He was pleased when I made my own decisions and he encouraged me to show my feelings. He was never impatient at my slow progress, even when I became impatient with myself. He accepted me as I was. Gradually his acceptance enabled me to accept myself; his confidence in me increased my confidence; he showed me that I was worthy.

To supplement Dr Goldblatt's psychotherapy, I organised my leisure time with a view to meeting my psychological needs. I went out with Peter a couple of times a week and he introduced me to other people. These people were happily married couples, and I was able to experience the friendly atmosphere of their homes. Some weekends I stayed at Pat's, and several times I went camping with Mary's family (she had visited me in hospital after my hysterectomy). I benefited from their affection.

During the last two weeks of October I began to feel much better. Phases of sadness came but lasted for only a short while. This respite was like a gift from heaven. For the first time since the onset of my illness I didn't need to drive myself mentally and physically. For short periods most days I complimented myself on my recovery. I enjoyed gazing out of the window and letting my mind drift, without having to analyse everything.

I discussed this new development with Dr Goldblatt thinking I was becoming lazy. He disagreed with me. He thought that by doing nothing from time to time I was making positive progress. We analysed my attitude carefully, and I began to realise that I always had to be doing something. I was compulsively active. I agreed with Dr Goldblatt that it was somewhat neurotic to be constantly 'on the go.'

After our discussion, I thought of a new motto for myself: 'Leave until tomorrow the things that don't need to be done today.'

For the next few weeks I reminded myself of my motto when I planned my visits, and I discovered it actually helped me. I became less anxious and better able to plan my job and my life. By clarifying the reasons for my visits I was able to go to people's homes in confidence. After each visit I would assess whether it had been worthwhile. Some tasks didn't need to be done immediately, so I left them. I became able to see myself and others in perspective.

One day I noticed that the clinic caretaker looked harassed so I spent a few minutes talking to her. I became more sensitive to the moods of my colleagues. It occurred to me that my depression had made me self-centred. My motto helped me to look beyond myself and I had time to consider the needs of others.

Dr Goldblatt reminded me on a number of occasions that it would be useful for me to relate to the opposite sex. My friendship with Peter was more platonic than close. We enjoyed each other's company and we felt safe with each other. According to Dr Goldblatt I should try to become more involved, but I argued that it was better for me to share a platonic relationship than a deep emotional involvement. I wanted to become more stable and to develop my own personal philosophy.

Dr Goldblatt accepted that it might be more sensible to remain friends, but he suggested that a platonic friendship would not continue to satisfy me.

He was right. By mid-November I became frustrated by Peter's casual approach. Although we were planning a holiday together in the February, there was nothing romantic in our relationship. Dr Goldblatt argued that if the relationship was unsatisfactory, I should take steps to change the relationship, or if I didn't think it worth the effort, I should look elsewhere.

I decided to modify my relationship with Peter. I felt safe with him, but our platonic friendship continued with little or no physical contact, not even holding hands.

I remembered my childhood and my mother's inhibitions, which prevented her from showing spontaneous affection. When I began to go on holidays without her she had kissed me goodbye, but it always seemed like a formality – a duty that was required. Kissing had been an expression of her duty, not of her affection.

My father was more demonstrative, but that had caused conflict in my mind. I had been taught I should love my parents equally, yet I felt I loved my father more. He had often sat me on his lap and given me a cuddle. I had enjoyed it, but I had felt guilty, because I loved him more than I loved my mother. I felt my mother would be jealous, so I tried not to respond too openly in my mother's presence. I thought that perhaps my childhood experiences might still be inhibiting me and could be the cause of the slow development of my relationship with Peter.

Peter and I had been friends for nearly four months, and Dr Goldblatt considered that in that time a man who had no anxieties about relationships would have made some advances. Dr Goldblatt suggested I should take the initiative and lead Peter on instead of waiting for him to 'break the ice' first. 'Kiss him goodnight,' Dr Goldblatt said, 'and see how he reacts.'

From mid-November until mid-December Dr Goldblatt encouraged me to take the initiative, and we analysed together why I was unable to do so. We discovered there were several things I was afraid of. To begin with, I was afraid that if I took the initiative Peter might be scared off. That could cause a major setback in my recovery and it could even bring back my depression.

Dr Goldblatt didn't share my fears. He said my friendship with Peter would be useless unless I could behave naturally with him. I had everything to gain by being daring. Dr Goldblatt told me to trust him. Whatever happened I could bring my anxieties to him, and he would help me through. He made me realise that in the long run my relationship with

Peter could prove to be more a hinderance than a help, unless the relationship could be developed into a healthy man-woman situation. On one occasion after a frustrating evening with Peter I explained my fears to Dr Goldblatt and he actually called me a prude.

I was startled by this response, because it was so uncharacteristic. I got the impression that Dr Goldblatt hadn't really meant to speak his mind in that way – momentarily he had forgotten he was my analyst.

'Take Peter's hand at the next opportunity,' Dr Goldblatt continued. 'Don't stop to think about reactions. Simply reach for his hand as soon as you are near to each other.'

Next time I went out with Peter I resolved to do as Dr Goldblatt had said, but I couldn't bring myself to act. Eventually I did speak to Peter about our strange relationship, and to my surprise he told me that he believed any move on his part would be taken so seriously by me that it might end the relationship altogether.

'You take everything so seriously,' he explained. 'I only make a pass at a girl if I think she'll take it the way it's meant – just as a bit of fun and innocent pleasure. You'd read too much into it if I made a pass at you.'

The next weekend at a party someone switched off the lights and suddenly Peter and I were in each other's arms.

When I next went to Harley Street Dr Goldblatt began by apologising. 'Last week I said things an analyst shouldn't say. I became over-involved and that affected my objectivity. Possibly it was because I was feeling unwell. I'm sorry.'

'It didn't matter,' I replied. 'In fact, it helped.' I told him about the latest developments in my relationship with Peter.

'You have taken a big step forward,' he said.

Frequently we discussed anger. I saw it as a destructive force, something to be avoided at all costs. Dr Goldblatt argued that there were occasions when it was reasonable to be angry. He claimed that within a sound relationship anger could be beneficial, and could increase the understanding between the people concerned. He said I should see anger in context: I should understand why people become angry and I should examine the effects of anger on groups of people.

I agreed with what he said, and I began to lose my fear of

anger. Rita was often angry and she showed it. I watched her carefully, and saw that as a result of being angry she felt better, and I could understand her more easily. I could see that anger was beneficial to her, but for my part I still preferred not to be angry about things, and if I did feel angry I preferred to resolve matters by logical argument. On the rare occasions I did get angry I told Dr Goldblatt and he became enthusiastic. I couldn't understand why it was so important to him, because compared to my other difficulties, a show of anger on my part seemed of little consequence.

By February 1968 I had learnt to overcome my depressions by using analysis and logical argument. I was also developing my personality. I felt more confident in all aspects of my life, and I was beginning to formulate priorities and standards of my own. My first priority was to become mentally stable, and on that foundation I could build my life.

# 17 Stocktaking Once More

(September 1967 - February 1968)

From September 1967 to February 1968 I continued recording my discussions with Dr Goldblatt – not from my original feeling of vulnerability, but because I sensed that Dr Goldblatt was giving me 'lessons for life' and I didn't want to forget what he was teaching me. Our relationship remained one of mutual trust, respect and cooperation. I looked forward to my sessions, I enjoyed them and I felt renewed afterwards. I usually took ideas away with me which I could apply in the intervening days.

In all respects I was improving, although I was still far from well. An examination of my symptoms shows the extent of my improvement.

I had unpleasant dreams every week or two, but those dreams didn't usually terrify me. In my dreams I was often unable to find my way; occasionally I was faced with difficult decisions. The dreams were easy to interpret, sometimes I actually interpreted the dream while I was still dreaming. In January 1968 I dreamt it was a Monday afternoon, I had left work early and driven to Harley Street to keep my appointment with Dr Goldblatt. As I drove along Euston Road and Marylebone Road I realised I had gone too far, so I turned off the main road and tried to get back to Harley Stret via the side streets. I kept thinking that the next turning would lead to Harley Street, but it never did. I drove up and down endless back streets. Eventually I gave up because my appointment time was past. Suddenly in the dream it became Wednesday. I drove again to Harley Street and this time I found the street, but I couldn't find the house number. After a lot of walking up and down I eventually found the building. I was just in time for my appointment. As I talked to Dr Goldblatt I realised that the weird journey of the previous Monday had been a dream. Dr Goldblatt asked me what I thought the dream meant. I said it meant I only thought I knew where I was going, but in fact I was lost; my life was without direction. Dr Goldblatt disagreed with my interpretation. He said that deep down I wanted to form a special relationship with him, but however hard I tried I couldn't get that relationship going. Suddenly Dr Goldblatt changed into my father. I woke up.

I told Dr Goldblatt about that dream, and he said both explanations were correct.

Occasionally I woke up in the night, terrified by a haunting dream, desperate to talk to someone. Then I would run downstairs to the phone and dial Peter's number. I knew he was a light sleeper, and fortunately for me he didn't seem to mind being woken up at two or three in the morning. Instead of trying to blot out my fears by drinking sherry, I was learning to cope with them by talking to other people.

During those six months I believe I had several attacks of 'night fits', but I didn't record when they occurred. I believe they were caused by overtiredness and tension. The fits were very unpleasant while they lasted. I was shaking all over, yet my body felt rigid, and I couldn't wake up.

Only once during the six months from September 1967 did I have a strong desire to withdraw from life. It happened towards the end of November, and the reasons were to be found in the preceding two weeks.

My father had severe chest pains on the night of 9 November. I told him it could be a heart attack, but he refused to listen to me, and on the following morning he went to work. On the train he had several more attacks and nearly died. By the time the train reached London he had recovered sufficiently to get a taxi home. It wasn't until I arrived home from work that evening that I heard about his attacks, but no doctor had been called. My parents didn't appreciate the seriousness of the situation so I called the doctor myself. Meanwhile my father insisted on walking about the house, and refused to take any advice. My father's attitude made me feel that he was rejecting me.

The doctor arrived and arranged for my father to be admitted into hospital immediately. He was placed in intensive care, and remained there for a week, critically ill. I drove to the hospital each evening, and I soon began to feel tired. It was a two-hour journey there and back. At first my father seemed comforted by my visits. He said my presence was soothing and restful to him. However, once he was out of intensive care he no longer wanted 'soothing and restful' visitors, and I began to feel unwanted. At the same time I felt unwanted by by Peter. For some weeks he had been calling on me on Saturday mornings. Usually we went shopping and then cooked a meal together. Suddenly he didn't show up, and I felt rejected. My long drive to the hospital each evening and my journey to Harley Street after a day's work had left me exhausted. In addition my father's off-hand manner and Peter's absence made me feel I didn't want to relate to anyone. This feeling lasted for about four days.

Throughout the whole of that six months from September 1967 I felt I was emotionally unstable, but my actual behaviour was quite stable. I had formed the habit of analysing my feelings, and I tried hard not to act on any irrational feelings.

My sense of dread and foreboding had lessened, but there was still a feeling of uneasiness, especially if I thought about my illness or if I imagined not seeing Dr Goldblatt again. Normally I tried to keep my mind off those things. Analysing my experiences and feelings each day was enough to keep me busy.

Compared with the previous six months my thinking was now transformed. By thinking logically I was able to understand most of my feelings and actions. I became dependent on logic, because I tended to interpret other people's attitudes towards myself in the light of my own feelings about myself, and this had to be overcome by logical thought.

I no longer imagined committing suicide. I became more optimistic as I realised I was recovering. However, I held the option at the back of my mind that I would prefer to die rather than face a renewed period of depression again. On the practical side I was determined to continue my treatment with Dr Goldblatt until I was sure my recovery was complete.

Occasionally my recovery took a lurch backwards. In the January my mother had 'flu and my father was ordered to rest as much as possible. I assumed responsibility for the day-to-day running of the home. At lunchtimes I drove home to prepare the meals. Soon I felt exhausted, and once, when I went to a supermarket, I suddenly couldn't think what to buy. I just stared at the packets and tins on the shelves: my mind was a blank. Eventually, in desperation, I went back to my clinic, and got one of my colleagues to help me. This was an isolated occasion, and it never recurred, but it scared me at the time.

I gradually learnt how to cope with my job. It was an effort, but since I understood my difficulties I was able to plan my work to my best advantage.

Comparing the middle part of 1967 with the six months following, my symptoms had greatly declined. The improvement seemed to begin during August and continued through September 1967. The first two weeks of October became very difficult, but during the last two weeks I felt really well. After that my symptoms varied according to my circumstances, but I didn't feel really well again for more than a few days at a time until my holiday in February.

Dr Goldblatt was assuring me throughout that I was improving. On 18 December 1967 he said I was making rapid progress, and on 5 February 1968 he told me I was becoming more secure.

I felt really encouraged, and when I left with Peter for a holiday in Majorca I was able to face the world in a normal, happy state of mind for the first time since my illness began.

# Part 3
# COMING TO TERMS WITH LIFE

# 18 The Final Months of Psychotherapy

(February 1968 - August 1968)

I returned from Majorca on 16 February 1968. The psychotherapy session which I attended on 19 February was the last I recorded in my psychotherapy diary. This was a definite decision.

My purpose in keeping a record of what Dr Goldblatt said to me had been twofold. I distrusted psychiatrists. I was afraid my mind might be manipulated while in a state of mental distress or weakness. Keeping a written record reassured me because it enabled me to look back on what Dr Goldblatt had said when I was able to think more clearly. If he was not an honourable man I hoped that my diary would help me to find out quickly, so that I could escape from his clutches. The nature of my illness was such that I felt unable to trust anyone completely.

My second reason for keeping a diary was to ensure that I was getting value for money. My psychotherapy was an investment to me. It involved financial sacrifice. According to Rita I was being treated by one of the best people in the profession. There was no way I could verify that, but I was happy to believe her, and the more I reflected on my treatment, the more I believed that Rita was right. The best way to obtain the maximum value for my money was to write up each session as soon as possible, so that the guidance I was being given, and the insight I received were not forgotten. I was paying for that insight, and I valued it.

The reasons for suddenly ending my accounts of my treatment were that I came to accept and believe in Dr Goldblatt's integrity and professional capability, and, after my holiday with Peter, Dr Goldblatt and I discussed aspects of my relationship with Peter that I didn't want to record in case my diary was discovered. I believed at the time that after a few weeks I would be well enough not to need further treatment, and it seemed no longer necessary to keep writing a diary.

My friendship with Peter and my thoughts about our holiday had taken my mind off my unhappiness at home, but once I was back to the ordinary routine of life I became restless. I looked into the possibility of buying a home but I had to admit that there was no chance while my spare money was being used on psychotherapy. I viewed some caravans on a site a few miles from my home but I realised I wouldn't be happy there. I considered the offer a friend had made several months ago of a room in her house, but she wished to mother me and I felt I no longer needed mothering. Dr Goldblatt had helped me through that difficult phase and enabled me to have my childhood needs met without reverting to childhood.

I didn't believe in precipitous actions, so I decided that for the time being, with my very limited means, I would have to stay at home with my parents, but live my own life as independently as I could. In the long run I was determined to leave home, but for a while I had to be patient. I don't think I discussed any of this with Dr Goldblatt. It was a practical problem which I was well able to sort out for myself. There were more important matters needing discussion.

I hoped and expected that once I had recovered from my mental illness I would feel on top of my job – a job I liked and from which I derived a great deal of satisfaction. However, as time went on I became increasingly disillusioned because I continued to have some difficulties. These difficulties arose in the area of work where I felt most confident: the clinic sessions. To my dismay I began to dread my mothercraft classes. These had always been the highlight of my week, and even during the worst time of my illness, I had been able to rise above my problems and I had run the classes satisfactorily. But the thought of the classes now made me sad and I wanted to cry. I thought about the mothers, happy to be pregnant, eager to learn all they could about their pregnancy, and keen to prepare themselves for childbirth. They asked me so many questions, they wanted to know so much, and I was just as eager to impart my knowledge to them, yet, unaccountably I wanted to run away and cry.

On one occasion, which stands out in my mind, the mothers were a particularly lively and outgoing group. They were exchanging notes about their babies' kicking activities. They found it an exciting experience, except when the babies wouldn't let them sleep at night! 'It's a marvellous feeling,' one of the mothers said. 'My husband loves to put his hands there and feel the baby's kicks.' As I listened I realised I would never have such an experience. My eyes filled with tears.

In one class we were discussing the actual birth of the baby and what it felt like. I explained the mechanisms of birth without difficulty, and then talked about how best the mothers could cooperate, and how they could work positively towards making the birth a rewarding experience.

'What does it actually feel like?' one mother asked me.

'I can't speak from personal experience,' I said, 'but I can tell you how mothers have described it to me, and I can tell you what impressions I have formed from my experience as a midwife.' Suddenly I felt the tears welling up. The force of my own words hit me. I couldn't speak from personal experience and I never would be able to. I couldn't choke back my tears. I stammered. 'Excuse me,' and fled from the room. I rushed to the toilet and sobbed. I longed to share their experience – to feel my own child develop and move inside my own body, to know the pangs of childbirth and enjoy the relief and thrill of the birth, to look forward to the joy of holding my own infant, to plan for the responsibilities and the pleasures of cherishing and nurturing my child through babyhood, of directing it through childhood, and giving guidance as it developed its own personality. I longed for an experience which I knew could never be mine.

I pulled myself together as quickly as I could, washed my face and powdered my nose, and then I returned to the mothers who were sitting happily together.

'I'm sorry,' I said. 'I must have eaten something that upset me last night. I've got an upset stomach. Let's get on to the relaxation.'

No one appeared to notice anything odd about my behaviour, and the rest of the morning passed without further trauma.

It was a mild day, so at lunchtime I decided to walk through a nearby park to shake off my gloom. I wanted to think positively about my afternoon visits.

'Accept what you can't change,' I said to myself, as I wandered slowly across the grass. 'What does it matter? There's far more to life than having a baby.' But my feelings didn't agree with my reasoning. My tears wouldn't stop.

Suddenly I heard my name being called. I looked up. On the footpath a mother was waving. She had a large pram with her. I recognised her as one of the mothers on my list. She had attended my mothercraft classes and had given birth two months previously. I walked to meet her. 'I'd better not get too close,' I said. 'I've got a wretched cold. How are you getting on?'

She was a mother who lived up to my ideal of what pregnancy, childbirth and motherhood could be. For her the whole experience was 'fantastic'. She told me how wonderful it was to watch her baby develop and to build up a relationship with him.

I couldn't bear it. I was hearing about something I longed for but could never have. Somehow I had to escape without offending her.

'I'm thrilled everything is so wonderful,' I said, quite truthfully, 'but I've got a dreadful cold and I don't want to risk passing it on to you, so I won't keep you. Goodbye for now.' I waved goodbye and fled to a lonely part of the park.

That afternoon I couldn't go visiting mothers and babies in case the longing came over me again. Instead I visited handicapped people who were living in a small block of purpose-built flats. They were always pleased to see me.

I told Dr Goldblatt about my depression. 'I can usually cope with my feelings of inadequacy,' I said, 'but now I'm becoming more upset when I'm with expectant mothers. When I talk to someone who is establishing a good relationship with her baby I feel pleased and happy for her but, at the same time, I have a feeling of sadness and my eyes fill with tears. Surely it's time I stopped feeling like this.'

'Your sadness is normal in the circumstances,' he said. 'Accept your feelings, and see them for what they are. For a long time you have been telling yourself that it doesn't really matter that you can't have a child, because you don't really want one anyway. Now you are admitting to yourself that you would like a child of your own, and all the experiences that go with it, but you are having to accept that it's impossible for you. Being with mothers who are enjoying the experience is bringing your loss home to you.'

'Sometimes I feel I can't stand it any more. I'm being tortured by my job. I don't know what to do.'

'It's necessary for you to grieve over your loss.'

'I suppose so,' I said, 'but it's hard to keep being reminded of it every day.'

'It's something you must accept. Don't run away from it. Let yourself mourn,' he said. 'In mourning you are reacting normally to the loss. Don't tell yourself it doesn't matter and you don't mind that you can never conceive a child. It does matter, and you do mind. Allow yourself to be upset, so that the healing process can take place.'

'I can't allow myself to be upset when I'm running a mothercraft class or visiting someone in their home. That would be unprofessional,' I argued.

'But you can express your feelings about it here with me, and with your friends. It's necessary for you to express your feelings. Don't suppress them,' Dr Goldblatt said.

At my sessions with Dr Goldblatt we continued to discuss my relationship with Peter, my feelings of inadequacy and my sadness that I could never have a child. Dr Goldblatt also encouraged me to get to know a few men friends, but the more I thought about getting to know men the more I worried about how I would cope with such relationships. Dr Goldblatt set about discovering the cause of my anxiety. We spent a lot of time examining what I was afraid of. I felt no one would want to know me, but Dr Goldblatt was not prepared to settle for such a vague explanation. Between Easter and Whitsun 1968 we at last traced my problem to its source.

Dr Goldblatt asked me about my feelings for Peter.

'Would you be afraid of a special relationship with Peter, if he were wanting that?'

'No,' I replied.

'Even though he has a weak heart?'

'That makes it easier for me,' I said.

'Why?' exclaimed Dr Goldblatt.

'Because I wouldn't feel I was depriving Peter of children, since his condition makes it inadvisable for him to father children anyway.'

At last we were making progress. I had to admit that my hysterectomy gave me a 'leper complex' as far as men were concerned.

'I feel inferior to other women,' I admitted. 'An important part of a married woman's role is to bear children, but I'm incapable of something basic and fundamental to a woman.'

'But bearing children isn't the most important attribute of being a woman,' Dr Goldblatt said.

'What other attributes are there?' I asked.

'You don't need me to list them. Look at the families you visit. Is bearing children the only thing for a mother to do?' he asked.

'No,' I said. 'I visit one family where the mother hasn't been able to conceive, and she has adopted four children. She and her husband are very happy together. They are proud of their children, and they both say that they feel as close to their children as if they were their own.'

'So a happy marriage is possible without the woman being able to bear children,' Dr Goldblatt continued.

'Yes, I can see that,' I said.

'You should look at yourself objectively,' said Dr Goldblatt. 'Think of the other attributes you have. Don't dwell on what you haven't got.'

I followed Dr Goldblatt's advice. It strengthened my self-image to think about the positive aspects of my personality and my abilities. But I wasn't totally freed from my anxieties. By bringing my disability into the open other anxieties followed. These I discussed with Dr Goldblatt at the next opportunity.

'I know there are other things in a relationship besides

giving birth to children, but even so, I feel a man has the right to be a father, and I would be depriving him of that right. How can I justify getting involved with someone who might want children, when I know it would be impossible?'

'It's possible to adopt a child,' Dr Goldblatt suggested. 'Some men need to have a child that's biologically theirs, but for other men that isn't important. You must accept there is more to marriage than having children. You need to look at the facts constructively. You can't give birth to children. You have to accept that. But if a man forms a friendship with you he will have a choice: he may decide that he needs you as you are. But if he decides that he needs children then you won't be for him.'

'That could be very hard to take,' I said.

Dr Goldblatt agreed.

'I don't want to get hurt by all this,' I said. 'I don't think even you realise the hell I've been through this past year. I could never endure anything like that again. It's as if I've been suspended over a forest fire with the smoke choking me and the sparks and the heat burning me. I'm terrified that another trauma might push me back to where I was a year ago. When I first became ill, I had no idea my agony would last for so long, so I kept struggling and fighting against my symptoms. If there is ever a next time, I would rather be dead.'

'My work with you has been towards preventing a recurrence,' said Dr Goldblatt. 'Mentally you are stronger now. You have insight into your mind and your emotions. Your chances of becoming mentally ill are far less than they have ever been.'

'I'm afraid to take the risks,' I said.

'I'm discussing these matters with you in order to minimise risks,' he explained. 'You can't ignore things which are bound to affect your life.'

'You are right to make me face the future,' I admitted.

We had a number of discussions about my need for relationships with men, and my fears of being hurt. I tried to think of ways of minimising the risks.

'If I meet a man, how soon should I tell him that I can't have children?' I asked.

Dr Goldblatt paused. 'At the moment the knowledge that you can't have children is uppermost in your mind. It's overshadowing your thinking. That's perfectly natural and normal.'

'But if I follow my inclination, I shall blurt it out to everyone I meet.'

Dr Goldblatt smiled. 'When you have it in perspective, it will not be a problem. You will be able to mention it at an appropriate time as a matter of fact. For some men it could be of no importance.'

I was greatly encouraged by what Dr Goldblatt said to me. He was a man himself, and he would understand. I knew that he was being honest with me. He was seriously trying to help me to bring my problem into perspective, and I felt reassured.

In May 1968 I began thinking about new directions. During my illness my life consisted of Peter, my local friends, my colleagues at work, my job, Pat, psychotherapy and my parents. Peter lived near me, and his friends were my friends, but for my own sake I knew I must break away from him as soon as possible because our aims in life were incompatible. I began to realise that the only way to get away from him would be to move.

The thought of moving appealed to me. I wasn't close enough to my local friends to miss them, and I hadn't confided in them as I had with Pat and Rita. They were pleasant company, but I could part from them without any regrets. I would also be glad to leave my home town. It held too many sad memories of my illness and of my brother's illness. I didn't want to be reminded constantly of my unhappy past.

With regard to my job, I believed I was as happy as I could be. I was becoming used to the idea of not being able to have a baby, and I was crying less often. In fact, I began to enjoy being with mothers and babies. Most of the mothers who came to the child health clinic I knew from my mothercraft classes. Many of them placed the babies on my lap. At first I found this upsetting, but gradually I enjoyed holding the babies week by week and watching them develop. I saw I had mourned enough, and the knowledge of my loss no longer hurt me. The mothers and babies were helping me recover, and I had the satisfaction of knowing that the mothers appreciated what I was doing for them.

Yet despite this new sense of wellbeing there was a strong drive urging me to move on. I also gradually realised that my reliance on my colleagues was in some ways preventing my further progress. They were sympathetic and understanding, and the temptation was always there for me to pour out my problems to them. That was no longer good for me because I was now capable of working out my problems on my own, and it was time for me to stand on my own feet. My relationship with Rita was also in need of a rethink. I respected and admired her, and without her help I would never have won through. I used her as my model and tried to become like her, yet I knew I was being childish and unrealistic. As far as our temperaments and personalities were concerned we were poles apart, and I needed to develop myself in my own way, and realise my own potential. I needed to see her as a colleague, on an equal footing to myself. Yet she had more than saved my life. I would always look up to her, and I would want to run to her for help. The more I thought about it, the more I saw that it was time for me to go.

I also thought about psychotherapy. In one sense Dr Goldblatt could always be helpful to me. I didn't consider that there was nothing more for him to do. But together we had achieved what we had set out to do. My illness was over. I had faced the consequences of my hysterectomy, and I was ready to continue to live my life. I had progressed. Dr Goldblatt had helped me to understand myself to a degree which I had never thought possible. He had also helped me to face the problems in my personality and begin to overcome them.

I knew I still had a long way to go, and I had many things to learn. My feelings of inadequacy persisted, but I recognised and understood those feelings. In addition, Dr Goldblatt had suggested ways in which I might build up my confidence from within, so that in time I would no longer feel inadequate.

There were also practical reasons why I should end my treatment. It was expensive, and economising was a strain. I had no money for new clothes, and I could only buy the cheapest food. As long as I needed psychotherapy I was willing to make the financial sacrifice, but I saw no point in prolonging my poverty any longer than necessary. Another reason for ending my treatment was my decision to start a new job.

By the time I had considered the various aspects of my life I decided that I would leave home, change my job, finish my friendship with Peter and stop psychotherapy as soon as possible.

I told Dr Goldblatt about my plans. 'Do you think it's sensible to change my job?' I asked.

Dr Goldblatt smiled, but made no comment.

'All I have to do is decide what job I want,' I continued. 'I feel as though I've had enough of health visiting for a while.'

'Think of what you would like to do best,' he suggested.

I let my mind wander. I thought of the jobs I had had in the past, and the training courses I had taken. 'I've got it,' I exclaimed. 'I'll go back to midwifery. I enjoyed that more than anything. A midwife's job is worthwhile, and it's a job that gives me confidence. At the same time my longing to be close to pregnancy, childbirth and babies would be satisfied.' I paused. 'Am I being neurotic?'

'No,' he smiled. 'It's an idea worth considering.'

I did consider it, and I decided I had nothing to lose. If it didn't work out, I could easily go back to health visiting.

I searched through the advertisements until I saw what I was looking for. It was a midwifery post in a residential home for unmarried mothers and their babies. The mothers went to the home about six weeks before the baby was due to be born, and would stay for about six weeks after their delivery. There was room for twenty mothers at a time. As a residential midwife I would have the opportunity to get to know the mothers and babies well. At the same time I would be leaving my home and making new contacts.

I talked to Rita about the new job. She told me to go for an informal interview. I did so and I took to the girls and their babies immediately. I would have one room at the home and share responsibility for running the place and supervising the girls in their domestic duties. However, I felt unsure about it. A few days later I received a phone call from the home, to ask if I wished to apply for the post. I said I'd decided against it because I didn't like the accommodation, and I felt the girls were required to do too much domestic work. The woman on the phone told me that a new matron had been appointed, and if I accepted the post, we could make any changes we wished.

I decided reluctantly to go for an interview, and I was offered the post. I was to start my new job at the beginning of September. Although I had misgivings, I knew I would be happy with the mothers and babies. Rita thought I should look for a more liberal and better staffed home, but I argued that I wasn't looking for a perfect environment, and I wanted a challenge.

Before deciding definitely to accept the job, I discussed the proposition with Dr Goldblatt.

'Why do you want to be a midwife for unmarried mothers?' he asked.

'The fact that they are unmarried is immaterial,' I replied. 'The job appeals to me because I shall get to know the mothers and babies. It will be good for me to become acquainted with the problems they experience.'

'Have you thought of the consequences of a residential job?' he asked.

'Yes, but it will enable me to leave home.'

'Can you see no problems in a residential post?'

'It will be difficult for me to continue with psychotherapy,' I said, 'but I'm hoping I won't need to continue after the summer holidays.'

'Are there any other problems?' he persisted.

'I might become overinvolved with the mothers and their problems, and it may be difficult to have a social life,' I said.

'Anything else?'

I thought for a moment. 'I suppose if I'm on call four nights a week I'm likely to have a lot of disturbed nights. Unmarried mothers away from home are going to be more frightened than most mothers. They'll probably wake me up at the slightest excuse. The babies will also keep me awake.'

'Do you think it's worth taking this job in the light of these disadvantages?' said Dr Goldblatt.

'I think the job satisfaction will outweigh the problems,' I said. 'I'm not committing myself for life. I could move on after a few months if the job proved unsatisfactory.'

Neither of us spoke for a while. Then Dr Goldblatt asked, 'Have you made your decision?'

'Not yet,' I said. 'There's something I must know before I decide. Do you think I'm mentally stable enough to cope with such a demanding job?'

'You have made great progress,' said Dr Goldblatt. 'If you continue as you are I shall not have any serious reservations.'

'Do you think I shall be ready to do without psychotherapy by the summer holidays?' I queried.

'We can work towards that end,' he said.

'Do you think it's possible that I shall be able to continue my life alone?'

'Yes, I think so.'

I didn't press him any further. It was enough to know that he thought it was possible. It was up to me to try to do without him by the summer. It was only mid-June. That gave me two more months of psychotherapy.

'I've made my decision,' I said. 'I'll accept the post and start at the beginning of September, and providing you feel happy about it, I'd like to continue with you until your summer holidays. What do you think?'

'It's your decision,' he said, 'and that's what's important. You don't need my approval.'

'You will let me know if I decide to stop the treatment too soon, won't you? I don't want to suffer from depression again.'

'Of course,' he said, 'as a psychiatrist I like to do the best I can for my patients. It's important for me not to conclude treatment until my patients are ready to continue without my help.'

Rita seemed concerned about my decision to accept the post. 'You need to make friends,' she said. 'You won't find an eligible man by shutting yourself up in a mother and baby home.'

'I won't shut myself up when I'm off duty,' I replied. 'I shall go out.'

'Where and with whom?' she demanded.

'I don't know,' I said, feeling hurt.

'Well, you'd better know before you start the job,' she said, and walked off angrily.

A few days later, Rita placed some literature on my desk. There was a leaflet about the Varsity club in London. I had never heard of it, so I read a few paragraphs and discovered it was a club for wining and dining, theatre going, walking, languages and many other interests. 'The languages and the walking appeal to me,' I said. 'Thanks.'

**14 August 1968**

It was my last psychotherapy session. Over the previous few weeks it seemed to me that Dr Goldblatt had left no stone unturned in his analysis of my thinking. I was satisfied with the service he had given me; if I had any unresolved conflicts I was sure he would have discovered them. Yet I felt apprehensive.

'Dr Goldblatt,' I said. 'I want you to tell me truthfully, do you think I am ready to face my new life without your assistance?'

'Yes, I do,' he said, quickly and firmly.

'Do you think I'm likely to suffer from depression again?'

'I can't predict the future,' he said. 'What I can say is that you now understand yourself better. You have learnt to accept yourself and your emotions. I have given you the tools you need, and I have shown you how to use them. You know the areas in which you need to concentrate.'

'Yes,' I said. 'I need to be less inhibited and more ready to show my feelings and speak my mind.'

'Those things are important for you as you make new relationships. Be yourself. Let people see you for what you are. Don't pretend you don't have certain feelings.'

'That's something I must keep working at, because my natural inclination is still to hide my feelings,' I said.

'Remember that your feelings are an important part of you,' he said.

There was a pause, then I said, 'I must admit I feel nervous about my new job. I'm still not as stable emotionally as I would like to be, and I'll be working amongst teenagers who are likely to be unstable, and going through an emotional crisis. It's going to be a difficult job. There'll be more to it than midwifery skills.'

'Do you regret your decision?' he asked.

'No, I have no regrets. I shall make mistakes and I shall have no one to lean on, but it's time now to take a few risks and to make a few decisions of my own, and to face the consequences. I shall do my best.'

'Don't push yourself too hard, or demand too high a standard of yourself,' he advised.

'I'll try not to.'

'And don't always take yourself so seriously. Enjoy yourself from time to time.'

'I appreciate all this advice you are giving me,' I said. I looked at him. I was sorry I wouldn't be coming to him again. 'I shall miss you.'

'You are ready to go, but if you ever wish to consult me again, contact me for an appointment.'

'Thank you,' I said. 'Do you think I will ever come back to you?'

'Do you think so?' he replied.

'No. Perhaps if a new calamity happened in my life I might need to see you, but otherwise I believe I will be able to cope on my own.'

Dr Goldblatt smiled. 'I'm glad you have confidence in yourself.'

There was one more thing I wanted to say to him. Words could never convey my feelings, but I had to try.

'I'd like to thank you for everything you've done for me. You've been so understanding and patient.' I glanced quickly at the couch. 'And you've given me so much advice.' I paused, searching for words to express all I felt. 'I can't imagine what would have happened to me if you hadn't undertaken to treat me. You have really saved me from a fate worse than death, and you've enabled me to start living a new life. I just can't thank you enough.'

Our eyes met. He held my gaze. 'It's what you yourself have done that has enabled you to recover,' he said. 'Without your determination to overcome your problems, and your perseverance, I could never have helped you. It isn't my achievement. It's yours.'

I thought of my song which had helped me through the darkest hours.

Dr Goldblatt's final words remained in my mind and strengthened my belief in myself. 'It isn't my achievement. It's yours.' If what he said was true, if the achievement was mine, then it was no mean achievement. I had overcome seemingly insurmountable problems in my illness.

It was time to go. I stood up, strengthened, confident, relaxed. 'I hope you have a happy holiday,' I said. 'Goodbye, Dr Goldblatt.'

'Thank you. Goodbye, Margaret.' He opened the door for me. 'I wish you well.'

I walked slowly down the stairs and into the waiting room for one last look. The room was full of memories: the mirrors I'd looked through when I had wanted the room to grow bigger, the comfortable armchairs, the huge carpet, the enormous doors. I walked through the doors into the cloak-room. How many tears had I shed in that room? I paused and then went back into the hall and out of the front door. I looked up at the majestic building. How fine the building was. I walked slowly to my car, along the familiar streets. I got into my car and drove slowly away. 'Goodbye Dr Goldblatt,' I whispered. 'And thank you, thank you very much.'

# Part 4
# APPENDIX

# 1 Practical Tips for Helping a Depressed Person

Unless we have experienced depression ourselves, we find it very difficult to begin to understand people who are depressed. It is easy to feel impatient with them, and expect them to help themselves out of their own depression.

However, depressed people themselves often don't understand why they are so depressed, and much as they would like to help themselves, they don't know how to. Friends or relatives should encourage anyone who can't overcome their depression to consult an expert. Normally the family doctor is the person to advise on this, but if the person with depression doesn't receive the necessary help from him, it would be advisable to arrange a consultation with a psychologist or a psychiatrist. Advertisements placed by people or associations offering psychotherapy appear in a number of professional journals, and some psychologists and psychotherapists have their names in the yellow pages. It is important to check the credentials of people who have not been personally recommended to you. Voluntary agencies and counselling services also give advice.

Obtaining treatment from an expert is only part of what is needed for recovery. Friends and relatives have an important part to play. If the patient agrees, they could ask the doctor or therapist how they might cooperate with the treatment.

From my own experience of depression, and from my contact professionally with people suffering from depression, I have formed opinions on how help may be given, which are now passed on in the following pages.

Depressed people feel lonely and afraid, and often ashamed of themselves for not being able to cope with their lives. Telling them to cheer up, reminding them there are plenty of people worse off, and explaining that they are a worry to everyone, is the same as saying that you don't understand, and that you don't care enough to try to understand.

Depressed people, like all other people, need to feel that someone cares about them, they need new experiences, they need self-confidence, they need to develop their own personalities, and they need a sense of purpose in life. It is in these five respects that friends and relatives can help.

I shall now discuss these five areas in turn.

### Feeling that Someone Cares

We can show a depressed person that we care by listening properly when they talk about their symptoms, and by showing that we appreciate how bad they feel. While being ready to give what help we can, it is important that we do not relieve them of their responsibility for their own life. We also need to bear in mind that once we have won someone's confidence, they are liable to turn to us whenever they feel desperate, and may even want to cling to us all the time. This problem needs careful handling. It is important not to reject them, but at the same time we should protect ourselves from being swamped by their demands. If we aim from the outset at an interdependent relationship, in which we try not only to understand their needs, but also to help them understand our needs, we should be able to set limits on their demands without spoiling the relationship.

### New Experiences

New experiences are especially important for people leading a sheltered or closed lifestyle because they need new ideas and to see new ways of doing things and to increase their chances of meeting people with whom they can form helpful relationships.

## Self-confidence

It is important for people to have confidence in themselves. If they can't do something they will be afraid to try, because failure will make them feel worse. We can increase people's self-confidence if we let them see that we have confidence in them. Show appreciation whenever they do anything for you, recognise their good points, treat them as equals and never let them feel small. Don't be afraid to let them see your own failings and weaknesses. If you are someone who needs to show off your own accomplishments, and you like to pretend you are superior to others, you are unlikely to be able to help anyone who is depressed.

## Personal Development

People are more likely to become depressed if their own personalities haven't been allowed to develop. We can help that development if we recognise that they are individuals with a right to choose for themselves in life. It can be particularly difficult for relations to help in this respect because parents sometimes try to map out their children's lives for them. Husbands and wives, too, can have set ideas about their relationships, and might resist letting their partner change or have more freedom. Relations and friends need to accept that a new and changing relationship might be necessary, and that they themselves might need to reassess their own attitudes and perhaps modify them. We can help further if we encourage depressed people to share their thoughts and show their feelings. This again can be disturbing to us. For example, we might do all we can to give them a happy day, yet they still say that they feel really depressed. This will probably make us feel rejected or annoyed because we haven't got the satisfaction of feeling that we have helped. We want them to show their feelings, yet when they do, we feel hurt. This difficulty must be faced. We must get our satisfaction from the fact that they are able to show their feelings to us, rather than looking for satisfaction in their appreciation. Depression can last a long time, and if we expect every effort to be rewarded by seeing the depression lift, we will soon be disappointed and disillusioned.

Another way to encourage the individual's personal development is to give them the opportunity to choose and to make decisions, however small. When they do choose to do something, don't tell them that they should have chosen something else. Their sense of achievement at making a decision is more important than whether the decision was the best in the circumstances.

## A Sense of Purpose

It can take time for people who are suffering from depression to begin to feel that they have a purpose in life. In fact, they have a most worthwhile purpose — to become mentally healthy. We are indeed privileged if we are able to play any part in helping them to work towards that end.

# 2 An Examination of the Psychotherapist's Methods from the Patient's Point of View

## The Couch

Dr Goldblatt preferred to work sitting out of sight with his patient lying on a couch. Not all psychotherapists have this preference. Some like an informal seating arrangement, while others discuss with the patient whether to use the couch or a chair. For Dr Goldblatt the couch was important. He was an analyst. He wanted to help his patients analyse their own thoughts without being influenced by his personality. Despite my protestations that the couch made it harder for me to say what I was thinking, Dr Goldblatt persisted with the couch for six months. I believe he did that in order to encourage negative transference, which is explained later.

## Trust

A relationship of trust between therapist and patient is essential if the patient is going to expose thoughts and feelings that in the past they have pretended not to have. They feel mentally vulnerable because they don't fully understand what is happening to them. If they didn't trust their therapist they would probably terminate treatment at the first sign of difficulty.

Friends can help establish trust in the patient. In my case, Rita won my initial trust. Her conviction that I needed psychotherapy became my conviction. She believed in Dr Goldblatt's ability and integrity, and that enabled me to risk entrusting myself to him.

## Self-acceptance

Self-acceptance is crucial to understanding oneself. Some patients don't accept themselves and have spent a lifetime concealing what they are really like. As long as they continue to be untrue to themselves they will not be able to understand why they are depressed. From the outset Dr Goldblatt encouraged me to be honest with myself and to accept the way I was. He set an example by accepting me. The first piece of advice he gave me was, 'You need to learn that it can be perfectly acceptable for you to be yourself and to act spontaneously.' Again in the second session he said, 'whatever you say is acceptable to me. You are acceptable.'

Self-acceptance doesn't come to a person merely through the intellect. It comes through being accepted by others. If the patient is lacking in that experience, the therapist concentrates on showing the patient that they are acceptable.

## The Developmental Viewpoint

In Freudian theory the child passes through various stages in the process of its development to adulthood. The child's experiences in the different stages affect its attitude to itself and to others. If difficulties or deprivations have occurred in a particular stage, the personality will be defective unless the difficulties can be resolved, and unless the essential needs are met. Analysing uncovers the difficulties and reveals the areas of deprivation, so that the difficulties can be sorted out and the unsatisfied needs can be met.

Dr Goldblatt soon discovered that I had not enjoyed being dependent as a baby, and as early as the third session he worked positively to meet my unsatisfied need of dependence. 'Depend on me. Express your needs to me as a baby does to its mother,' he told me. At the same time Dr Goldblatt encouraged me to learn more about the nature of a baby's dependence by observing the mother/child relationship first hand.

## Resistance

Resistance to treatment is common. The patient has devised ways of protecting themselves from being hurt by avoiding potentially hurtful situations or hurtful emotions. The therapist encourages them to face those things, but they are frightened to do so.

For some time I resisted depending fully on Dr Goldblatt and later I resisted thinking about my 'rights'. Even when I had consciously broken down my resistance, unconsciously the resistance remained. Having decided to tell Dr Goldblatt my dreams, I promptly forgot them.

## Transference

Experiences in early years play an important part in moulding a person's attitudes to themselves and to others. If a child is brought up in an atmosphere of hostility and criticism it will tend to interpret other people's attitudes towards itself in the light of its early experience, and will tend to feel that people are hostile and critical of it. In other words, we often 'transfer' our feelings and attitudes which we developed in childhood into new, similar situations. The phenomenon of 'transference' is used by the therapist. The patient projects their feelings on to him, and he can then draw attention to what is happening, and help them to understand how they misinterpret other people's actions. When the feelings are favourable, the transference is called 'positive'. When the feelings are of hate or rejection, the transference is called 'negative.'

Negative transference occurred early on in my treatment. I felt that Dr Goldblatt was bored or irritated by me, and that he didn't care how much I was suffering. The experience confused me, because when I could watch him I could tell he was concerned, and listening to me. Despite a mass of evidence to the contrary, however, I continued to feel he was indifferent to my problems. The negative transference usually went when I sat in a chair and watched him, because then the visual evidence was sufficient to inhibit those feelings. Hence my dislike of the couch, and my resentment at his lack of flexibility in that respect. I believe Dr Goldblatt might have wished to remain out of sight so that the negative transference could be used in his treatment. I needed to show anger and resentment, and to understand those feelings in myself.

Gradually the patient learns to examine their feelings in the light of the actual evidence to them. In this way they can unlearn, and then relearn from their experiences with the therapist.

## The Ego and Superego

The ego can be described simply as the non-physical part of ourselves that we are aware of. It develops its character by finding a balance between the natural impulses the person has, and the expectations of society and its own conscience.

The superego is in the unconscious part of the person. It develops through early relationships, particularly with parents, and it works as a conscience. It causes guilt and anxious feelings to occur when the ego wishes to satisfy inclinations that are considered unacceptable. In some people the ego is so dominated by the superego that the personality is unable to develop satisfactorily. Ordinary harmless pleasures might cause such distressing feelings of guilt that the person turns to a life of duty. They become dominated by what they 'ought' to do, and behave as they think they are expected to behave. The person might not even know what they like or dislike, because they feel guilty if they consider their own wants. Decisions are made on the basis of right and wrong, or what is expected of them. In situations where it isn't a question of right or wrong, and it isn't clear what is expected, they have difficulty in making a decision, because they feel guilty if they choose on the basis of their own enjoyment.

My problem, too, was that my ego was dominated by my superego. Dealing with the problem was frightening, because I was fighting my conscience and I was changing the basis of my thinking.

## The Therapist/Patient Relationship

The relationship between therapist and patient is of the utmost importance. Like all worthwhile relationships, it develops and changes to meet the changing needs of the people concerned. If a sound relationship is formed the patient has the reassurance that they have someone who genuinely cares about their wellbeing, and has the ability to guide them through. When they no longer need the relationship, they can terminate it with a clear conscience, knowing that the therapist has been working towards that end.

# 3 Factors Influencing the Outcome of Psychotherapy

The extent to which a patient benefits from psychotherapy doesn't only depend on the skill of the therapist. The patients themselves, friends and relatives also influence the outcome of the treatment.

## The Patient

It is important that the patient realises they need psychiatric help and want that help. When they meet the therapist they should like him and feel he is trustworthy, otherwise they won't be able to break down the distrust and fear they are sure to have. Once they have committed themselves to treatment, perseverance is essential. If they give up when faced with difficulties, or if they allow themselves to be influenced by every doubt they have, they are unlikely to continue with the treatment long enough to benefit.

Certain personality traits might help or hinder progress, but the skilled therapist can help various personality types. Distrust makes treatment difficult, but Dr Goldblatt was able to continue to help me, despite my deep distrust of psychiatrists.

The ability to express one's thoughts and feelings helps, but again the skilled therapist can work with an inhibited patient. I was more inhibited than nearly everyone else I had known, but Dr Goldblatt told me that I was giving him enough to work on. In retrospect, I believe that my lack of trust and my difficulty in showing my feelings prolonged my depression, but through the patient and painstaking work of Dr Goldblatt I eventually overcame those problems sufficiently to recover.

Logical thinking helps the patient to understand their depression and to plan ways of overcoming it. However, I don't think that highly intelligent, logical thought is essential or necessarily helpful in severe depressions. It was trust, interdependent relationships, self-acceptance and self-expression that enabled me to recover. I didn't learn to trust, accept myself and express myself by logical thinking. I learnt by experiencing a trustworthy, accepting therapist and caring friends. Psychotherapy uses the intellectual method as a vehicle to reach the emotions. If the emotions aren't reached I believe that the therapy will not achieve its goal. True progress is dependent on the patient learning from their emotional experience.

All through childhood, adolescence and early adulthood I had used logical argument to cope with my inner feelings of being unwanted and unloved, but those feelings remained. For years I tried to believe that God loved me, yet, despite constantly reading and studying the Bible, and despite sincerely trying to live up to its teachings, and following every formula I was given, I never felt within that God was a loving God. I had the head knowledge, without the inner experience. Through psychotherapy I gradually obtained the inner experience. The accompanying knowledge of Freud's theories I believe was incidental to my recovery.

## Friends and Relatives

By their attitudes friends and relatives can both help and hinder the patient's progress; see Appendix 1: Practical tips for helping someone who is depressed.

# 4 Table of Symptoms, Causes and Coping

The table overleaf outlines some of the symptoms I experienced during my illness and includes the probable causes of these symptoms and explanations on how I tried to cope with each symptom as it arose.

It should be noted that this table only describes my own experiences.

# TABLE 1

| *Symptom* | *Probable cause* | *How I coped in the short term* | *How I coped in the long term* | *Source of help* |
|---|---|---|---|---|
| Nightmares | My disturbed mind<br>Guilt feelings<br>Fear of the future<br>Conflicting ideals and beliefs | Sleeping tablets | Psychotherapy<br>Self-analysis<br>I shared my fears with Peter by phoning him in the night | Dr Goldblatt<br>GP for sleeping tablets<br>Personal effort<br>Friends |
| Shaking and rigid fits at night | Extreme tiredness<br>Anxiety | Sleeping tablets<br>I forced myself to relax | I tried not to think about them<br>I avoided becoming overtired | GP for sleeping tablets |
| Withdrawing from people | Fear of letting people see that I was ill<br>Other people's happiness emphasised my own misery | I forced myself to meet people even if I did not want to, because I feared schizophrenia<br>I refused to go on the sick list, and carried on at work | Psychotherapy<br>Self-analysis | Dr Goldblatt<br>Friends<br>Colleagues |
| Feelings of isolation | My awareness that my family did not understand me and were unable to help<br><br>Recovery meant discarding my childhood beliefs and attitudes | Psychotherapy and contact with friends | Psychotherapy | Dr Goldblatt<br>Friends<br>Colleagues |
| Elation | Relief at being cured of possible cancer<br>Temporary freedom from my unhappy environment | Librium tablets | Psychotherapy<br>I acted out my elated feelings when circumstances allowed | Dr Goldblatt<br>Self-control |
| Emotional instability | I had turned away from my strict religious upbringing and I was uncertain about what I wanted and what I stood for | Librium tablets<br>I analysed my feelings and acted on them only if it seemed reasonable | Psychotherapy<br>Forming relationships | Dr Goldblatt<br>Friends |
| Dread and foreboding | Fear that I might become more seriously ill in the future and fear of being unable to cope with life | I had to bear it | Psychotherapy | Dr Goldblatt |
| Panic attacks | Cause unknown | I telephoned friends | Psychotherapy | Rita<br>Pat<br>Dr Goldblatt |
| Shopping phobia | Fear of taking something from a shop without paying<br>Difficulty in concentrating | I did not use a shopping bag for shopping<br>I kept to the same meals nearly every day<br>Occasionally I had help from colleagues | Psychotherapy | Myself<br>Colleagues<br>Dr Goldblatt |
| Imagining committing suicide | My illness and my future seemed to be so dreadful that I sometimes contemplated suicide as the only escape from my misery | I forced myself to avoid danger. For example I only ran two inches of water when I took a bath<br>I drank sherry | Psychotherapy | Dr Goldblatt<br>Myself |
| Crying fits | Despair<br>I came to regret that I could not have children | If I felt a crying fit coming on I moved away from people | Psychotherapy | Dr Goldblatt |
| Confused thinking | The way of life which I had believed in since childhood was being challenged | Sleeping tablets<br>I drank sherry<br>I phoned Rita | Psychotherapy<br>Discussions with friends | Dr Goldblatt<br>Rita |